BOOK COVER AND END SHEETS DESIGNED BY VERN NELSON

collector's history of
THE AUTOMOBILE

The Development of Man's Greatest Means of Transportation

by
Peter Roberts

edited by
Horace J. Elias

BONANZA BOOKS
a division of Crown Publishers, Inc.
One Park Avenue
New York, N.Y. 10016

Contents

To the legion of private persons, organizations and companies who have contributed their time, cooperation and assistance on the preparation of this book, the author, editor and publishers extend their deepest gratitude. Quite literally, the book could not have come into being without them.

International Registration Letters

established by international conventions and/or as notified to the United Nations

A	Austria	H	Hungary	RCB	Congo (Brazzaville)
ADN	Democratic Yemen (formerly Aden)*[1]	HK	Hong Kong*	RCH	Chile
		HKJ	Jordan	RH	Haiti
AFG	Afghanistan[2]			RI	Indonesia*
AL	Albania	I	Italy	RIM	Mauritania[2]
AND	Andorra	IL	Israel	RL	Lebanon
AUS	Australia*	IND	India*	RM	Malagasy Republic (formerly Madagascar)
		IR	Iran[2]		
B	Belgium	IRL	Ireland, Republic of*	RMM	Mali
BDS	Barbados*	IRQ	Iraq[2]	RNR	Zambia (formerly Northern Rhodesia)*[1] [5]
BG	Bulgaria	IS	Iceland		
BH	British Honduras			ROK	Korea, Republic of
BR	Brazil	J	Japan*	RSM	San Marino
BRN	Bahrain	JA	Jamaica*	RSR	Rhodesia (formerly Southern Rhodesia)*[1]
BRU	Brunei*				
BS	Bahamas*	K	Khmer Republic (formerly Cambodia)	RU	Burundi[2]
BUR	Burma			RWA	Rwanda
		KWT	Kuwait[2]		
C	Cuba[2]			S	Sweden
CDN	Canada	L	Luxembourg	SD	Swaziland*
CH	Switzerland	LAO	Laos	SF	Finland
CI	Ivory Coast	LAR	Libya[2]	SGP	Singapore*
CL	Sri Lanka (formerly Ceylon)*[1]	LB	Liberia[2]	SME	Surinam (Dutch Guiana)*
		LS	Lesotho (formerly Basutoland)*	SN	Senegal
CO	Colombia[2]			SU	Union of Soviet Socialist Republics
CR	Costa Rica				
CS	Czechoslovakia	M	Malta*	SWA	South West Africa*[2] [4]
CY	Cyprus*	MA	Morocco	SY	Seychelles*
		MAL	Malaysia*	SYR	Syria
D	Germany[2]	MC	Monaco		
DK	Denmark	MEX	Mexico	T	Thailand*
DOM	Dominican Republic	MS	Mauritius*	TG	Togo
DY	Dahomey	MW	Malawi (formerly Nyasaland)*	TN	Tunisia
DZ	Algeria			TR	Turkey
				TT	Trinidad and Tobago*
E	Spain (including African localities and provinces)	N	Norway	U	Uruguay
EAK	Kenya*	NA	Netherlands Antilles	USA	United States of America
EAT	Tanzania (formerly Tanganyika)*[1]	NIC	Nicaragua		
		NIG	Niger	V	Holy See (Vatican City)
EAU	Uganda*	NL	Netherlands	VN	Vietnam, Republic of
EAZ	Tanzania (formerly Zanzibar)*[1] [3]	NZ	New Zealand*		
EC	Ecuador			WAG	Gambia
ET	Arab Republic of Egypt	P	Portugal (including Angola, Cape Verde Islands, Mozambique*, Portuguese Guinea, Portuguese Timor, São Tomé, and Príncipe)	WAL	Sierra Leone
				WAN	Nigeria
F	France (including overseas departments and territories)			WD	Dominica*[2]
		PA	Panama[2]	WG	Grenada*
FJI	Fiji*	PAK	Pakistan*	WL	St. Lucia*
FL	Liechtenstein[2]	PE	Peru	WS	Western Samoa*
		PI	Philippines	WV	St Vincent (Windward Islands)*
GB	United Kingdom of Great Britain and Northern Ireland*	PL	Poland		
		PY	Paraguay	YU	Yugoslavia
GBA	Alderney*			YV	Venezuela
GBG	Guernsey* } Channel Islands	R	Romania		
GBJ	Jersey*	RA	Argentina	Z	See RNR
GBM	Isle of Man*[2]	RB	Botswana (formerly Bechuanaland)*	ZA	South Africa*
GBZ	Gibraltar			ZR	Zaire (formerly Congo Kinshasha)
GCA	Guatemala	RC	China, National Republic of (Formosa)		
GH	Ghana				
GR	Greece	RCA	Central African Republic		
GUY	Guyana*				

WD Dominica*[2], WG Grenada*, WL St. Lucia* } Windward Islands

* In countries marked with an asterisk, the rule of the road is drive on the left; otherwise drive on the right.

Notes
1. Established under former country name
2. Not included in the United Nations' list of signs established according to the 1949 Convention on Road Traffic
3. The letters EAT are also used
4. The letters ZA are also used
5. The letter Z is also used

List of Abbreviations

A.A.A.	American Automobile Association	irs	independent rear suspension
bhp	brake horse power	NACC	National Automobile Chamber of Commerce (USA)
cc	cubic centimeters		
cu in	cubic inches	ohc	overhead camshaft
cv	cheval vapeur	ohv	overhead valves
fwd	front wheel drive	RAC	Royal Automobile Club (GB)
G.P.	Grand Prix	sv	side valve
ifs	independent front suspension	T.T.	Tourist Trophy

Note: the abbreviation in parenthesis following a caption indicates the automobile's International Registration Letters. See the preceding page for list of abbreviations used.

DAWN OF THE
AUTOMOBILE AGE:1769~1885

*From the ancient Greeks, through the time of
Leonardo da Vinci, to the steam pioneers of the late
eighteenth century, it had been the impossible dream of
man to improve on the energies whipped out of a horse,
ox, steer, or other beast of burden and by mechanical
means to provide transport that either utilized forces in
natural state, or a fuel that, when brought under control, would furnish a fleeter chariot than the next.*

*To hot air, falling weights, clockwork, wind power,
passenger muscle, and gunpowder they applied their
wits—Jesuit priests of the fifteenth century, physicists
from Holland, noblemen of Switzerland, and engineers
of Italy. All labored, with varying degrees of failure, to
uncover a method of propelling a vehicle capable of
carrying its inventor. But the names of Huygens; of
Volta, who succeeded in igniting a gas mixture with an
electric spark; of Frenchman Lebon; of Englishman
Murdock; and of de Rivaz, who was granted patents as
early as 1807 for a combustion engine for road vehicles, are set in the halls of history and fame as pioneers
whose efforts edged us ever nearer the machine age. We
must honor them for their work. Perhaps we must also
forgive them, for they knew not what legacy they were
leaving us.*

*Stationary steam engines were fairly commonly used
for winches and pumps by the time the first genuine
road vehicle was built in 1769 by Nicholas-Joseph
Cugnot and offered as an innovation to the French
army—"a carriage moved by the effect of steam produced by fire." That Cugnot built his wagon for the
army is undoubted fact. The various reports of what
happened after it started to rumble its dinosaur way
down the Paris streets, on test, is now a confusion of
legend, but it almost certainly demolished a garden
wall en route.*

*Shortly afterward the clanking, steamy dawn of
motoring moved to England and Cornwall, where engineer Richard Trevithick fabricated something between a mail coach and a railway locomotive. In 1801
(the year that Cugnot's machine was finally consigned
to the Musée des Arts et Metiers in Paris, where it still
resides) Trevithick took out a party of friends in his
contraption. One described the journey thus: "We
jumped up, as many as could, maybe seven or eight of
us, when we see's that Captain Dick was agoing to turn
on steam... 'twas a stiffish hill but she went off like a bird,
and up the hill as fast as a man could walk." However,
Britain's first motorist absent-mindedly left the boiler
fire on one night, and the whole thing went up in smoke.*

*Thence to the steam-bus companies that first used
Britain's improved post-Napoleonic War roads, setting
up a network of relatively fast transport by around
1830. By 1835 they were being forced out of business,
as stagecoach and railway companies put on parliamentary and private pressure that caused the tolls*

*for steam business to be levied at something like twelve
times those for horse-drawn vehicles. In France steam
was also being developed, but without the crippling
legislation that England stamped on its first "automobile" ventures.*

*Stationary engines using coal (town) gas had been in
regular use since 1861, at first operating somewhat
feebly without a compression stroke. Efficiency was
vastly raised in 1876 when German engineer Otto built
in a fourth stroke for squeezing the mixture before ignition, giving us the conventional four-cycle unit. At the
Gasmotoren-Fabrik Deutz in Germany, then beginning
to produce the new Otto four-cycle engine, thirty-eight-
year-old Gottlieb Daimler was chief engineer.*

Dawn of the Automobile Age: 1769-1885

The use of steam for power was not new—even the ancient Greeks had a go at it. What *was* new was the application of steam power to propel a vehicle. 1769 is the date generally assigned for the debut of the first mechanically propelled road vehicle. A Frenchman, Nicholas Cugnot, was commissioned by the French Army to build something to tow heavy field artillery. While it certainly was not an automobile, a person or persons *could* ride upon it. Two years after the debut, Cugnot improved on his original, and had the dubious honor of participating in the world's first motor accident. It ran into a wall!

In the automobile's dawn age, new models didn't appear every year. It was some 15 years after Cugnot's first tractor that the Scottish engineer James Watt, who had been making stationary steam engines, and his assistant Will Murdock, built a steamer and tried it out in 1784.

Eighteen more years went by. Then another Britisher, Richard Trevithick, entered the scene with a high-wheeled steam coach that looked more like a locomotive than a carriage—but the contraption *worked*! It survived a journey from Cornwall to London in 1802—but to no particular enthusiasm from the public. It went to a fiery grave when Trevithick forgot to extinguish the boiler fire one night!

Cugnot Steam Tractor, 1769 (F).

Then, during the 1820's, the British began improving their primitive roads. Apparently, this was all the encouragement various entrepreneurs needed. Steam coach companies were formed, and for the next 15-20 years Britain had a network of regularly operated steam coach lines. But the railroads and horse-drawn coach companies got into the act, put pressure on Parliament, and were able to force through a set of tolls which, in some cases, were 12 times as high for the steamers as they were for the horse-drawn stagecoaches. Naturally, the steamers were driven out of business.

The drive for mechanical locomotion wasn't completely quenched in England. Smaller steam cars began to appear, usually operating in defiance of the law.

On the other side of the English channel, no such ruinous restrictions were placed on steam coaches. The twelve-passenger masterpiece shown on this page was christened "L'Obeissante," the obedient one. The French Minister of Works allowed it on the highway, provided Amédée Bollée, who built it as a sideline to his regular business of bell casting, gave three days advance notice of any journey he might undertake!

Also in France, the passenger car (steam-driven, of course) was beginning to take shape. The Comte de Dion had purchased a miniature steam engine. It fascinated him—and he searched out the manufacturer—one Georges Bouton. Together, they began to make steam cars through the 1880's—many of them quite successful. ·

Bollée Steam Coach, 1873 (F).

The Years of Promise:
1886-1899

Karl Benz was the complete automobile engineer and a practical businessman. He had worked on an engine designed to be an integral part of the total design of a road vehicle. Gottlieb Daimler was an equally skilled engineer, but had directed his efforts to an engine of universal application. He installed his first engine in a motorcycle, then a carriage. The following year, 1886, a small, self-propelled riverboat could be seen on the Neckar, and later a Daimler-engined airship made a maiden flight of four kilometers (2½ miles).

By means of a license to build Daimler engines, a death in the family, and a subsequent marriage, the French company of Panhard and Levassor became the first gasoline-engined automobile manufacturer in France — closely followed by Armand Peugeot, who built a car around the same power unit. By 1892 both companies were selling their products, and by 1894—the year of the first motor-sport event—motoring was established in France as a fashionable method of taking one's morning constitution in the Bois.

Benz had been on the French scene even earlier. One of his early models had been bought by Emile Roger, Benz' representative for stationary two-cycle engines in France (and who, curiously, kept it at the works of Panhard and Levassor), and in 1888 he started to sell, then assemble, Benz cars in France, under the name of Roger-Benz.

It took very little longer for American engineers to catch the fever, although for more practical reasons than the leisured European motoring set. Reliable transport over the vast reaches of the American continent was desperately needed, and "could transform life both social and commercial, if only the roads could be improved to accommodate the new vehicles," as one writer put it in 1897. The roads were not improved, but by 1900 no less than 8,000 private cars used them.

Britain needed a sort of gentlemanly revolution to get its automotive industry off the ground. An Act of Parliament that restricted speeds to 4 mph demanded that a pedestrian with a red flag should precede all vehicles, reducing their use to merely another way of saving boot leather. The Act was repealed in 1896 because of popular pressure in Parliament, but until that date it had delayed any serious participation in the infant industry that was to change the face of the world.

And so to the twentieth century. The years of the dreamers were over; man could now travel under a power many times superior to that of the horse—although, as often as not, he was less certain of reaching his destination. Mechanical layout was already that of the modern car—the 1891 Panhard had pioneered this—and the motor car actually worked. By the end of the nineteenth century the motor men were beginning to think not simply in terms of making the thing go, but of making it go well—there and back again.

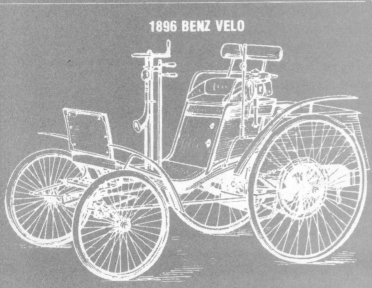

1896 BENZ VELO

1896 BENZ VIKTORIA

Karl Benz, 1844-1929.

atler Petrocycle, 1888 (GB).

Gottlieb Daimler, 1834-1900.

While the middle 1880's did not signal the death knoll of the steam-powered car, they did mark the beginning of a new power source which would take the automobile out of the playtoy class and develop it to one of the most potent social and business forces in the history of mankind. The power source was gasoline, called variously petrol, benzol, benzoline, etc.

The actual parentage of the automobile is obscured by many names. However, two men are recognized as the first to build practical gasoline-driven cars: Karl Benz and Gottlieb Daimler in 1886 built actual, working automobiles.

Benz's first was a four-stroke, 1-cylinder engine, which delivered less than 1 horsepower at 250 rpm. Daimler put his engine in a four-wheeled vehicle based on a carriage body. Actually, many years elapsed before the automobile stopped looking like a vehicle to which a horse should have been harnessed.

Daimler had the foresight to see the gasoline engine as a multipurpose tool. He powered a motorcycle with it, a motorboat, and in 1888, he flew it successfully in a primitive airplane, for 2½ miles!

The English were wakening to the possibilities, also. Edward Butler, son of a Devon farmer, took out a patent as early as 1884 "for the mechanical propulsion of bicycles", and actually produced his first in 1888. It traveled at 12 mph and possessed a 4-stroke engine with double rotary valves and an advanced jet-spray carburetor—years ahead of its time.

The Years of Promise: 1886-1899

By 1889, Gottlieb Daimler had concocted something which looked a little like a four-wheeled bicycle—a contradiction in terms. It was a light-weight two-seater which broke away from the carriage tradition. It used a dual-purpose tubular frame construction—first for strength—and second, the water which cooled the engine actually circulated through the tubular steel!

The public relations men were busy even in those days. In response to an early Benz piece of publicity entitled "A Complete Substitute for Carriage with Horses", the *Scientific American* ran an editorial in their January 5, 1889 issue which stated: "This motor is driven by gas which it generates from benzine or analogous material . . . the motor . . . is placed in the rear of the three-wheeled carriage over the main axle, and the benzine . . . is carried in a closed copper receptacle secured under the seat from which it passes drop by drop to the generator . . ."

Rene Panhard and Emile Levassor were partners in a woodwork machinery business. Then Levassor married the widow of the only Daimler licensee in all of France, and the state was set for automobile production in that country. Their first attempt was the dos-a-dos seen on this page. The bearded boulevardier on the extreme left is Rene Panhard.

By June of the following year, the second Panhard-Levassor car was ready. A contemporary report had it as follows: "With Levassor conducting (sic!) as far as Etratat . . . and home again without much trouble. His average was 10 km/h, sometimes touching 17 km/h in spite of pertrol that did no good to the sparking plugs." The car had one feature which should go into the annals of auto-dom: a front-mounted engine—the very first. And they're still mounting them there—80-odd years later!

Panhard-Levassor, 1890 (F).

In the meantime, another Frenchman, Armand Peugeot, bicycle-maker by trade, had seen what Panhard and Levassor had done with the Daimler engine, procured one, and installed it in a vehicle of his own design. By the time Panhard-Levassor's second car was on the road, Peugeot's was sufficiently practical to follow a bicycle race from Paris to Brest and back—some 650 miles as the crow flies. Peugot's quadricycle car averaged a spanking 10 mph, which was less than most of the bicycle racers—but the trip made history as the longest journey undertaken by an automobile to that date.

In his first year of production, Peugeot managed to turn out a total of 5 cars. Then a new company, called Les Fils de Peugeot Frères, was organized and developed the elegant vehicle on this page. The Victoria was a four-seater, had a twin-cylinder power unit (1282-cc), a leather cone clutch and boasted a claimed top speed of 30 km/h, which translates to 18½ mph. If true, it was pretty good boasting, since that speed put it in a class all by itself. The factory (at Beaulieu-Valentigney) built 18 of these beauties.

Early on, Panhard-Levassor had developed a layout: vertical front engine, followed by transmission, and rear wheel drive—which soon became famous as the "Panhard System." His partner, Emile Levassor, coined a phrase about their cars which went down in the annals of motor history: "C'est brusque et brutal, mais ce marche!" ("It's rough and brutish, but it goes!"

Peugeot Victoria, circa 1892 (F).

The Years of Promise: 1886-1899

In 1892, Daimler began to install a twin-cylinder, in-line power unit in his cars, supplanting his earlier V-twin.

In Mannheim, Germany, Karl Benz was busily engaged with his Viktoria, his first four-wheel model. The car, incidentally, was not named for the then current Queen of England. He chose the name because it reflected his victory over certain basic streering problems inherent in 4-wheel vehicles. His patent noted that it was a "steering mechanism for a car with steering circles set at a tangent to the wheels". It was what we know as "kingpin steering," and had been developed earlier by the coachbuilder to the royal court of Bavaria.

Two years later, in 1893, Benz had a collection of firsts in the Velo, which emerged from the Viktoria. As will be apparent from the photograph, it was a small car. That in itself was a first. Additionally, it was the first standard production car, and a good-sized step toward the goal of later manufacturers—a "people's car". It tootled along at 12 mph, and soon became the best-known of the Benz cars. And, it proved a stimulus for the entire industry on a world-wide basis.

One year later, a French newspaper, *Le Petit Journal*, had a bright promotional idea. They organized the world's first motor-sport event. The contest was a trial of reliability and was designed to encourage the use of automobiles as a means of arriving at a destination, as well as to promote the joys of traveling. The route was from Paris to Rouen, some 79 miles in all. Over 20 entrants left the starting line and the prize was

Benz Velo, 1893 (D).

divided between a Panhard and a Peugeot as the two most economical and reliable vehicles. A footnote: one entry, a 9-passenger steam bus, spent much of the trip picking up drivers of disabled vehicles!

As a second footnote of the historic Paris-Rouen trial, another steamer, a de Dion, came equipped with a passenger trailer! It arrived first in Rouen, but was placed second because *it needed a crew of two! Le Petit Journal,* in announcing the results of the race, said "Second prize (2000 francs) awarded to Messrs. De Dion, Bouton et Cie, for their interesting steam *tractor* which draws a carriage like a horse, and develops a speed beyond comparison, especially uphill"!

The 1894 Daimler shown was a vis-a-vis (face-to-face seating) and was one of the first cars imported into Britain. Its belt-drive gave it an unusual quietness in running and flexibility when starting or changing speeds. In 1896 an English friend of Daimler's gave the Prince of Wales, later Edward VII of England, his very first ride, in one of Daimler's belt-drive cars—a ride which stimulated the first real interest in motoring in Britain. The one in the photograph had a two-cylinder engine and could move along at 25 km/h-15½ mph.

In France, Leon Bolèe, son of the builder of "L'Obeissante", suffered from a cardiac disorder, and was told by his doctor to stay off his bicycle. He compromised by adding a third wheel and a 1-cylinder gasoline engine and called the result a "Voiturette". At the same time, in England, the general manager of a sheep-shearing company went him one better in the matter of cylinders, and came up with his own version of something small and light which would run. *His* name was Herbert Austin—which is still firmly entrenched in the international automobile world.

Daimler belt-drive, 1894 (D).

1895 Duryea (USA).

The car illustrated was the second effort of the two men who built America's first gasoline-engined automobile. Numero uno was seen for the first time in operation in Springfield, Massachusetts on September 21, 1893. The car in the picture, with Frank Duryea at the tiller, was photographed during the first American motor race, from Chicago to Evanston on Thanksgiving Day, 1895. The original was a 4 hp, 1-cylinder high-wheeler.

All sorts of oddities crop up in the history of the automobile in the pre-1900 years. In Surrey, England, a man named John Henry Knight had built steam cars during the late 1860's. By 1895, he had a contraption which looked like the front end of a haymower, but which contained a one-cylinder, water-cooled engine. With it, he could barrel along at 9 mph. He did just that and was arrested and fined for speeding in 1896. It's not strange that he was arrested—since he was driving at over *twice* the speed limit—which was 4 mph! In addition to the speed limitation, Parliamentary law required a pedestrian to precede, carrying a red flag!

Those Daimler engines were proliferating by this time. In addition to the cars bearing Daimler's name, Panhard had them in *their* cars—and they must have proved eminently worthy and valuable, because in 1895, they were in Panhard delivery trucks on the streets of Paris. In the same year, Panhard's partner, Emile Levassor, unofficially won the great Paris-Bordeaux race in a two-seater, Daimler-engined Panhard.

In what could have been called the first instance of mass production, Les Fils de Peugeot managed to produce 87 cars of one model during 1895-96. It was their 4-seater vis-a-vis,

Lanchester—1895-96 (GB).

with a twin cylinder horizontal engine, 1,056-cc capacity, with three forward speeds plus reverse. It moved along at 18½ mph, using 18 liters of gas every 100 kilometers. That translates to 15 miles to the gallon. Not exactly a gas guzzler—but in those days, just *traveling* 15 miles by car was an accomplishment!

The French, noted for volatility and elan, were not about to sit still after their first great race in 1894. The very next year, they were at it again, this time from Paris to Bordeaux and return. And it was a *real* race—not a test of reliability. It was this race that was unofficially won by Emile Levassor in a Panhard-Levassor two-seater.

From the notes of Marius Berliet, motor manufacturer of Lyons, France: "1895: I constructed a first small car with two seats in tandem, which succeeded in travelling from Lyons to Villefranche and back." The distance? 40 miles—and the small car was a quadricycle, with a rear horizontal engine. This was perhaps the very first example of a back-seat driver—because that's where the controls were!

In those middle 1890's, another name destined to become somewhat of a hallmark in the automotive world entered the scene in England. The car illustrated is the prototype Lanchester, and it was the first commercially successful 4-wheeled gasoline car to be made in the British Isles. Originally, it was steered with a tiller, but then converted to a steering wheel. About F. W. Lanchester, a modern editor said, "In my view, he is the only engineer in the early history of motoring. All the others were just mechanics." It *was* a sophisticated vehicle that Lanchester built, without reference to stationary engine tradition or horse-drawn carriage design.

In 1896, a clever promoter, one Edward J. Pennington of Chicago, managed to take advanatage of a situation which existed in England at the time. A newly formed organization called the British Motor Syndicate was attempting to come as close to cornering the market on automobile patents as was

The Years of Promise: 1886-1899

humanly possible. Pennington had designed a vehicle, a three-wheeler, which seated its 4 passengers on bicycle-type seats mounted on a skeletal frame. Pennington made highly exaggerated claims for his 2-cylinder, 2 hp 1868-cc unit, and the British Motor Syndicate had themselves a lemon.

There were probably as many failures in the early days as there were successes, since it seemed as though everyone was trying mightily to "get in the act." And, because it was a completely new industry, no one had any real experience with the finished product. Carriage-makers, stationary engine manufacturers (even men like Herbert Austin, who was general manager of a sheep-shearing company), bicycle makers—all leaped into the arena. One of the latter category was Alexandre Darracq. He sold his French bicycle company, turned to self-propelled vehicles, and began to turn out motorcycles, tri-cars and quadricycles. One of his three-wheelers bore a strong resemblence to a wheelchair—and all of them seemed to show bicycle parentage. He very likely regretted his abandonment of the bicycle business after a rather conspicuous failure in his attempt to build and sell an electric car.

Probably unbeknownst to the motor car antheap in Britain, Germany and France, some monumental thunder was building up across the ocean.

In Detroit, Henry Ford began tinkering with a gasoline engine (on his kitchen table, according to legend) as early as

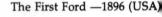

The First Ford —1896 (USA)

1893. In June of 1896, his first car was finished and running-with what consequences we all know.

Ransom Eli Olds came up with *his* version in the same year. One year **later**, R. E. Olds formed the Olds Motor Vehicle Company, thus becoming the oldest (no pun intended) automobile manufacturing company in the United States. Alex Winton moved into the picture in 1897 with an experimental car which delivered a very creditable 33.7 mph in a one-mile run. In Newton, Massachusetts, the Stanley Brothers had their first steamer in action the same year (1897) that Olds became a company. Stanley and Winton are long gone, of course, but Ford and Olds managed well enough.

It is not really surprising that Ford was able to achieve success. Even though his first car was a twin cylinder mounted on a frame suspended on four bicycle wheels, he had one big thing going for him—a lack of competition. In those years, new cars were erupting constantly in Britain and Europe. (Renault and FIAT were looming on the near horizon also). However, it is doubtful that what was going on in Europe had reached the American community in more than nebulous form. So, in the USA, the Fords, Olds's, Wintons, Cadillacs, Buicks, etc., were able to pursue their goals without comparison with or competition from their peers from the other side of the Atlantic.

In Germany, Benz and Daimler were the dominant early names. But another man—Lutzmann—built and displayed his wares in 1896-97. However, he found his real niche when another new name arrived—Adam Opel. The Opels had made sewing machines as early as 1862, later turning to bicycles. In 1897, they acquired production rights to the Lutzmann car. The following year the first Lutzmann-Opel rolled from the factory. It was a real whizzer: the single-cylinder engine cruised at 19 mph-and it was rumored to have a top speed of 30 mph on level ground.

Take a cane chair, stick it on a frame, add four mudguards, wheels, headlamps, and a two-cylinder, rear-mounted engine and presto—a Wartburgwagen. Oddly enough, it sold very well in Germany at the close of the nineteenth century. Perhaps the fact that the 765-cc engine, which developed 5 hp at 1000 rpm and pushed it along at nearly 25 mph was responsible for its success. The question remains, what sane person would ride in this flimsy contraption at that speed? Any why was it called by that awkward name? Because the Eisenach Company, which built the car under a Decauville license, was located in Wartburg, Germany!

One question which was asked in the fledgling days of the automobile doesn't get asked today: will it run? Once this was established, another question popped up: Very well, it runs—but how far? And then finally, when a certain amount of belief in the automobile's ability to travel somewhere and *return* had been established, the age-old question which had been asked of practically everything that moved: how fast will it go? By 1898 in Europe, cars were speeding from one place to another, setting new records every day. In France, a Peugeot raced from Marseilles to Nice and back—some 146 miles—at an average speed of 32 mph. When you stop to think about it, that's better than the average of a modern-day motorist driving into downtown from the suburbs of a major city! In the same year, international racing began with the

20

race of the year from Paris to Amsterdam and return. The airline distance is over 500 miles. Heaven only knows what a good odometer would have registered as the total mileage for the trip. Even longer was the Paris to Marseille jaunt—over 800 miles.

A Frenchman established the very first *world* speed record on December 18, 1898, in an *electric* car! He was the Comte Gaston de Chasseloup-Laubat and the vehicle, looking more like a farm cart than an automobile, was a Jeantaud. This Parisian company, after building an experimental car as early as 1891, had been in production since 1893. The record the Comte established over a 1 km course (about 6/10 of a mile) was 39.24 mph. As any sports fan will tell you, records were made to be broken. This one was, and promptly, by one Camille Jenatzy, who built another electric car to his own design. A few weeks later, the record was recaptured by the Jeantaud—and this time it was pushed up to 43.69 mph.

Jeantaud Electric, 1898 (F).

The Years of Promise: 1886-1899

Two more new names stepped on the stage of the automotive world in 1898-99. A garden-shed tinkerer named Louis Renault built a small car based on a de Dion tricycle, tested it on Christmas Eve of 1898, and had himself a fine Christmas present in the shape of a dozen orders from friends. His next effort was a four-wheeler, and was based on nothing but his own ideas. His contemporaries couldn't quite make up their minds about him—he was called a poet, a dunce and a genius. However, M. Renault did start a business that became the largest of its type in France. One of the reasons for Renault's success may have been the fact that he had some compunction for those who were to ride in his cars. He was the first to attempt a sedan. Odd-looking it may have been, but it was the very first time a car was offered with permanent, built-on protection against the weather.

The other name? Fabbrica Italiana Automobili Torino. Would they have become the Italian automobile colossus if they hadn't shortened it to F.I.A.T.? Suffice it to say that the first one was a 3½ hp, 2-cylinder, rear-engined, 679-cc, chain-driven vis-a-vis typical of the period. Perhaps no one minded riding backwards in those days!

By 1896, Humber was in the automobile business. And in 1899, they came up with a four-wheeler which more or less reversed things—a front-wheel drive, with rear-wheel steering!

Fifty-seven cars went on display at Old Deer Park, Richmond, near London, for one of the first Automobile Shows in England. The entertainment included, among other events, a zig-zag post race and a backwards race. Exhibitors included an Automotette, a de Dion, and Orient Express and a Vallee racing car. The damsel on the poster is in a Léon Bollée, followed by a golfer in what was probably a de Dion Bouton tricycle. Golf cart—in 1899?

Steam power, in contrast to electricity, fared rather well in the matter of longevity. It was used as motive power for automobiles into the 1930's, in the shape of the rather sophisticated Doble. The Stanley Brothers made their first steamer in 1897—and sold over 200 of them in their initial year. And in 1899, they built one that actually made it to the top of Mount Washington in New Hampshire.

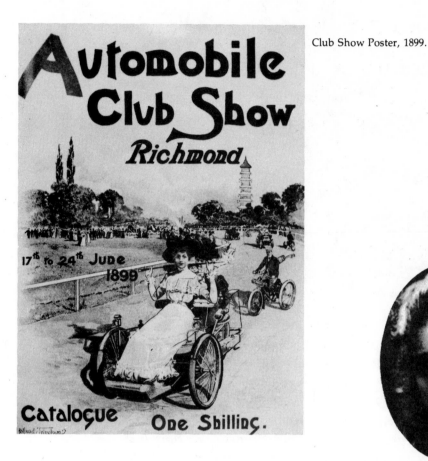

Club Show Poster, 1899.

Mercedes Jellinek

By 1899, top speeds were pushing higher and higher. A Cannstatt-Daimler with a 5-liter, 4 cylinder power unit could do a very respectable 50 mph. This was one of the first cars designed for competition. Emil Jellinek, Daimler's representative in Nice, France, had suggested the idea of a competition car. Its speed was satisfactory, but it proved to have a dangerously high center of gravity. Noting this, Jellinek suggested that the center of gravity be lowered, along with other modifications. His suggestions were followed, and when the new model needed a name, Jellinek further suggested it be named for his daughter. Her name just happened to be—Mercedes!

Daimler, 1899 (G B).

The picture is from 1899, and the result was a long-lasting love affair between the British Royal Family and Daimler. The bearded gentleman is Britian's Prince of Wales, and in 1900, he bought a Daimler. Daimler's patents had been purchased by an Englishman, J. R. Simms—and he made the first British Daimler in 1896. Apparently he couldn't meet the demand, because Daimlers were still imported into England until 1900. The car illustrated is a 12-hp, 3-liter vehicle.

Karl Benz was convinced that automobiles were basically brittle and self-destructive. It seems an odd viewpoint for a man who created such a lasting impression in the world of automobiles. However, he was quoted as follows: "A car which can attain a speed of over 60 km/h (about 37 mph) will soon rattle itself to pieces." All of this didn't prevent his 1900 racing car, which produced 20-30 hp, from winning the first international track race at Frankfurt, Germany over a 30-mile course. He could have been quite correct in his thinking, though, because racing cars are built not for endurance, but for speed—and racing cars in the turn-of-the-century era, driven at top speed over the roads of the period would undoubtedly have left bits and pieces of themselves all over the landscape. A road constructed for horse-drawn vehicles, which proceeded at 3-5 mph, was hardly a superhighway.

Merry Olds To Limited

In 1900 the French were leaders of the automotive world. Their industry had moved into commercial success more rapidly than the Benz and Daimler concerns in Germany and were flooding a small but eager market with products labelled Panhard, Peugeot, Bollée and de Dion Bouton. The first two were using the Daimler-designed engine built under licence; various members of the bell-making Bollée family were offering light cars, and Count de Dion and partner Georges Bouton were making popular voiturettes.

Benz had produced some 2,000 cars and Daimler's engines were in demand for various purposes, some unconnected with transportation, but de Dion was making and selling some 200 vehicles a month by 1900—more than the combined production of Britain and Germany together.

The following year was to change the balance. In March, Daimler's new car, called Mercedes after his agent's daughter, showed the world a vehicle that heralded a new era of motoring. In a week of sporting competition in the South of France it rendered all other entries obsolete.

In Britain 1900 ushered in the Thousand Mile Trial, a round-Britain motor cruise that introduced the automobile to the people, most of whom had never before seen a self-propelled vehicle.

In the United States the first ten years of the 20th Century saw the rise—and the eclipse—of the Curved Dash Oldsmobile, the 'Merry Olds' that offered mobility to drummers and doctors and, with its go-anywhere construction and light motor finally broke through the 'horse-barrier' and took America into the motoring age. The decade saw the progress from this light 'one-lung' buggy to the famous Oldsmobile 'Limited' a 60 hp vehicle of great sophistication and elegance.

This gentle era also saw the rise of the marathon races. Since the end of the century European sportsmen had pitted their ever-growing cars against each other in long, transcontinental races—from Paris to Marseilles—Paris to Berlin—to Vienna, to Madrid (where a tragedy cut short the event and ended major road racing, forcing contests to be modified to take place on closed circuits). The Vanderbilt Cup was first run at Long Island in 1904; the French Grand Prix and the grueling Targa Florio in 1906, the American Prize in 1908. In Britain the world's first racing circuit, Brooklands, had been opened in 1907. The World Land Speed Record had been bitterly fought over, and by March 1910 American Barney Oldfield had recorded 131.72 mph at Daytona in a Benz.

Although most cars still used chain drive well into this period several manufacturers had produced shaft driven vehicles; engines had long since settled down at the front end of the car, most transmissions followed the conventional pattern of clutch, gearbox, final drive. Wheels, until around 1906, were not detachable and every flat tire had to be levered off with the wheel in situ.

The years through 1909 were those in which auto engineers turned their energies from 'making it go' to 'making it go well' and by 1909 the role of the car had changed from that of a toy to that of economic transportation with a secure place in the domestic and commercial scene.

1900-1909

FIAT, 1900 (I)

Here it is—the car that began an automobile empire. This was the same basic layout as the 1899—2 cylinders, 1,082-cc, 6 hp. One year later, FIAT upped the horsepower to 10, without changing the mechanics. Judged by today's standards, it isn't good for much more than a laugh or two—but it did the job in the early 1900's.

In addition to the Daimler-British Royal Family billing and cooing, another element, also in 1900, got the British interested in the automobile. Prior to this event, the car was almost a legend in the Isles—it's probably safe to say that at least half of the population had never seen one.

The famed English newspaper proprietor, Lord Northcliffe, had seen what exploded in France as a result of the contest held by Le Petit Journal of Paris in 1894 and succeeding years. He proposed a 1000-mile trial for reliability as well as speed, and got sponsorship from the Automobile Club of Great Britian and Ireland. (This later became the Royal Automobile Club.) The whole affair was an unmitigated success, both in numbers of cars entered, and even more important, numbers of cars finishing.

An outfit called the Motor Manufacturing Company produced, also in 1900, a car which, 53 years later, was driven from John o' Groats in Scotland to Land's End in the Southwest corner of England in ten days—and on solid tires. If nothing else, it says something about the durability of the passengers! The car, incidentally, was a 6-hp, twin-cylinder with no protection for driver or passengers—and the trip was made in cold weather.

Columbia Electric, 1901 (USA).

This little electric car carried concealed beneath its not-very-attractive exterior nearly one ton of batteries. It must have worked, and worked profitably—they were New York City's first taxis—and were seen everywhere on Gotham's streets. It was marketed in England also, under the name City and Suburban. Queen Alexandra, wife of King Edward VII (he was the one who, as Prince of Wales, was bitten by the Daimler bug) bought one of the City and Suburban electrics for use in her garden at Sandringham House.

In 1901, Karl Benz was having his problems. He moved his engines to the front and lengthened his driving belt, and in general, updated his designs. But a new star was rising in Europe. The car named for Emil Jellinek's daughter had challenged Benz's designs with many new advances—and Benz's sales began to drop. It wasn't that Benz wasn't still making a good car, (his 1901 Spider still had a top speed of 37 mph), but Daimler's Mercedes was a better one. This, of course, is part and parcel of the history of the automotive industry. As one of the characters in *Alice in Wonderland* so trenchantly remarked, "It takes all the running you can do to stay in the same place!"

1901 was a strong year for FIAT. In his swan song with FIAT, the original company engineer produced a 2-cylinder front vertical engine. The company entered eight of this model in the first Tour of Italy (the course covered 1,000 miles) and all eight actually finished! Then FIAT added a four-cylinder model with a honeycomb radiator. The 12-hp, 3.7-liter unit developed 16 bhp, and ran at a maximum of 43 mph.

No wonder it hit the industry like a runaway train! With its 5.9 liter engine and a power output of 35 hp at 8,000 rpm, the Mercedes was the first car to have mechanically operated inlet valves, which meant considerably increased engine efficiency. Its 4 cylinders were cast in pairs (each pair fed by a jet carburetor), and engine speed could be regulated by a hand lever within a range of 300 to 1,000 rpm by altering spring tension on a governor. These and other advances moved the Mercedes far ahead of others on the market at that time. And besides, it *looked* like a car, not a variation of a horse-drawn vehicle.

In the spring of that year, the first Mercedes racing car won the steep Le Turbie (a village on the mountainside above Monte Carlo) hill-climb at an incredible average of 31.9 mph—which would be difficult to duplicate even today. Mercedes cars won almost every event that week, prompting one Frenchman to write "Nous sommes entrés dans L'ère Mercedes" (We have entered the Mercedes era.).

Steam had a strong following at this time, and the French *automobile a vapeur* by Serpollet was one of the more advanced. By 1901, an American named Gardner bought into the company, and a Gardner-Serpollet broke the world's speed record at Nice in 1902. How fast? As amazing 75.06 mph! One of the reasons for the popularity of steam was undoubtedly the fact that its speed seemed to be limited only by the size and compression limitation of the boiler. By 1900, Serpollet numbered the Shah of Persia and the Prince of Wales among his customers.

One of the reasons the curved-dash, motorized buggy was a big success for Oldsmobile was probably the fact that it *looked* as though it should have had a horse attached to the front end! Timorous would-be buyers seemed to welcome the familiar look and feel of something they'd been used to all their lives. The one-cylinder engine, according to the stand-up comics, gave "one chug per telegraph pole". But Oldsmobile built and sold 15,000 of them!

Oldsmobile, 1901 (USA).

One of the real oddities in automobile construction turned up at about this time. It was a Sunbeam Mabley with oddball wheel positioning, which forced the driver, at the rear, to sit facing the passenger in a sort of curved love-seat arrangement. No one ever would use the vehicle as a getaway car for a robbery—the tire tracks were unique. One rear wheel, one front wheel, two middle wheels—but the front and rear wheels were offset! Since they were not in line with each other (or with the two middle wheels) the car produced 4 separate and distinct tire tracks! And the whole thing was steered by a spade-grip tiller, which hopefully turned the offset front and rear wheels at the same time. Quite deservedly, this Sunbeam-Mabley went to an early grave.

Between August and November of 1902, the world speed record was broken three times—by the same car, but with 3 different drivers. The car was a French Mors, and the first driver, American Willis K. Vanderbilt, took it up to 76.08 mph. The next, a Frenchman named Fournier, pushed it a notch higher at 76.60 mph, and twelve days later, another Frenchman, this time named Augieres, got it to 77.13.

Cadillac Model A, 1902-1903 (USA).

We all have to start somewhere, and the prestigious name of Cadillac began with a 1-cylinder, 5 × 5 inch, 9.7 hp offering. Two passengers, and included were *patent leather* fenders at no extra cost! Brass lamps, horn, etc. were extras. The magazine *Horseless Age* said of the new Cadillac: "The vehicle is of the runabout type, but is probably heavier and stronger than the average representative of this type." That padded seat was rather more of a necessity than a luxury—the driver sat directly over the engine!

An American, George Cannon, built a contraption that looked a little like a wheeled two-man bobsled with a steam boiler between front and rear. In 1902-1903, "Flyer", which was his term for the home-built steamer, set several class records. It was a full-time job for the front and rear men—front steered, and rear handled all the other controls, which was a sort of throwback to the English steam buses of the mid-1800's.

At about the same time the first of the completely German Opels appeared, in the form of a 10-12 hp tonneau, housing a 1.8 liter, 2-cylinder engine. Very advanced features: automatic lubrication, gear shift on the steering column, and (very, *very* advanced) shaft drive.

Panhard went all out to capture the Paris-Vienna race in 1902. Their cars were huge, even by today's standards—13 liter engines, no less. But Renault won the race in a car which was smaller, lighter and faster, as evinced by the fact that when the Renault hit the finish line in Vienna first among 117 competitors, it was so far ahead that officials at first refused to believe the car was even *in* the race!

Stanley Steamer, circa 1902 (USA).

The Stanley steamer was the product of two brothers who were formerly photographic plate workers. After the model in the picture was produced, the brothers introduced a non-condensing engine, with a front-mounted boiler. Start-up speed, always a problem with the early steamers, must have been pretty good on these cars. Evidence of this is noted in the fact that Stanleys were much used by American police and fire department forces. The reference to photographic plates is not an idle one—that's George Eastman (of Kodak fame) and friend out for a spin in a 1902 Stanley.

There is in existence right now, somewhere in England, a one-cylinder, 5 hp two-seater Peugeot from 1902. It was imported at that time from France to Britain and sold to an owner who crashed it—then got rid of it on the ground that it was "quite uncontrollable". Someone rediscovered it in 1935, restored it (at heaven only knows how much expense, time and trouble) and today, this crashed, uncontrollable antique takes its present owner to rallies all over Europe!

During this 1902-1903 period, a new American name appeared on the rolls—only the man who bore the name was a native Scotsman who had emigrated to the USA and worked as a plumber and engineer in Detroit. The man was David Buick, and his first effort was a 2 cylinder, 2.6 liter, valve-in-head (ohv) engine mounted under the seat. He made sixteen of them before another man, whose promotional abilities made him famous, took over. The newcomer was William C. Durant, and the first thing he did after grasping the production reins was to institute a dramatically drastic price hike, taking Buick out of the "cheap car" category for all time.

Mercedes, 1903 (D).

Is it a freight car? A bus? History doesn't tell us—but the pictured Mercedes was probably designed for a private owner with a *very* large family, or equally probable, a pick-up limousine for a swanky hotel. At any rate, it boasted not only a 65 hp, 9-liter, 4-cylinder engine, but 10 windows, plus windshield and rear window. In case of an accident, think of the bill for glass alone!

1903 was the year of a race which had probably the highest mortality rate in the history of the automobile. Paris to Madrid was the course—over 750 airline miles, via the miserable country roads of France. Speeds as high as 85 mph were recorded on those roads, and the air was filled with wrecked parts (and bodies). Drivers, mechanics and even spectators died. So widespread was the carnage that the race was stopped after the first leg. And fortunate it was for the survivors, for the death toll might have been monumentally higher, had the cars attempted the Pyrenees mountains and the even rougher roads of Spain. Among those who died was Marcel Renault. His brother Louis was also in the race, but survived.

Another first in 1903—the first Vauxhall. A light car with chain drive, it proved popular with its forty owners—the entire first year's production. It was powered by a single-cylinder unit, horizontally mounted, with coil springs. Two forward speeds—but no reverse. Just keep going and don't look back!

32

The first Daimler vehicle, 1885. A 'single track'
machine of one cylinder and one-half horsepower. (D)

Karl Benz built this three-wheeler, his first machine,
in 1885 and patented it in January 1886. (D)

Gottlieb Daimler's first 'motorwagen', 1886. Four wheels and 1.1 horsepower. (D)

Peugeot vis-à-vis, 1892. (F)

Opel Luzmann, 1898. Single-cylinder, 19 mph. (D)

Benz Landaulet-coupé, 1899. Straight out of the carriage era. (D)

Cannstatt Daimler 1899. (D)

Daring De-Dion publicity, 1899. (F)

Renault single-cylinder voiturette, 1899.

The Ford 999, 1904 (USA).

91.37 miles an hour—in 1904, no less! With the famous racing driver Barney Oldfield at the controls and Henry Ford by his side (in the picture, not during the run!). The 999 had no gears, no clutch, no body—just a flat bed, wheels, an engine and a steering tiller. But on the surface of a frozen lake near Detroit, this monster did a mile at that incredible speed. Question: at 91.37 miles per hour, on ice, how did Oldfield stop the thing—even if it had brakes?

More civilized, albeit a lot slower, was the 1903 FIAT. It was a tonneau with a fold-back canvas—very handy if the rain came straight down! Developing 16/24 hp with an engine of just over 4 liters, it was highly sophisticated for its day, even though armored wood frames were still used in construction. Surprisingly, it was a six-seater and could cruise at 35 mph.

Another new name from 1903—Colonel Albert Pope. His Pope-Hartford of that year was a "one-lunger", conventionally designed and very popular. The company ceased to exist in 1914, but holds a surprisingly firm place in American automobile "folklore".

In England, also in 1903, the Standard Motor Company came into being. Its aim was to produce "a car to be composed purely of those components whose principles have been tried and tested . . . .". Sensible, indeed—when fledgling manufacturers were building wildly impractical vehicles in the first flush of enthusiasm over motor design.

Merry Olds To Limited: 1900-1909

Buick, 1904 (USA).

Even though the 1904 Buick was considerably more advanced than the earlier car, owners were not out of the woods in regard to repair, maintenance and breakdowns en route. The catalog for 1904 listed "horn, lamps, tool-box with sufficient tool equipment, *mats and rubber aprons to go under the car.*" In spite of the melancholy which must have been inspired by those italicized items, the 2-cylinder engine proved to be a winner and was continued almost without change in some Buick products until 1910.

This paragraph is included solely because of the name of an English company which first made quadricycles in 1898, then progressed to a shaft-driven, single-cylinder 7 hp 3-seater. Almost as remarkable as the name is the fact that nearly seventy years after its manufacture, at least one was still running. The name? Alldays and Onions Pneumatic Engineering Limited!

Time to mention another British manufacturer which had progressed, by 1904, to the point where two factories were necessary. Humber produced its less expensive models at Beeston in Nottinghamshire, while the higher-priced cars were made at Coventry, which was the real cradle of the British automotive industry.

That land speed record set by Barney Oldfield on the ice didn't last long. In the same year, 1904, it was broken twice. First by a Darracq at 104.52 mph, and then by a Gabron-Brillie at nearly 1 mph faster. Not long before the 100 mph barrier was breached, scientists argued that man could not breathe at over 70 mph!

No wonder FIAT became the colossus of the Italian automotive industry—3 months after opening for business, they had entered motor sport and actually won a race with a 75 hp, 14-liter, 4-cylinder Corso (racer) at an average speed of 72 mph. The car was driven by Vincenzo Lancia, who was later to build his own cars—very fine ones, indeed.

xwell, 1904 (USA)

The car pictured is the very first Maxwell—a roadster with a 2-cylinder 8-hp unit and planetary transmission. The company was formed by a sheet-metal worker, Benjamin Briscoe, and a mechanic, J. D. Maxwell. That first year—1904—they produced the rather remarkable total of 540 cars. Four years later, annual production had reached 8,000. How many would they have sold if Jack Benny had been available in those days?

In France, the Compagnie Parisienne des Voitures Electriques was producing, quite naturally, an electric car called the Krieger. It had *two* electric motors—each driving one front wheel, which gave the driver a sort of power-assisted steering. And (remember—this was 1904!) four-wheel brakes. 15 mph was top speed, and it could go 50 miles before the batteries needed a charge—or at least so claimed the Compagnie!

In the town of Staines, near London, an American named Wilbur Gunn founded the Lagonda Motor Company. Early on, they made a steam launch, then motorcycles. By 1904, they started production on twin-cylinder tri-cars. Gunn, a stickler for precision, insisted that with the exception of the carburetor, every part (even down to nuts and bolts) be made in his own factory. The result was some very reliable Lagondas, as may be imagined.

The French Mors was a genuine luxury car in 1904. Heavy, with a 4-cylinder, 24/32 hp plant, the Roi de Belges model was big enough and luxurious enough to be named after the King of the Belgians. Rumor had it that the Belgian monarch ordered one of these lavish, elegantly styled vehicles at the behest of his mistress.

5 Opels—Carl, Wilhelm, Fritz, Ludwig, Adam

They only *look* like a vaudeville act—the "five Rus-sellsheimers", as they were known at the time. Each of the five was active in the Opel company. The car is a racer (shown with Fritz Opel at the wheel) which, for a brief time, held a world speed record in 1904 at 105.1 mph. By this time, the Opels were one of the leading German manufacturers, as well as living advertisements for bowler hats, wing collars and cigarettes. (Adam was a little too young to smoke!)

Rolls-Royce? Certainly—but there was a Royce car before the Honorable Charles Rolls, son of Lord Llangattock, hitched his name in front. Henry Royce completed his first car in 1904—a 1.8 liter, 2-cylinder model at his Cooke Street works in Manchester, England. Later that same year, Rolls and Royce got together, and the most famous hyphenated name in automotive history was born.

More than 100 different makes of steam cars had been manufactured in the USA by the time the Doble died in 1932. One of the most popular was the 1904 White. It was highly successful in the Glidden Tours (first held in 1905; 870 miles from New York City to the White Mountains and back) and had achieved a "perfect score" in the 650 mile reliability trials held in Britain. The company sold steam cars until 1911, although by 1909 they had added a gasoline car to their line. In 1906, after the disastrous San Francisco fire and quake, Whites were used to speed rescue operations and transport anti-looting troops throughout the area.

Opel rennwagen, 1904 (D).

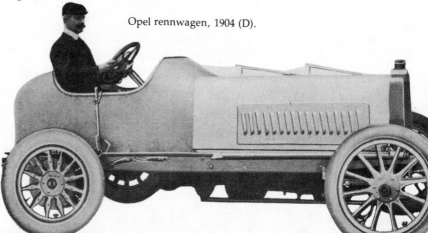

Model B Cadillac, early 1905 (USA).

Later in the year in which the Cadillac pictured was produced, the company made a move in the direction it was to go and flourish. They went to multi-cylindered cars, in spite of the success of their one-lungers. The Model D was a four-cylinder effort using a 30 hp unit. Some curtailment of production of the single-cylinder model was involved, but Cadillac was convinced that multi-cylinder cars were the wave of the future and put its money into them.

The following year (1905) Ford jumped into the 4-cylinder pond, with its model B, using two-speed planetary transmission. Even though the engine was under the floorboards, Ford hung a dummy hood in front to give the car the front-engined look demanded by an increasing number of buyers. The model B Cadillac used the same devious approach.

The first Volkswagen was called a "Volksautomobil", and was produced by this jawbreaker: Suddeutch Automobil-Fabrik at Gaggenau in Germany. It was a pee-wee: 1-cylinder, 1.4 liters, 4 hp, and 30 km/h (18-plus mph). Suddeutch was bought up by Benz in 1908.

The Vanderbilt Cup race, in its heyday the greatest thing in motor sports, had to be abandoned eventually because the spectators became uncontrollable. The race was so well-known and well-publicized that a Broadway musical was named for it!

Oldsmobiles, 1905 (USA).

By the time 1905 rolled around, the curved-dash Oldsmobile was the best-known small car in the United States. R. E. Olds, however, was always interested in publicity, so that when a public roads official suggested a transcontinental race by these cars, Olds readily agreed.

The event started from New York City on May 8, 1905 and ended at Portland, Oregon, over 4,000 miles of poor roads and multiferous emergencies. The roads were "wet, sticky and treacherous", according to contemporary accounts by the contestant drivers. Gasoline cost more per gallon as the cars trekked westward, (twice as expensive in Wyoming as Ohio) and the competitors either had to search it out or arrange with stagecoach drivers to have tins left at preselected spots. An example of the kind of ingenuity required in those days: in an earlier race, when the tires gave trouble and began losing air, the drivers merely filled the tires with oats—and kept on rolling!

Old Scout, the car on the left in the photograph, arrived in Portland forty-four days after the start. This doughty vehicle is still in running condition today.

A certain amount of business intermarriage went on in the early days of this century. The German Opel, using a French Darracq chassis to support its own Opel body, produced a 4-cylinder, 16/18, watercooled car with a claimed top speed of 60 km/h (37 mph).

Late in 1905, the first Standard Six—a six-cylinder engine, 18/20 hp was fitted to a low-slung touring car. A Standard was exported from Britain to Canada in that same year and caused excited headlines in the metropolitan Canadian dailies.

Model K Ford, 1906, (USA).

In 1906, Ford took a flying leap into the luxury market with his 6-cylinder, 6-liter Model K. He undoubtedly came to wish he had kept flying lower and slower, since the K soon developed transmission troubles, which led to sales troubles, which in turn discouraged the sage of Dearborn so badly that he abandoned six-cylinder cars for over 30 years. As a matter of fact, the K sold so badly that Ford had to double his dealer discount, just to get dealers to handle this ill-fated model. Well, you can't win 'em all!

For the very first French Grand Prix, held in 1906 at Le Mans, France, tar had been laid on the 65-mile Sarthe circuit. However, someone forgot to take into account the weather, which was hot. The tar melted, and flying blobs of the gooey black stuff became the order of the day. As a result, several of the drivers were temporarily blinded, since racing cars don't use windshields. One of the drivers who fell victim to this mishap actually continued in the race—and won it, no less!—in a Renault at an average speed of 62.8 mph, in a total 2-part time of 12 hours, 46 minutes, 26 seconds. Many drivers today seem to be similarly afflicted.

Did you know that the American Reo got its name from the initials of R. E. Olds, of Oldsmobile fame? Olds quarreled with his partner, (who was the majority stockholder) left the company which bore his name and went into business for himself. The result was the Reo, which, alas for Mr. Olds, failed to outlast his original company.

One of the most famous cars in automotive history first appeared in 1906. Henry Royce and Charles Stewart Rolls had finally gotten together with a working agreement late in 1904. In 1906, the Silver Ghost emerged. As was to be the case during the entire history of the company, it was the product of Henry Royce's continued quest for mechanical perfection.

The aluminum-painted touring body gave the car its name, which was used for almost twenty years. The 40/50 hp side-valve engine had 6 cylinders, 7-liter capacity and a phenomenal degree of silence was achieved by having a special expansion chamber for each cylinder.

In 1907, after a year of use, the car was driven *non-stop* for 14,000 miles. When torn down and examined after the non-stop run, it was found to need very few replacements. No one really knows how many miles a Silver Ghost will run, or how many years one will last—the car illustrated (the original) has travelled over 500,000 miles, and has no intentions of retiring.

In January of 1906, just before the first Austin appeared on the roads of England, Herbert Austin announced to the world that his cars would be "the embodiment of all the best features in modern automobile construction." Granted, it was an ambitious statement, but Austin's earliest production models were *not* experimental machines, but full-fledged cars. The Austin factory opened in 1906, and in a little over two years, produced no less than seventeen different models!

A man named Alanso P. Brush built single-cylinder light cars until 1907. Then his company merged into U.S. Motors, which, in turn, disappeared in 1913. But Brush had another

40

The First Hillman—1907 (GB).

arrow in his quiver. He designed the first Oakland, which became a part of General Motors, but alas, the Oakland name, after a number of honorable years, was finally dropped by GM.

Louis Coatalen was in his mid-twenties (a British Louis Renault?) when he designed the first car for William Hillman in 1907. It turned out to be a 4-cylinder, 25 hp built for the Tourist Trophy race of that year. It was not until 1912 that the company, still producing in small numbers, turned to the light car, a 9 hp model, that set the pattern of Hillmans for many years. The designer is at the wheel in the photograph.

On June 11, 1907 possibly the most wildly imaginative race in automotive history to that date was begun.

Five cars left Peking (China!) to "race" to Paris—10,000 miles away. Believe it or not, someone actually won the race—and 4 out of the 5 cars finished! The winner was a huge 4-cylinder, 40 hp Itala, driven by Italian royalty—no less than Prince Borghese was at the wheel. It took sixty days of untold trials and provocations, crossing deserts and swamps, rivers and mountains, rainstorms, windstorms and, of course, the enormous wasteland of Siberia, but finally the victorious Italian car pulled into Paris. It was three weeks later before two de Dions and a Dutch Spyker got there. History doesn't record what make the fifth car was, or what its fate. Possibly it was eaten by Chinese dragons.

One last sidelight on the race: the Prince must have been a lineal descendant of the Medici. He outsmarted his competitors by driving across Siberia on the *roadbed* of the trans-Siberian railroad, reasoning that bumping along across railroad ties was preferable to taking to the local Siberian roads. His biggest problem during this section of the race was avoiding being pot-shot by the extensive bandit population of the region!

Merry Olds To Limited: 1900-1909

The Model A Cadillac shown here, considerably gussied up by the addition of auto club insignia, a lone headlamp and a butler serving coffee to S. F. Bennett at the wheel, was so successful that it was produced until 1909. However, a bit of Cadillac memorabilia from 1908 is noteworthy. In that year, Bennett organized a test. In England, three later model Cadillacs (Model K's) were totally dismantled, the parts thoroughly mixed up, and from the disassembled parts, three cars were re-assembled and track-tested. They all worked perfectly. It might be difficult to duplicate this feat today!

Ford Model A (USA).

Another Model A was introduced in the year of the Ford Motor Company's incorporation. It was sold on July 22 of that year, to a Dr. Phennig of Chicago, much to the relief of the very nervous stockholders. Their nervousness was occasioned by the fact that the company's bank balance was dwindling to the point of extinction. The Model A Ford could be had with a detachable tonneau that clamped to the back of the vehicle, which increased the passenger capacity to four. For those finicky about being rained upon, there was an optional leather top with side glass portholes. The car housed a flat-twin engine mounted under the floor, and was described (by the company) as "so simple a boy of 15 can run it".

The White Sewing Machine Company of Cleveland got into automobiles when the three White Brothers bought a steam vehicle for study, decided they could do better, and went into business in 1900. By 1903 they had a 2-cylinder, 10 hp vehicle which bore a strong resemblance to a gasoline-fueled car. This model was built with a front engine and a steering wheel—the first of their line to have these features.

Cadillac Model A (USA).

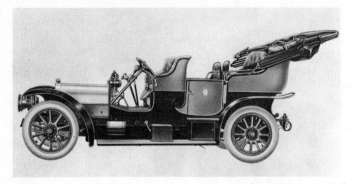

Laurent Klement (CS).

This Type E, 4-cylinder 4½-liter, 24-hp beauty was stylish enough to belong to a European monarch of pre-World War I days. L&K was yet another company to have a go at the Royal Automobile Club's nonstop run between London and Holyhead in North Wales, a distance of 265 miles to be negotiated without one single engine stop. Two Bohemian cars succeeded in the attempt. Bohemia became part of Czechoslovakia after the war. In 1925 Laurin and Klement was taken over by an arms firm, and the product became known as Skoda.

Also in 1907, Brooklands Motor course, the world's first genuine permanent race track, was opened. In June, a month before the first race, Selwyn Edge took a stripped-down 6-cylinder Napier and drove it single-handed for 24 hours around the course at an average speed of 65.91 mph. High speed, indeed, for those fledgling racing days.

The pre-war German empire, not to be outdone, had its own annual big race—the Kaiserpreis. In 1907, two Opels driven by two Opel brothers finished third and fourth, and the 8-liter model received the *"Besten Deutschen Wagen"* award.

The 1907 International Tourist Trophy was captured by a 20-hp Rover. This is Britain's oldest race (first run in 1905) and one of the first to be run on a regular basis. The Rover Tourer that won in 1907 beat out a number of much better-known cars: Darracq, Mettalurgique, Berliet, Humber and sixteen others. The Rover completed the Isle of Man course in 8:23:17, an average of 28 miles per hour. The chances of several close contenders were blown sky-high when they ran out of fuel nearing the finish line!

If there seems to be an inordinate amount of emphasis on racing in automobiling's early days, blame it on the desire of the manufacturers for an edge—any kind of edge—on the competition. Racing was a proving ground in those days, when the vast majority of the public was dubious about the automobile as a reliable means of transport. If you, as a manufacturer, could boast that your car had won a race of any size, it offered solid proof that the darn thing *could* run, *would* run, and with some degree of reliability. No such hesitance exists today—quite different standards apply.

Riley, a British manufacturer, had made nothing but tricars until about 1907. Then, in that year, they took their 2-cylinder 60-degree V-unit of just over 1 liter and put it into a four-wheel sporting model with quarter-elliptic suspension, direct steering, wire-spoked wheels and three-speed transmission. At least one of that model is still in existence in England and is trotted out regularly at antique car rallies.

Model 24 was one of the first 4-cylinder cars made by Rambler of Kenosha, Wisconsin. The picture, taken in 1907 in front of the old Marietta Country Club in Marietta, Ohio, gives some idea of what Ramblers, women, drivers and golfers of the period looked like.

Rambler, 1907 (USA).

Sunbeam—1906/7 (GB)

Pictured is the side-valve, 4-cylinder, chain-drive, 16-20 Sunbeam first introduced in 1906. It had completed the reliability run from Land's End to John o' Groats and back again without an engine-stop to prove its qualities, and had become a popular car in Britain. The car was designed by Sunbeam's chief engineer, who also drove it in the long-distance run.

Rolls-Royce's managing director, Claude Johnson, apparently had a strong promotional sense. At a spot called Cat and Fiddle Hill near Buxton in Derbyshire, he demonstrated the R-R ability at hill-climbing by gathering up handsful of early R-R owners and persuading them to climb Cat and Fiddle, a notoriously difficult task for those early cars. Naturally, the R-R's barreled up the hill with ease, where others failed. And to this day, R-R owners regularly perform the same feat—using those vintage cars!

In the Edwardian age of the automobile, it seemed that limousines tended to look very much alike—almost as though the designers had all used the same master plan. Wolseley, one of the better-known makes of the era, fell into this mold. By 1907, they were making vertical-engined fours to the designs of engineer J. D. Siddeley. Herbert Austin by that time had left the company over a disagreement: he had wanted to continue the horizontal, rather than vertical units.

Standard Motor Company, despite a shaky financial position, *didn't* fall into the standardized trap. In 1907, their Roi des Belges model was a highly impressive 30-hp, 6-cylinder car that would have looked quite at home in the entourage of the Belgian King.

Wolseley, 1907 (GB).

Produced from 1908 to 1912 and extremely modern in appearance for its day, with its near-torpedo bodywork the Benz shown was a modest 4-cylinder family car of 10/18 hp. At this time, in stating horsepower, the first figure represented the power developed at 1000 rpm and the second figure, the power developed at maximum engine speed. The definition was changed in later years.

Also in 1908, FIAT delivered a thunderbolt into England. The thunderbolt was named "Mephistopheles", and it was a racing car—their SB4—an 18,146-cc affair built to be matched against a British Napier at the new Brooklands track. It won the challenge at an average speed of 119.9 mph. Its subsequent history is interesting: its owner blew up the engine sometime after World War 1. The engine was replaced with a real monster-a FIAT airship unit of 21,714-cc. Its new owner, Ernest Eldridge, drove it to a world speed record in 1924 at 146.01 mph.

If there was a legitimate challenge to Rolls-Royce in this period, it came from France in the form of the Delauney Belleville. Its exterior was unmistakeable, because of the fat, round hood, a throwback to their early boiler-making business. Actually, the hood was copied by several manufacturers of the period, hoping for some sort of sales spin-off, due to the motoring public's respect for the car. Many considered it to be an even finer car than the Rolls-Royce.

Ever wonder at the derivation of the term "pit stop" in automobile racing? In 1908, at the Grand Prix in Dieppe, France, servicing teams were allocated a number of trenches dug alongside the track for speed in handling repairs and tire changes. Hence—"pits"!

Benz, 1908 (D).

Model T Ford, 1908 (USA).

Probably the most famous car in the entire history of motoring. The first one was delivered in October of 1908, and was described as "homely as a burro and friendly as a pair of shoes". In the first year, an amazing 10,000 were sold, and by mid-1927, when the "Tin Lizzie" was discontinued, nearly 15,500,000 had been delivered. The car weighed only 1,200 pounds, and was propelled by a 20-hp, 2.9-liter, 4-cylinder engine. It had a high ground clearance (10½ inches) necessitated by country roads, with pedal-operated planetary transmission and two forward speeds. It could do 45 mph and go 20 miles on a gallon of fuel. The use of vanadium steel wherever possible allowed a light but strong construction and gave the car a "go-anywhere" reputation. That it could and would go just about anywhere was proved conclusively in 1909 when a Model T was driven 4,100 miles from New York City to Seattle, Washington in appalling weather conditions over roads so poor that some had almost ceased to exist.

Another Model T came along at about this time: just about the last of the "one-lunger" Cadillacs. The resemblance of the early Model A Cadillacs to (believe it or not!) early model Fords was attributable to the fact that Henry Leland, who formed the Cadillac Motor Company, was associated with Henry Ford in his early days in the industry. By the time the Model T Cadillac hit the streets, the resemblance was no more.

48

Racing, racing, and more racing. Napier built a model to the order of racing driver J. E. Hutton, called it by his name and entered it in the two places it had been designed specifically for: Brooklands and the Isle of Man Tourist Trophy. It was successful in both places. And then *Le Matin* of Paris sponsored a race even wilder than the incredible Peking-Paris race in 1907. This time, they said let's go from *New York* to Paris—a mere 13,000 miles! No details, but the race was won by an American 60-hp Thomas Flyer. Panhard, on the other hand, had practially no success with their giant 18-, 15.5-, and 12-liter entries in Grand Prix racing in 1906, 1907, and 1908. Their philosophy (and that of certain others, including FIAT) that "the more liters—the more successes", proved a resounding flop as legions of smaller Renaults and Mercedes went thundering by the elephantine Panhards, et al. As a matter of fact, Panhard-Levassor probably heaved a huge sigh of relief when Grand Prix racing practically died for the next few years.

The shape is identical, or nearly so, with other vehicles of its class. But this car, a 10/20 hp Mercedes, was one of the first shaft-driven cars from the Daimler works in Germany. This was a development of the drive first used for the 6-cylinder racing cars of two years earlier. The old chain drive soon became a back number, and after 1908 was used on only one or two larger models. There is extant a picture of Czar Nicholas and Czarina Alexandra of Russia visiting their troops in a car which is almost a twin of the one pictured here.

Mercedes did very well in racing that year, also. One of their entries won the French Grand Prix at an average speed of 69 mph, and another set a new lap record at 78.6 mph.

Mercedes, 1908 (D).

This snappy number appeared in the same year that Olds-mobile became a part of General Motors, not long after Buick became a charter member. The car, called the Model M Toy Tourer, was more luxurious and stylish then its predecessors, bearing no resemblance whatever to the earlier "curved dash" models. Only 1000 of the Toy Tourers were made, but in 1908, one of these 3½-liter, 4-cylinder numbers completed the 1,669 miles of the Glidden Tour with a "perfect" score.

Olds made another version of the Toy Tourer and rather grandiloquently called it the "Palace Tourer". Their literature stated that the Toy and Palace, along with other contemporary models, were designed "on French lines". Translation: they had moved the engine up front under the hood from a spot which they called "the engine room"—under the body of the car. Even in those days the Madison Avenue mind was hard at work!

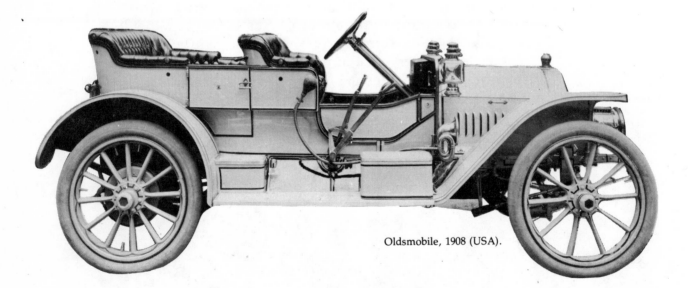

Oldsmobile, 1908 (USA).

Oldsmobile Model Z, 1908 (USA).

How they got from "M" all the way to "Z" in the same year is a mystery-but later that year, Olds unveiled a Model Z in Madison Square Garden, no less. The Z was their first 6-cylinder model, and at 8 liters, the first of their really large ones. The Z incorporated another Olds first—the use of nickel plating, which had been recorded the previous year.

Another "O" firm—Opel of Germany—brought out their elegant 10/18-PS "Doppel Phaeton" in 1908. Statistics: 4-cylinder, water-cooled engine; timed valves; magneto ignition; dredge lubrication; three forward speeds and reverse; gate-type gearshift; top speed of 60 km/h (37 mph). And yes, it sold very well in Germany.

Merry Olds To Limited: 1900-1909

That New York to Paris race previously mentioned must have been an enormously trying experience for those with enough hardihood to enter. The occupants of the Italian Zust seem ready for almost anything, even though they seem not very happy at the trip facing them. The weather in New York was what you see in the picture. (posed before the start of the race.) The trek took them across the USA, Russia and Europe in the absolute worst of weather conditions. The trip, which took 168 days for the winner, prompts two questions: who was the genius who decided the race should start in the dead of winter? And—if the weather was like that in New York, what was it like in Siberia?

The preceding paragraph brings something else to mind: in the early days of the twentieth century, with automobile design being improved upon almost daily, why did just about every manufacturer insist on a design feature which can only be termed, "Freeze the Chauffeur"? Nearly every make had a brougham, a landaulet or a whatever-you-are-pleased-to-call-it with the poor chauffeur sitting out in front, getting rained upon, snowed upon, and in general, subjected to extremes of weather! Addenda to the above: even the London taxis were designed that way!

Of course, it should be remembered that, even as late as 1910, not all models had even as much as a *top*! Many of the so-called touring cars didn't have a fold-back top—and the owner of any sports car worthy of the name wouldn't be caught dead with one!

Zust, 1908

Sunbeam, 1908 (GB).

Two very different approaches to British motoring in 1908. Sunbeam called it a brougham, even though it was in truth an open tourer with a detachable top. Style terms of the period were almost impossible to sort out in this transitional time when carriage-body style terms were being used as nomenclature for motored transport. The Sunbeam was still chain-driven, with a 4-cylinder engine developing 20 hp. A magazine of the day decided, and rightly so, that "It cannot be called graceful, the abrupt square form that rises abruptly behind the front seats . . . nor can the owner of such a vehicle take the wheel himself without looking as if he were a coachman." Pistols at 20 paces in Hyde Park at dawn, perhaps?

The 20-hp, 4-cylinder Vauxhall, on the other hand, began a long series of sporting successes for the Vauxhall company. In the Royal Automobile Club and the Scottish Reliability Trials of 1908, it became the first car in the world to complete 2,000 miles without an involuntary stop of any kind. Designer, due to the departure of Herbert Austin, who left to or- for all sporting Vauxhalls that followed.

Also in 1908, Wolseley had to go looking for a new designer, due to the depature of Herbert Austin, who left to organize his own business. Wolseley found him in a young designer, J. D. Siddeley, who began producing vertical-cylinder engines for the firm. By this time, Wolseley had a large range of vehicles in production and a backlog of experience in racing.

Vauxhall, 1908 (GB).

"Blitzen" Benz, 1909 (D).

This one became a legend. It was the 1908 Grand Prix Benz, but now cowled and streamlined. Blitzen (Lightning) Benz had a 21.5-liter, 4-cylinder engine and a claimed 200 horsepower at 1,600 rpm. In 1909, it captured the world speed record at 125.95 mph. Then Barney Oldfield took it in hand and clocked a flying-start mile record of 131.7 mph at Daytona, Florida. It achieved still further world-class record successes in the hands of another American race driver—Bob Burman by name.

Much more down-to-earth, another landmark appeared in 1909—the first Austin Seven. The 1922 model became more famous, but the seven of 1909 (the earliest "Baby Austin") was an attempt to do in Britain what Ford was doing in the United States: produce a really low-cost, low-powered automobile for the new motoring public. However, it wasn't a true Austin—Swift of Coventry made most of it and also sold an almost identical car under their own name.

Austin was also in production with a wide variety of styles, including what the company was pleased to call a Park Phaeton—which looked like a carriage with a grafted-on back end. If you wanted an Austin, you could have one in 10-, 15-, 24-, 40-, and 50-hp sizes—something for everyone, it seems!

Merry Olds To Limited: 1900-1909

The first Hudson advertising appeared on June 19, 1909, which beat the completion date of the first Hudson car by fourteen days. It can be imagined that the first one came through in a big rush to meet the demand created by the advertising. The picture was obviously taken in the winter of 1909-1910, and displays one of the originals—Model 20, a 4-cylinder, 20-hp vehicle with a top speed of just under 50 mph. That year the first mile of concrete road was built in rural America—in Wayne County, Michigan—and a woman drove cross-country from New York to San Francisco in fifty-three days. The placement of that mile of concrete road was, of course, occasioned by the fact that Detroit is in Wayne County.

The fashionable Cadillac roadster of 1909 was, in fact, a masterpiece of quality. Its four separately cast cylinders were copper-jacketed, and, said the inevitable brochure, the car was "truly a marvel for noiselessness and smoothness in action . . . with a power of 28.9 hp." Over 5,900 were made in 1909. (and were relatively inexpensive in standard form.) A total of 66,939 were sold by the end of 1914. The year 1909 also saw Cadillac become a part of General Motors.

Benz brought out a new 14/30-hp model in 1909, based on earlier engine designs, plus the knowledge gained through racing. This one had its 4 cylinders cast in one block, with a bore and stroke of 90 × 140 mm. It developed 35-hp at 1,500 rpm.

Hudson, 1909 (USA).

Kissel Kar, 1909 (USA).

Twice restored (and now in superb condition) this 1909 Model L-D9 Kissel Kar shows little evidence of the farm-machinery background of its manufacturers. A 4-cylinder, 30-hp tourer, this well made vehicle underwent exhaustive bench-testing before leaving the factory—and would be rejected if the unit developed less than the stated horsepower. The company held an enviable reputation for workmanship throughout its existence from 1903 to 1931. To quote Kissel Kar advertising: "Noiseless, fast and powerful . . . has shown immense reserve time and again in the severest hill-climb tests".

Another one of the legion of American cars which sprouted but failed to survive was Lozier. H. A. Lozier and Company had begun by making steam trucks off a British design in 1896. Entering the passenger car field, they built a few experimental steam cars. By 1905 they were into internal combustion engines and showed their first model at Madison Square Garden. It was one of the finest quality American cars as it developed; but it didn't save them from the automotive graveyard in 1917.

Still another very early bloomer which didn't last was the Mitchell. Mitchell Wagon Co. made horse-drawn vehicles as early as 1834, entered the automobile field in 1903 (with the help of a bicycle engineer named John W. Bates) and stayed for thirty years. The company was finally liquidated and its buildings sold to Nash Motors.

These are but three of the long, long list who didn't stay the course. In the history of the automobile, there were hundreds and hundreds that tried and missed—some abruptly, some whose death rattle wasn't heard until rather recently. Each one, however, added something to the nearly two-centuries-old history of powered vehicles.

Humber, 1909 (GB).

The snappy little two-seater, apparently designed to appeal directly to the younger set, was a part of Humber's strategic bid to capture a share of the lighter car market. It was fitted with Dunlop tires, side and tail lamps, horn, hood and tool kit. Just the thing for tootling off on a Saturday night date—and don't forget the tool kit!

The overly-vertical Lion Peugeot was a product of the Beaulieu-Valentigney factory, an old Peugeot plant used by Robert Peugeot to build his own cars after a disagreement with the original company. By 1910, Peugeot was reunited with the family firm, and by 1913 Lion-Peugeot ceased to exist. The vehicle in the picture, looking as though it were designed on the drawing boards of Walt Disney Studios, was a 9-hp cabriolet.

1909 was the year members of the Automobile Association in Britain mounted an ambitious effort: to transport a battalion of soldiers from London to Hastings on the south coast of England. It must have successful—fifty years later they did it again, using cars of the same period in what was termed a commemoration run.

Prince Heinrich of Prussia was an automobile enthusiast. (This seemed almost epidemic among European royalty—Britain, Italy, Germany—all had *aficionados* among the royal families.) In 1909, his big effort was the Prinz Heinrich-Fahrt. (Prince Henry Trials) Who gained the glory? Opel, of course—first, third, fifth, sixth and tenth places!

Lion-Peugeot, 1909 (F).

Merry Olds To Limited: 1900-1909

The "Doktorwagen" (doctor's car) was offered especially to physicians to (as the advertising put it) "safeguard harassed country doctors from the hazards of unsurfaced byways." It was a bright idea that caught on in several countries. Medical doctors were among the first to appreciate the speedy mobility of the car and were eager buyers in pioneer motoring days. The Opel pictured had a 4-cylinder, 1,029-cc engine. Remember house calls?

In New York, in 1909, a 24-hour, 1000-mile race was run over an oval dirt track. One of the contestants, a driver named Raffalovitch, took his 4-cylinder, 35-hp Renault once around, then by pre-arrangement, drove it for a pit stop. There, he had mud-guards fitted on his front wheels for protection against flying stones and dirt *from his own wheels!* He had kept quiet about his intentions (except for his arrangements with the pit crew) and his strategy proved so successful that he won the race with his "secret weapon"!

In these days when a production run must be in the high thousands to even be considered as practical, it's a little difficult to see how certain early makers managed to keep their financial heads above water—but many of them did. Peugeot, still a prominent French manufacturers today, had a car (Type 113) in 1909—35-hp, 4-cylinder motor of 7½ liters, with 4-speed transmission plus reverse, cone clutch, chain final drive and a top speed of 104 km/h (64½ mph). They offered it in double-phaeton, coupe, landaulet or limousine. History doesn't reveal how many were sold but the production run was a grand total of 95—in all three models!

Opel "Doktorwagen", 1909 (D)

Rambler, 1909 (USA).

Two elements in the picture make it irresistible: first, the 4-cylinder Rambler is toting around the United States of America's heavyweight champion President, William Howard Taft. Second, and vastly more important in automotive history, kindly note the item mounted on the right running board. Yes—it's a spare tire—and Rambler was the first American company to offer a "fifth wheel", thus taking a giant step in simplifying tire changing. Note also the lighting arrangements: gaslight, no less, with gas supplied from the brass carbide generator just forward of the spare tire. A very close look will discover another feature: the throttle was a ring placed just under the rim of the steering wheel.

When the modern-day driver goes anywhere in his car, a hill is just another place on the road. Not so in the early 1900's. Hills were a real challenge to *every* car up to and including the illustrious Rolls-Royce. Hence, find a steep hill, (if you were a manufacturer of motor cars) take a picture of your car climbing it, and send it along to whatever newspaper or magazine that could be persuaded to publish it, along with your carefully written description of the ease with which your car climbed it. Neither picture nor story, of course, made any mention of the coughing, wheezing, sputtering and jerking which were additional features!

Clement-Talbot, Ltd., of London imported French cars into England dating from 1903. From 1906 on, they made their own in England. In 1909, they offered, among other models, their Talbot 4T, with 4-cylinder, side-valve engine, transmission brakes at the rear, plus 4-speed transmission.

59

Merry Olds To Limited: 1900-1909

Stanley Steamers weren't the handsomest cars ever built—but they were easy to maintain, cheap to run, (no gasoline!) and could out-accelerate anything powered by any other fuel. By 1909, Stanley had adopted its "traditional" shape, had an unexplodable boiler, high seating, very reliable performance, and could travel over 50 miles on a single fill of water. Of course, no manufacturer could please everyone— but one of the complaints offered about the Stanley falls into the "Believe it or Not" class: it was too quiet! Why was this cause for complaint? Because unalert pedestrians wouldn't hear it coming and might be struck down! The Stanley pictured is the 10-hp Touring version.

Vauxhall, in the final year of the first decade of the twentieth century, was into two widely varying areas of motoring. First, among their models was a landaulet with a full window directly behind the chauffeur. The window, naturally, was designed to give the populace a chance to envy and admire the occupants within. You may be sure no one envied the poor chauffeur, who, as usual, sat outside, at the complete mercy of whatever elements were operating at the time. Comfortable inside, even luxurious—it cruised amiably at 30 mph, and could be pushed to 45. It drank a gallon of fuel every 30 miles or so.

Vauxhall's other venture was a 3-liter affair with a long, narrow body and christened KN. This was a very bad pun—KN stood for cayenne pepper—very hot stuff. However badly named, the KN became the first car of its class to reach the "ton". It recorded 100.08 mph over the kilometer, and put up some very fast times at England's Brooklands track.

Stanley Steamer, 1909 (USA).

America: The Big Store

Henry Ford had built on the production expertise of Ransom Olds and in 1910 some 20,000 Model T's, using methods pioneered by the Lansing manufacturer were made, increasing to 200,000 by 1912, just two years after moving to his Highland Park plant which he had equipped with advanced mass-production machinery.

At the 10th National Auto Show in the U.S. the new torpedo shape made its debut, the high-sided tourer with a line that was followed for many years on both sides of the Atlantic. Standardization was apparent at this time, many manufacturers modifying their suspension, transmission and final drive to come into line with others who had found more efficient systems. All-steel bodies began to appear, developed by Budd and first seen on a Hupmobile; automatic transmissions, introduced as early as 1904 on the Sturtevant were becoming more popular. Electric self-starters appeared in 1912, pioneered by former cash-register engineer Charles Kettering. The system flew round the automotive world and within two years was almost universal. Many historians declare that this development was one of the most significant in the motoring world, allowing women to take the wheel in numbers for the first time by doing away with manual starting, and providing a sharper stimulus to female emancipation than any political legislation could have done.

The First World War, which began in Europe in 1914, soon forced Allied automotive plants over to war production. But it was not enough. French and British factories could not produce in sufficient quantities for their own needs (the British Army did not possess a single unit of mechanical transportation in 1914) and America—a non-belligerent until 1917—became the great supplier of the Allies, shipping over, amongst other war goods, many thousands of automobiles. It was noticed that by this time American design had, astonishingly to many, caught up with and even surpassed that of European vehicles, from where it had been thought all knowledge stemmed. Amongst the vehicles to arrive during those three years were the V8 Cadillac and the V12 Packard and although these were not a new concept by 1915, their operation was a challenge to the most expensive of European models.

Although the war halted private car production, its urgency pushed technical development along at breakneck speed, teaching more in four years than the industry had learned in two decades. Aircraft production was the key, and when aircraft engine technology was applied to post-war products a new generation of vehicles appeared.

Road systems and surfaces, which had been lamentably slow in development, particularly in America, had been given a boost in 1913 when the Lincoln Highway plan had been launched. With a continuous road from New York to San Francisco (it took fourteen years to complete) the ocean-to-ocean Highway encouraged other states to build up their inter-city links, creating a badly-needed network of roads over the North American continent, the lack of which had earlier made it 'easier to sail round then to travel over'.

1910-1919

Oldsmobile, 1910 (USA).

This is another "landmark" car. The Oldsmobile "Limited", first introduced in 1910, became one of the most famous automobiles of the period. It sported a big 60-hp, 707-cu. in. power unit with 6 cylindrs, and was big in other dimensions as well—it needed two mounting steps to get on board! With a cruising speed of 65 mph, the "Limited" was, in its day, the ultimate in fast luxury motoring in America. So famous did it become that it was immortalized in a painting depicting a crack New York Central express train!

Rallies were great social and sporting events in the years generally termed the "Edwardian Age". Hudson, who seemed to have a rather strong promotional sense, would send a whole fleet of one model, each with a pretty girl and driver-escort to a Sunday afternoon rally in America's automotive Mecca, Detroit. In 1910, however, despite all the promoting, Hudson ranked only 17th among American makes in registrations.

A very impressive racing record was compiled by the (then) Bohemian form of Laurin and Klements during the 1908 through 1911 years. One of their more successful efforts was a big 4-cylinder (85 x 250 mm) vehicle which gained a number of European victories. How well L & K did may be judged by the fact that in the years mentioned, they had fifty-seven firsts, twenty-five seconds and eleven thirds in motor sport events.

Not long after this 5-seater touring car was offered to the public, Packard, already known for quality, produced a model in the new style—a "Torpedo". Seen first at the 10th National Auto Show, the "Torpedo" (in this case) was a high-sided open car with a clean line from windshield to rear end, with the dashboard brought closer to the driver by means of a cowl. But why is this nice Packard driver being stopped? Driving without a windshield? Or perhaps the police officer is lost and needs directions!

The Renaults of 1910 were characterized by a rather curious radiator placement. Instead of the radiator up front, where it could catch outside air, Renault placed their radiator behind the engine, where any air reaching it would have first been heated by the engine. This was probably a help in very cold weather, but those engines must have been burning up in summer heat!

That year, R.E. Olds' Reos were moving well. In addition, the company was now turning out a line of trucks, called Speed Wagons. The Speed Wagon was designed as a most-for-the money delivery truck.

One of Sunbeam's failures was one attempt at a racing car. The engine was satisfactory (OHV) with 4 valves per cylinder operated by pushrods and rockers. But an attempt at streamlining the nose (it came to a sharp point) resulted in some rather troublesome overheating.

Prince Henry Vauxhall, 1910 (C

The car shown is the prototype of the most distinguished vehicle in Vauxhall's history. It was destined to become internationally famous in the sporting world. First seen in 1910, this 3-liter car became public property at the 1910 Motor Show in London. Shortly thereafter, three were entered in a Swedish rally; one of them won the event. Fifty were built in 1912 on a 9-ft., 6-in. wheelbase, after which the engine was enlarged to 4 liters and the size of the chassis was increased. The Prince Henry was built until 1914, made a name in record-breaking and racing and was the immediate ancestor of Vauxhall's famous 30/98.

In the primeval days of the automobile, cars were stored in strange places. Probably the strangest hiding place of all was discovered in 1953, when an old house was demolished in France. Behind one of the panels was the wooden chassis of a 1910, 12-hp Sizaire-Naudin voiturette, a car which had been manufactured in France since 1905, and one which had won an important race for small cars in 1906. The car was restored after its rediscovery. It should have been well-mellowed, after over 40 years in the wood!

Henry Austin was one of Britain's automotive greats—but he had some rather unusual, not to say eccentric, ideas. For example—his 4-cylinder, 15-hp Town Carriage of 1910 placed the engine inside the cab, a la modern-day buses. The result was a snub-nosed vehicle, with the passenger compartment looking like the back end of a coach-and-four.

1901 Pieper voiturette. (B)

Opel tonneau, 1902, with 2-cylinder engine. (D)

Lanchester 1903. Twin-cylinder, 12 hp. (GB)

Fiat Corsa, 1902. Four cylinders, 23 hp and a racing
speed of 60 mph. (I)

Touring Mercedes, 1903. (D)

A 1903 Clement Talbot at a recent London- Brighton Commemoration Run. (GB)

Winton, 1903. (USA)

Aristocratic Edwardian; a 20-hp Thornycroft. (GB)

One of the most popular models of its time,
a 1903 de Dion Bouton. (F)

Daimler 'Detachable' 1905. The roof could
be removed. (GB)

Vauxhall, 1904. (GB)

Brush Runabout, 1911 (USA).

The "one-lunger" Brush was, the advertising said, "Everyman's car". Priced inexpensively, it was indeed good value for the money, with a tough wooden frame and helical suspension on all four wheels. See if this next company claim doesn't make you groan, in view of today's prices: running costs were advertised at "less than a cent a mile." How'd you like to be able to drive 5,000 miles for less than $50? As an afterthought, upon looking at the weather in the picture, perhaps it wasn't really such a bargain, if you added in the time lost because of frostbite, head colds and pneumonia!

Berliet, by 1911, was using shaft drive and four-speed transmissions on all their cars produced in the Berliet Lyons factory. Even with those improvements, the car's mechanics were uninspired, although in appearance it was at least three years ahead of its time, with a long low line which gave it the desired "racy" look.

The 1910 Riley sported the fashionable cylindrical hood spawned by the aristocratic Delauney-Belleville. Under the hood, the changes were many. The engine (a water-cooled twin-V unit of 10 hp) had been moved there for one thing, plus these added starters: mechanical inlet valves, trembler coil ignition, cone clutch and three-speed transmission.

America: The Big Store: 1910-1919

Looking like a cross between a moon buggy and half of a V2 rocket, the elephantine S76 was an incredible record-breaker. The monumental overhead valve engine of 28,353-cc (it had a stroke of 9.67 inches!) produced some 300 hp at 1,900 rpm. Built specifically to take the World Land Speed Record away from Germany's "Blitzen Benz", the S76 was sent to Britain's Brooklands to be tried out by Pietro Bordino; later, at Saltburn Sands, it reached 124 mph. It actually set a world record in Belgium with French driver Duray at the wheel, but the recorded 137 mph was never confirmed because of suspect timing equipment.

Louis Chevrolet, who had come to America from Switzerland to sell wine pumps, entered motor sports, won several events, became a Buick team driver and designed an experimental car. All this by 1911. Then he got together with W.C. Durant and formed the Chevrolet Motor Car Company of Michigan, which began production with the 4.9-liter T-head Classic 6. The date? November 3, 1911.

A French company from Luneville in Lorraine, De Dietrich is part of the fabric of motor history from its earliest days in 1897, when Baron de Turckheim obtained a license to build cars on the "Systeme Amédée Bollée." He later built Belgian cars under license, following with the Turcat Méry. Ettore Bugatti also designed for the company. In 1908, the firm name was changed to Lorraine-Dietrich.

FIAT S76 (I).

, 1911 (I).

Standard, 1911 (GB)

It is readily apparent that FIAT was getting to be very nearly ubiquitous: aside from the monstrous racer, the car kept turning up in all corners of the globe. That's the President of Chile (on the streets of Lima, one presumes) riding in the Type 2 15-20. This car, with a 2,612-cc engine, was made in various forms until 1920 and was the first car to be adopted by the Italian armed forces during the Libyan campaign.

Included in our VIP notes from all over: King George V and Queen Mary in India during the Delhi Durbar of 1911. The car is a 6-cylinder 20-hp Standard Landaulet. At least 70 Standards were sent to India to convey various groups attending the celebrations.

It would be interesting to see the results of a sales gimmick used by the Regal Company if it were tried today. After their first year, they took back every car they had sold, and replaced them with the next year's model. Needless to say the offer was not repeated the following year— or ever again !

The first Indianapolis "500" was held on May 30, 1911, and was won by a 6-cylinder Marmon Wasp driven by Ray Harroun, who led the race for about 300 miles. He averaged 74.59 mph and covered the distance in 6 hours and 42 minutes.

Mercedes "Knight" (D).

Still more "mobility among the nobility": Nicholas, Czar of all the Russians, visiting maneuvers of the Kaiser's army in Germany, this time accompanied by his daughters. (One of them is said to be the mysterious Anastasia) The car is the Mercedes "Knight". The company used Knight sleeve-valve engines in several models after the Daimler Company of Coventry had proved their worth in a series of tests and had used them in the British production cars.

In 1911, a disastrous fire almost completely destroyed the Opel plant at Russellsheim in Germany, but Phoenix-like, the company rose from the ashes and built a completely new and far more sophisticated plant. Result: a newer, more sophisticated line of cars.

The 40/50-hp Gobron-Brillie Landaulette was produced by a French firm which began operations in 1898 with the intention of offering cars that were free from the number one plague of automobiles of that date: vibration. The opposed-piston system (2 pistons per cylinder) they used certainly made for smoother running. The brochure explained, "As the pistons draw apart, a charge of gas is drawn into the cylinder through the inlet valve. This charge is compressed by the pistons coming together again and then fired, the impulse being transmitted to the crankshaft by the lower and upper connecting rods. On the next upward stroke, the exhaust gases are disposed of through the exhaust valve in the usual way." All very clear and succinct, but it must have been just as bewildering to the average motorist then as it would be to his opposite number today . . .

FIAT Tipo Zero, 1912 (I)

FIAT, FIAT, FIAT. Wherever you looked, there it was again. The open tourer shown was one example of what circumstances can do to even the most enterprising and popular entrepreneurs. The Tipo Zero was conceived as a popular car for the motoring masses and was intended to be produced in quantity. But a happening known as World War I got in the way—and after all the expensive tooling up for a major production run beginning in 1913, only a total of 2,000 were made by 1915. The car could be considered the first small, inexpensive FIAT to be manufactured in a large single series. At first only one body (the one shown) was offered. Engine: 1,846-cc, 4-cylinder, developing 19 bhp at 2,000 rpm.

1912 had *some* good news for FIAT, however. Their S61 (4-cylinder, 10,087-cc) racing car won the American Grand Prix at Tacoma that year. This car, driven by Teddy Tezlaff, was made in Grand Touring form as early as 1908; the competition model developed from it was produced specifically for the North American market.

The Lancashire Vulcan Motor & Engineering Company of Britain first went into passenger automobile production in 1902 (after making a name for itself in commercial vehicles) with a single-cylinder light car. By 1911, the company and the product had matured to the point where they offered a large 6-cylinder model, with a choice of 2.4- or 3.6-liter engines.

Between 1912 and 1914, Hillman made a small, 13/25 hp, 6-cylinder model in its Coventry factory. Designed, it was claimed, for the "sporting family", its torpedo shape was quite clean and modern for the times, looking somewhat similar to contemporary FIATS.

One that got away: Austro-Daimler was formed in 1899 when Gottleib Daimler built a factory in Austria to produce Daimlers. However, by 1906, the company became independent of the German and British company. The 4-cylinder, 6/25 personeauto was a light "Alpine" shaft-driven vehicle with two-wheel brakes, four-speed transmission and magneto ignition. A smart tourer from Vienna, it was made by Austro-Daimler from 1912 to 1914 and again from 1919 to 1920.

The most successful air-cooled car in the United States, the Franklin, reached that pinnacle because, as the company claimed, they had "done away with the plumbing". The phrase sold a lot of cars for Franklin prior to World War I. The case for air-cooling was a strong one in pioneer days—no radiator, no leaky hose, no water pump—and a lot of weight saved.

The Model T Ford was growing up into something approaching luxury with a car which Henry Ford would probably not have been willing to admit was a landaulet. The monoblock, 4-cylinder, side-valve unit still chuffed along at around 45 mph maximum, and little change had been made in the planetary transmission. But—in 1912, the plant at Highland Park covered 60 acres!

The rugged Hudson was seen in many odd corners of the planet. In India, Europe, Africa—you name it—Hudson was there. During 1912, precisely 5,708 Hudsons were shipped overseas from the United States.

Daimler, 1912 (A)

Maxwell, 1912 (USA).

The writing on the windshield of this Maxwell says, "Perfect Score, Winner Glidden Tour AAA 1911," and if the terrain under the car is any indication of the type of ground covered in the 1911 event, it says much for the car. The scene is Northern Mississippi and the caption seems to indicate that this is part of the 1912 Glidden Tour, also won by a Maxwell, perhaps even the one in the picture. The varied Glidden Tour was over a total of 1,272 miles through Detroit, Indianapolis, Louisville, Memphis, Baton Rouge and New Orleans in twelve days.

In 1912, the Peugeot 7.6 Grand Prix cars heralded the demise of the giant racing cars of earlier years. At 7.6-liters they were small by racing standards of the time—cars of 14 liters had been entered for the French Grand Prix. The smaller Peugeot, reputedly designed by Swiss engineer Henry (before doubt was cast on his ability to do so) had twin overhead camshafts and four valves per cylinder; stroke and bore were 110 X 200 mm, and the unit developed 135 bhp at 2,200 rpm. The car won the two major races of 1912.

For a company that began life in Canada making sleighs, the transfer to the automotive world seems unusual. However, the Ontario-based firm of McLaughlin produced a sturdy, high-sided vehicle using a 4-cylinder Buick engine and various other parts by agreement with W.C. Durant. The bodies were Canadian-built, and at first the wood-framed coachwork was considerably different from the Buick products. About 1912 the firm began to use the name of Buick coupled with its own, but the practice was discontinued when sales fell off.

Renault Tourer (F).

This was elegance in the pre-World War I years. On the boulevards of Paris, on the Grand Tour. One of the larger Renaults, this 6-cylinder, "carriage-trade" open tourer with coach work by Gache developed 40 hp under that distinctive hood. Renault's layout continued to place the radiator behind the cylinder block until 1930. Don't be silly—of *course* the chauffeur got rained on, frozen and heat-struck!

Everyone, it seemed, was making an attempt to crack the very-low-cost market. British designer Leslie Hounsfield built a prototype with a two-stroke, 4-cylinder, 1,523-cc engine which chugged out an unimposing 10 hp and had chain drive and solid tires. He called it "Trojan" and mounted the modest engine vertically between the two seats—which were all the seats the car afforded.

On the other hand, Oldsmobile took the high road with a much more grandiose effort called the Autocrat. This was built as a companion car to the great Oldsmobile Limited, and was part of a short-lived effort on Oldsmobile's part to enter the up-market.

After Opel's disastrous fire in 1911, the firm produced a car as dainty in appearance as it was nicknamed—"Puppchen"—Dolly. You could have it in 2- or 4-seater version with a 5/14 hp engine.

72

Cadillac, 1913 (USA).

1912 saw the introduction of one of the great steps forward in automobiling. In that year, Cadillac introduced the electric self-starter, plus electric lighting and ignition. If any one thing did, this finally confirmed Cadillac as one of the great leaders in the automotive world. Women drivers who had found the crank an almost insurmountable obstacle were now able to drive without the aid of a strong male arm. The car shown is the 48.7-hp Model 30, with torpedo body. Production run: 15,017.

In the interest of mechanical silence, numerous makers had attempted to tame chattering valve gears. There were many, many bizarre attempts to emulate the virtually noiseless Rolls-Royce and other high-quality cars. One that got there was called the Valveless, using a two-stroke engine of 2 cylinders. It sold successfully until 1914, when presumably World War I put it out of business.

Austin made a smaller edition of its big luxury 6-cylinder, 50-hp Laudaulette. They called the scale-down (10-hp, 1.6-liter) the Aylesford Cabriolet and sales results proved it elaborate enough for most. 1913 also marked the excursion of Austin into yet another field of powered vehicles (their engines had already powered a motorboat) when they built and marketed a 20-hp, 2-, 3-ton truck.

Just before World War I, FIAT opened the doors to coachbuilders who wanted to use the Zero chassis for their own designs. Prior to this, they had offered only one type of body with the Tipo Zero—and of course, the Tipo was FIAT's entry into the "people's car" field.

Hillman 2-seater circa 1913 (GB).

Morris-Oxford, 1913 (•

Pictured are the two prime competitors for the inexpensive car-buyer's money in Britain. William Morris was a former cycle-shop owner who began production of his own cars in 1913 with the light car illustrated. He bought his parts (rather then making them) including the 1-liter engine. Read the rhapsodical maker's own tribute: "The consumption is from 50 to 55 miles to the gallon, and tires and lubricating oil are upon an equally economical basis. Speeds range from 5 to 55 miles per hour in top gear on average roads."

Now—Hillman's self-adulation for their "drop-head coupe", which offered 9-hp in a 4-cylinder, 1,357-cc runabout: "Nine—and Fine! Never was a better two-seater than this 9-hp Hillman at the price . . . on June 21 last the Hillman was FIRST in short handicap at Brooklands, attaining an average speed for three miles from a standing start of 60 miles an hour. And the Hillman is only 9-hp!" Well, you pays your money, and you takes your choice. Both were highly successful.

Peugeot had themselves a big year in 1913 racing. They won at Indianapolis at an average of 75.93 mph, then pushed up the world one-hour speed mark to 106.22 mph at Brooklands in England. They followed this with a 1-2 finish in the G P de L'A.C.F., (Grand Prix de L'Automobile Club de France) still the official title of the French Grand Prix. One they didn't win was the German Prinz Heinrich Trials. Opel grabbed that one with its 260-hp *rennwagen*, sporting a 4-cylinder, 12-liter power plant, water-cooled with a single overhead camshaft. Top speed for the *rennwagen* was 141 mph.

Mercer Raceabout (USA).

A classic American sporting car in the days before World War I shattered the tranquillity of the Edwardian era, the Mercer Raceabout was the envy of all who owned anything else. With its slow-revving, 5-liter, T engine (58 bhp at 1700 rpm) it loped along at speeds much faster than passengers appreciated. The car had a top speed of about 75 mph (at just 2,000 rpm); the only disadvantage was that its brakes were not of similarly interesting specifications. The company called it "The most talked-about car in America", and it held that reputation for many years.

Renault, in 1913, made only the mechanics and chassis for their cars, preferring to farm out the body work to coach makers. At that time, many Renault clients still preferred to have car bodies constructed to their own specific desires and needs. Expensive? Very!

Frank Duryea had built American cars since 1892, but by 1902, he found himself in need of capital and entered into an agreement with the Stevens Arms and Tool Company. The first Stevens-Duryea models came off the line in March of 1902. Then followed some alphabet soup: Models H, L, R, S, U, X, XXX, Y, and AA. By 1913, a model C had arrived (what happened to "C" the first time around we don't know) in the shape of a 6-cylinder car with a choice of 131- or 138-inch wheelbases.

Lord Baden-Powell founded the Boy Scouts. In 1913, he married. His wedding present was a 20-hp 6-cylinder Standard Laudaulette, purchased by Boy Scouts with voluntary contributions—limited to one penny each!

One of the most prolific companies in variety of models before World War I was Adler of Germany. Between 1910 and 1914, almost 12,000 cars in thirty different models came off their Frankfurt factory lines.

This simple little runabout, made to Ettore Bugatti's designs, was the pretty little "Bebe" Peugeot. It was seen in fair-sized numbers in France (3,095 were produced at the Beaulieu-Valentigney plant from 1913 to 1916). More, of course would have been produced had not the war reared its disruptive head. The model shown is the Type BP1, with an 855-cc, 4-cylinder motor of 6 hp, a two-speed transmission and a *vitesse macimum*—top speed—of 35 mph.

The big breakthrough for Chevrolet came in 1914, with the advent of a touring car and a roadster called respectively Model H4 Baby Grand and Royal Mail. They both sold well and established Chevrolet as a serious contender in the automotive market.

That same year, Buick introduced its first 6-cylinder model, along with a total of five other models all designated by the initial "B". Total production for Buick in 1914 was their highest ever to that date—32,889, from no less than *twenty-eight* plants! Torque tube drive and electric starting equipment, introduced the previous year, were now standard on all Buicks.

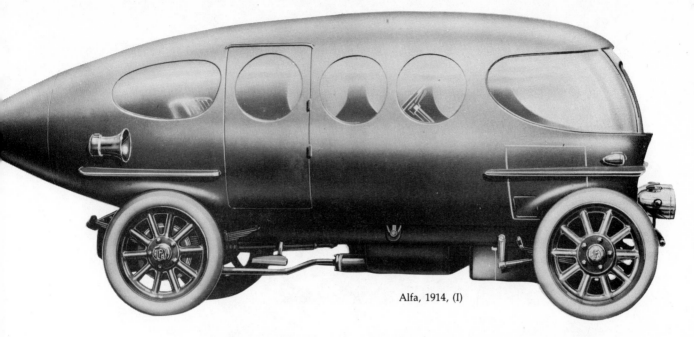

Alfa, 1914, (I)

Do you believe it? Yes, it was designed in 1913 and built in 1914 by Italian coach-work designer Castagna. The proof is in the archives. An amazing essay into streamlining, this 4-cylinder, 40 / 60-hp, 6,082-cc six-seater looks like something en route to the moon rather than a custom-built sedan constructed to the order of an important client, Count Ricotti. Top speed was 139 km/h (86 mph).

The Baker was one of America's more popular electric cars prior to 1917, when America got into the European conflict. Most of the electrics of the day used a dummy hood in front which housed batteries. Baker, like so many manufacturers, was a war casualty. Others fared better: Detroit Electric Company, for example, survived until 1942. The major reasons for the popularity of electrics in the early going were simplicity of operation, freedom from smelly fumes, and probably most important, no cranking to start up. This latter was one of the major problems which held back woman drivers: the crank was simply a chore with which most women (and in fairness, a great many men) couldn't cope. Certainly their top speed of 15-20 mph was conservative enough to attract even the most timid of women. The serious disadvantage (then and now) was that they couldn't travel more than about 50 miles without elaborate arrangements to recharge their array of batteries. In spite of this obvious flaw, which must have been a time-consuming, expensive nuisance, Detroit Electric produced (and presumably sold) about 1,000 cars a year from 1907 to 1914, and as noted, survived until 1942. That latter date sounds suspiciously like they escaped oblivion in WWI only to fall victim to WWII.

Austin Landaulet (GB).

Obviously taken at a time when women's lib first surfaced in Britain under the suffragette banner, the passengers of this early Austin reveal the Edwardian version of female militancy. Also revealed is Herbert Austin's early Landaulet, a 4-cylinder model that preceded his great luxury car of 1913. The 1913 car was a 50-hp, 6-cylinder model. Austin also made Gladiators during 1908-1909 for Frenchman Clement. These were pure Austins in all respects—save the nameplate!

Argyll was one of the few cars made in Scotland. The Argyll Brougham, a 16/20-hp, 4-cylinder cab, was used as a "station car" for some years. However, its extraordinary control system (a long, tortuous path of control linkages) made it a quite troublesome vehicle to maintain.

In addition to his production models, Herbert Austin also designed 3 special Austin Racers in 1908 for the French Grand Prix. In spite of his previous experience in building racing Wolseleys a few years earlier, the cars did not distinguish themselves in the race. However, the two-seaters, which used a 100-hp, 6-cylinder unit of 9,677-cc and were shaft-driven with 4-speed transmissions, were the only British entries to finish. Benz racing cars took second and third places, even though plagued by tire trouble (it was not at all unusual for all four tires to suffer punctures more than once during a race, making numerous pit stops a necessity).

Marius Berliet had been making automobiles in France in 1895, had made a modest excursion into racing, and in 1908 won the Targa Bologna. He had, in his production line, a very distinguished-looking C2 double phaeton, and in that same period, first offered compressed-air starting on a larger 6-cylinder car.

Ford Roadster, 1910 (USA).

Ford built this Model T roadster for six years-through 1915. According to contemporary advertising, Ford was slightly ashamed of its looks, (or feared that the buying public would be!) since the ads proclaimed that the car was disguisable in many ways—"by means of a streamlined hood with radiator shell and crown fenders", said one ad. Many accessories were available from an early date in the roadster's history: floor mats, canvas top, seat covers and pads, side screens—even a radiator cap with "Baby Lincoln" on it!

1910 was a turnaround year for FIAT. Its range was considerably revised, plus the production of a new series of models: Types 1 through 6, ranging from 1,846-cc to the type 6's 9,017-cc power unit. Type 4, for example, housed a 5,699-cc engine. Several styles of bodies were offered, among them a rather old-fashioned (even for 1910) landaulet.

One year before, British Daimler had adopted the "Silent Knight" engine for all their cars. Knight, an Englishman who had emigrated to the United States, had built a sleeve-valve-engined car that had impressed Daimler's manager when he saw it on a visit to the USA. By 1910, the company's smooth, silent cars were a byword in the industry, and remained so for many years.

The 18/24-hp Austin of 1910 would have been considered a pee-wee compared with Austin's 40, 50 and 60-hp models. This wasn't Austin's smallest, since the previous year saw the first "Baby" Austin, a one-cylinder model. Early Austins, by and large, were sound, reliable vehicles, although rather more conventional and uninspired in appearance. However, they were the solid foundation of the manufacturing empire that came to maturity after World War I.

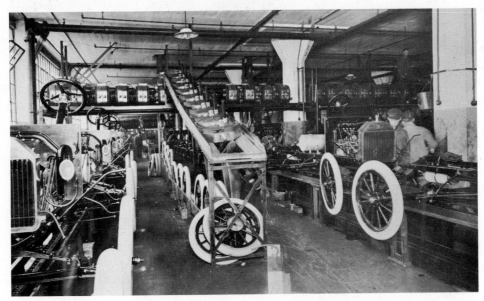

Ford Highland Park Plant, 1914 (USA).

This was a Ford assembly line in 1914, showing the pioneer flow-line system that helped drop the price of the Model T progressively. That year, an interesting statistic emerged: Ford made *one-half* of all the cars made in the U.S.—but it required only *one-sixth* of the nation's automotive manpower to do it!

One of the earliest French pioneers, Hurtu made a single-cylinder, small vehicle for the first fourteen years, then built cars with "dashboard radiators" behind the engine in Renault style. Borrowing another feature, they used a hood shape which could easily be confused with earlier de Dion-Bouton products. The company finally called it quits in 1929.

One name which didn't quit was Audi. Doctor Adolph Horch left his original company after a disagreement and began to manufacture the Audi (which was a Latin translation of Horch) in 1910. There is some sort of parallel here: remember R.E. Olds, the Oldsmobile, the disagreement, and the resulting REO—Old's initials?

In Belgium a firm with the warlike name *Fabrique Nationale d'Armes de Guerre* was the exception to the Belgian rule of manufacturing expensive automobiles for export, mainly to Great Britain. Their F.N. two-seater with a power unit of 1,245-cc, developing about 10 hp, was a rival to a number of smaller cars being produced in Germany and elsewhere.

Tourer (USA).

The Dodge brothers—Horace in the left rear, John, right rear. They are shown taking delivery of the first car from the production department of the Dodge assembly plant at Hamtramck, Michigan. This four-seater found a ready market, since the Dodge name was familiar to the car-buying public through its reputation earned by supplying transmissions, axles, and other parts to Ford and Olds for several years. Why neither of them looks particularly pleased is not a matter of recorded history.

Forty-one cars of fourteen different makes from six different countries took part in the French Grand Prix of 1914, the race which ended an era of motor racing. Five of the forty-one cars were entered by Mercedes. Using team tactics (almost unknown at the time, since multiple entries were hell-for-leather, every-man-for-himself affairs) Mercedes came in one, two, three. The cars, designed by Paul Daimler, had single overhead camshafts in 4½-liter engines which developed 115 bhp at 3,200 rpm. Their only serious flaw was in cornering, due to the fact that they had rear-wheel brakes only, in contrast to other entries which had braking on all four wheels.

Although better known for commercial vehicles (they built a steam wagon in 1835) Maudsley made several attempts at private transport. Their first cars arrived in 1902, (3-cylinder) but they went on to make fours and sixes—as well as more threes. In 1914, they adopted a one-model principle which caused their larger cars to vanish, leaving only the 17-hp (Sweet Seventeen, they called it!) which had first been produced in 1910. The Maudsleys were apparently badly bitten by the automobile bug—another branch of the family formed the Standard Motor Company in 1903.

Renault, 1914 (F).

S.A. des Usines Renault had been building medium and large cars for some years, and the car in the picture is considered one of their smartest: a 20 CV, 4-cylinder sports torpedo with body by Labourdette. Also fashionable in 1914 was a single-studded, anti-slip tire shown here fitted on the left front wheel. Smart it may have been, but that curious seat arrangement must have been constructed for a menage-a-trois! (husband, wife and mother-in-law?) Louis Renault, of course, was to build even larger cars for the luxury market.

The renowned "Silent Knight" engine caused one of two reactions among a number of reputable companies in Europe and the United States. They either used it, or scurried frantically to develop new mechanics to compete with it. By 1913 Itala (of Italy, naturally) had made a successful rotary-valve engine which they installed in road cars and some racers.

A little-known car in the history of the industry was the British Jeffery, made from 1914 to 1917. Perhaps their lack of success was due to the fact that their "button-backed" coupe looked dated. (in spite of an aluminum body—a rare bird in those days.) The car was named for the company's founder, Thomas B. Jeffery, who built the first Rambler in 1897 and went on to head that company.

The Simplex "semi-racing runabout" was one of the more distinguished American cars of its time. In 1914, the company offered 38-, 50-, and 75-hp models of 4 cylinders, and a 6-cylinder 50-hp. That last was one of the fastest cars in the country, and was very probably the last chain-driven car made in the USA.

london: Summer, 1914

England's King Edward died in 1910, but the Edwardian era is generally accepted as ending in August of 1914—the onset of the war. The photograph was taken in Regent Street that summer and gives some idea of what traffic was like in a metropolitan center in those days. Motor buses, private cars, taxicabs—even horses!

There was another Puppchen (Dolly) nearly a year before Opel's. This Puppchen was by Wanderer, another German firm. Theirs was a 3-seater, 1,145-cc, 5/15 PS and was made at a real jaw-breaker: Wanderer Werke at Schonau bei Chemnitz.

Another company that graduated from sewing machines to automobiles, (they progressed through bicycles and motortricycles on the way) Swift of Coventry first made small cars. But by 1914, after offering a better-than-most cycle car, they settled down to a 4-cylinder, 10-hp model. This was good enough to be continued in various modified forms until 1931 when, sadly, Swift of Coventry bit the dust.

Cadillac again—1915. The first U.S. manufacturer to offer a V-8 water-cooled engine in a production car. (this discounts the 1910 Coyote and an abortive Marmon venture) Also—the first to use thermostatic cooling, thus setting the pattern for every quality carmaker in the United States.

Rolls-Royce Silver Ghost (GB)

This car was made for nineteen years—from 1907 to 1926—first in Manchester, then in Derby from 1908. Late in 1920 a factory was opened in the USA at Springfield, Massachusetts, where Ghosts were made until 1926. Rolls-Royce reinforced its claim as "the best car in the world" when in 1913 a team of Silver Ghosts won the Austrian Alpine Rally with ease against the best Europe could muster. Shortly afterward, James Radley, one of the victorious RR drivers, drastically reduced the London-Monte Carlo record (1,000 miles) from 33 to 26 hours in his Silver Shost Alpine Eagle, the car in the picture. In view of all this, how did the RR get a reputation for being almost everlasting, quiet, etc—but a lumbering car with no top speed of consequence? (Note: another Silver Ghost picture *is* redundant, but we couldn't resist another glimpse of this magnificent vehicle before the arrival of the war years plunged Europe into a period where cars became war materiel.

During the retreat from the Somme in France, the roads were packed with refugees on foot, and cars full of British and French soldiers being transported back to new defense lines. Taxis, private vehicles, all were pressed into service in a war in which, for the first time in recorded history, motor transport was to play an important part.

Daimler, Vauxhall, FIAT, Crossley and a legion of others (just about every German make, it can be assumed) played their roles in the massive movement of men and materiel. Every branch of the service of every country involved made use of the automobile in one form or another.

FIATS, 1915 (1).

A fleet of 1915 FIATS is shown here assembled for troop-transport work. By 1915 this model, first seen in 1912, was fully equipped with electric lights and a starter operating through a starter ring on the flywheel. With a maximum speed of about 50 mph and seating for five, this type of massed motor transport began to change the methods of war at both tactical and strategic levels. Engine: 4-cylinder, 4,396-cc developing 40 bhp at 1,800 rpm.

Crossley mounted various types of bodies on their 20 hp chassis, from light trucks to ambulances. The Royal Flying Corps, a fledgling in those days, used many of them. The RFC Crossley, as it became known, used a 4-cylinder, 4.5-liter engine, and was the big brother of the 3-liter, 15-hp model supplied to other of His Majesty's armed forces.

Vauxhall built nearly 2,000 vehicles (staff cars, mostly) for the British War Office, cars that saw rough service in many theaters of war. General Allanby rode one on the occasion of his entry into Jerusalem in 1917.

American cars were seen, also—Eddie Rickenbacker, America's top flying ace in World War I, used a Hudson Super Six in Paris to be greeted by French generals.

But in America in general, it was Europe's war—and business as usual. Ford brought out a closed body in the Model T, called the Tudor. And for a slightly larger model—well, what else could they call it but a Fordor? Still the same gutsy engine—still push pedals to change gears.

Packard, 1915 (USA).

In September of 1914, Cadillac brought a V-8 engined car off the production line. Three months later, on New Year's Day of 1915, Jesse Vincent (the man who took Packard into the upper-bracket market) began to design his 12-cylinder engine. One year after the Cadillac V-8's debut, the first 6.78-liter Packard Twin-six was unveiled. This was a quantum leap, at a time when 1- and 2-cylinder cars were still seen in abundance!

Sweden's Scania-Vabis was an amalgamation of two rival companies—Vabnfabriken and Scania. Their thrust was mainly in the commercial vehicle field, but they did produce a number of passenger cars. How many? Probably the lowest annual production rate of any automotive firm that lasted more than a few years. Between 1906 and 1924 they made 485 cars. Between 1925 and 1929—exactly 4. A little computer time will tell you that's an average of just under 20½ cars per year!

Hudson, in 1916, sent one of their seven-passenger tourers on a round-trip transcontinental trek—a first ever. San Francisco to New York took just 5 days, 3 hours and 31 minutes. The return trip was made almost as quickly. Since a crew of 5 was aboard it can be assumed there were no overnight stops on this remarkably fast trip.

The same year, the same firm brough out a genuinely elegant Six-40 Town Car. Among the elegances offered was (rare for the time) your choice of colors; India blue, dark Brunswick green, light beige, or light Orriford Lake.

Pierce-Arrow, 1916 (USA).

In 1916, President Woodrow Wilson had three Pierce-Arrows in his White House garage. You may be sure none of them looked like the one in the picture. Built along the sportive lines of the Mercer and the Stutz, this speedster was a stark twin-seater, and uncompromisingly fast. The great 66 was discontinued in 1917 (a war casualty, no doubt) and thus the largest production car built in the United States to this date disappeared. They were often sold with two bodies, a closed one for winter use and an open one for fair weather. The respect that surviving Pierce-Arrows command says much for a company which once made bird cages. So prestigious was the car and so well-known was it by the *cognocenti* that its name was not even displayed on the radiator except for one year—1928. One question arises from the picture: were the tires (or the roads) so undependable that *three* spare tires were necessary?

With no extras to buy, the Maxwell was more economical than most cars. The company from which the Chrysler giant was to grow in the middle of the next decade produced their cars of this period on a strong economy basis. Their advertising and promotional pieces often listed the extras that purchasers would be forced to buy for other cars, showing that those extras alone would cost a third of the price of a Maxwell.

By 1917, electric lights and starters became standard equipment for Chevrolet—and that year they also introduced a closed tourer, the very first closed body in the Chevrolet line. The first V-8 engine was fitted into the 1917 D-series, an ohv unit of 288 cu. in.

87

Oakland, 1918 (USA)

Unlike the major producers of Europe, whose output was devoted almost 100% to the war effort, American manufacturers, while pulling their load for Uncle Sam (after April, 1917, when the USA declared war on Germany) found space, time and material for private car and commercial vehicle production. The Model 34 touring coupe from the Oakland Company of Pontiac, Michigan is an example: 35,000 were produced and sold in 1918. This rather conservative vehicle, using a 6-cylinder Northway Power unit of 177 cu. in., and which developed 41 bhp at 2,500 rpm sold extremely well in the middle market price class.

Others producing for civilian use in America included Buick, with their Model E-4-34, a 27-hp 2-seater, Studebaker, which offered a 50 hp model in either a four or a six, some of which still sported hickory wheels with demountable rims (the last Studebaker four was made in 1919); Cadillac, which sold 20,000 T57's in various body styles during 1918—one of them being an ultra-fashionable town limousine which developed a comfortable 60 bhp; and a Cleveland Company, Baker Rauch and Lang, which came up with an uncommon idea, which they claimed "banished the commonplace." If you can believe it, the car was powered by electricity—and was called the Owens Magnetic. But instead of using storage batteries as a source of electricity, the car was equipped with a standard 6-cylinder gasoline engine which *generated* the electricity! The electricity thus generated delivered about 33 hp to the rear roadwheels, employing an electro-magnetic automatic transmission system developed in 1915.

Dodge Sedan, 1919. (USA)

Dodge came up with the sedan in March of 1919—4 months after the war's end. On a wheelbase of 114 inches, it offered a standard 4-cylinder, 35-hp engine of 212.3 cu. in., with a compression ratio of 4 to 1. The 1919 Dodge is on the right; on the left is their 1914 car.

After a couple of years of flirting with V-8's (ohv), Chevrolet went back to 4-cylinder models in 1919. They stayed with the fours exclusively until 1929.

By 1919, engineer Andre Citroën, who had been making shells for France through the war years, had moved into motor manufacture and presented his first car, the Type A 10-cv torpedo designed by Jules Salmon. This 1.3-liter model, the first in Europe to be mass-produced and delivered complete, was available to the public from July, 1919. Production started with a run of just 30 cars, but under the delightful pressure of success, 27,000 were made and sold in just eighteen months.

In England, Humber solved the problem of what to do for its first post-war car very simply and easily. Since their 1914 10-hp model was rather advanced for its time, they simply picked up where they had left off—and re-manufactured it! FIAT, on the other hand, produced a model completely new in shape and mechanical design. This one had an outstanding success record—45,000 were sold by 1926.

Lancia Tourer. (I)

Vincenzo Lancia's company had already established its name for quality when the Theta, his outstanding car to date, was introduced in 1913. The 4-cylinder, 4,940-cc, 70 bhp Kappa in the photograph was a development of Theta, plus innovations such as a variable steering-wheel rake, electric engine-starting controlled by a pedal, and a central gear lever instead of an outside one as in past Lancias. Top speed was around 75 mph.

Like the Coventry firm of Humber, Singer had made a highly successful Ten immediately prior to the war—a two-seater with a channel-steel chassis, 4-cylinder power pack, and the transmission in unit with the back axle. After the war the company, not yet retooled after making wartime vehicles, continued with the popular Ten, now with complete electrics and some styling modifications. The 1,100-cc car sold well, although post-war inflation pushed up the price. Singer overcame the price resistance at least partially by giving away a free insurance policy with each Singer Ten sold.

As a final note for 1910-1919: Mercer didn't make a lot of cars, but they made them to move fast, safely, and to last—a difficult combination. They were, however, expensive, and war's end began a slow decline for Mercer, when public demand was for practical transport at a practical price. The elite and the sports car fanatic didn't exist in sufficient numbers to keep Mercer alive. 1925 was the last year a new Mercer was manufactured.

The Open Road

It had been said that there was probably more enjoyment to be had in motoring between the end of World War I and the Depression which arrived in 1929, than ever before or since. Roads were relatively empty in both Europe and the United States, vehicles were past the pioneer stage and reasonably reliable, service stations had started to appear; long-distance travel at domestic level beckoned seductively.

New models poured from the factories in ever-differing varieties. Cycle cars appeared again, fragile 'wire-and-bobbin' objects that were often well below minimum safety standards. 'Assembled' cars with their bought-out components from common sources creating finished products that were near-identical, sold well. To persuade the would-be owner to buy this product in favour of that, Madison Avenue engaged top gear and advertising went rhapsodic, led by the master of them all, Ned Jordan, whose lyrical 'West of Laramie' ads and others finally became better-known than his flagship, the Jordan Playboy.

In Britain the cycle car met its end when Herbert Austin put his tiny Austin Seven on the road in 1922. It was to be his 'Model T' and at £165 swept most of the competition away even while attracting jokes such as 'Buy two—one for each foot'. In France former munitions maker André Citroën had turned to cars in direct competition with Renault, whilst French aircraft makers Voisin and Farman produced quality cars. Marc Birkigt's Hispano-Suiza, previously known as a luxurious and well-built car, now drew heavily on its designers' wartime aero engine experience and was given an entirely new and admirable image. The Hispano H6 had a six cylinder unit using many aero-engine features—lightweight alloy block, steel liners, overhead camshaft—and was without doubt the most advanced car of its time.

The U.S. found that in spite of its larger and more thirsty cars (and the fact that gasoline was expensive in Europe) American vehicles could compete with European products despite heavy taxes, and in 1920 no less than 33,000 were exported to Britain alone.

In the American homeland while Ford, Dodge and Chevrolet set the popular trend, specialist companies such as Duesenberg were capturing a small but lucrative market, and established names like Packard, Peerless and Pierce Arrow came back strongly into home and overseas trade. Henry Ford, as usual, led the rest of the industry in cutting prices, improving conditions, encouraging sales. His Model T ceased production in 1927 in favour of the Model A, but not before Henry had given more than 15-million people an unlovely but rugged and reliable vehicle that had changed the way of life of every one of them...

Germany, no slower than any other country to recover from hostilities, had by the mid-twenties become once again a force in Europe, with Opel's Laubfrosch, a little 1 litre car that was a near-copy of the Citroën, appearing in 1924, leading the mass sales in that country. Opel were to become part of General Motors in 1928; similarly the founder firms of Daimler and Benz were to merge in 1926 to become Daimler-Benz, one of the great quality-producers of the automotive world.

From October 1929, economic blizzards blew thousands of small producers into the void, leaving only the strong to continue the slow climb back to prosperity after the crash.

1920-1929

Berliet, 1920 (F).

In 1920 the Lyons company of Berliet confined passenger-car production to one model, the 15CV VB which had the almost unmistakable stamp of an American car and indeed was called the "Fake Dodge" by many in France. Dodge motors had the same idea at the same time, and took legal action against Berliet. Under the hood of the car pictured: a four-cylinder, 3.3-liter unit, with three forward speeds.

Under the recently-established stewardship of businessman Nicola Romeo (whose name had been added to the radiator badge and the company), Alfa-Romeo resumed production in 1920 with several modified pre-war models, including a 4-cylinder, 4,084-cc 20/30 and the 6-cylinder G-1 (which was shown in 1921). The sporting version of the 20/30 hp won its spurs in hill-climb and racing fields after the war, and 1920 saw the start of a long line of Alfa Romeo successes.

Opening for business in 1914, Guy Motors of Wolverhampton, England showed a genuine luxury car at the 1920 Olympia Motor Show. Built of semi-polished aluminum, it had a V-8 unit, and incorporated a first—automatic chassis lubrication, operated by a cam on the steering lever every time the car was turned on extreme right lock. This was a forerunner of a system used in later commercial vehicles.

92

Lesseps Snow Vehicle. (F)

This is what happens when automotive engineers and designers have too much free time on their hands. It was a DeLesseps creation based on Renault design with a 70 cv, 8-cylinder Aero-engine. Yes, that *is* a propellor on the rear end. Could this have been the first snowmobile?

1920 saw Chevrolet win the Indianapolis 500, with Gaston Chevrolet at the wheel of a Monroe-Frontenac. They were called by that name because Monroe built them (seven identical 2,982-cc cars) at the Monroe works in Indianapolis, and Frontenac because that was the name Chevrolet chose for the corporation formed to make them specifically for the 500. Chevrolet's winning speed averaged 88.62 mph.

The Model T Ford had, up to 1920, been used for just about every form of transport. Down on the farm they had the tractor version, and the tourer was pressed into service as a power saw, milking machine, etc. So—in 1920, the Model T turned up as a station wagon—Ford's first venture into the multi-seater private car.

FIAT, as one of the arms of the automotive octopus it was, had one model designed specifically for taxicab work. It looked like an overgrown matchbox, developed only 18 hp at 2,000 rpm, could do only 37 mph at top speed and couldn't climb a grade steeper than 15%. But—it traveled 24 miles on a gallon of gas, and Rome was loaded with them!

Dodge, 1920 (USA).

This is very likely the car which the Berliet "Fake Dodge" resembled so strongly that it caused legal action by Dodge. This incredibly rugged vehicle had been for a long time the platform on which Dodge's prosperity was founded, and it kept right on being so until 1927. With a slow-running unit (3⅞ X 4½ in bore) pushing out about 25 hp (N.A.C.C. rating) and still with the back-to-front gear change, it had one new feature in 1920—a slanting windshield. The wheels were still wooden, although the company had flirted with wire a couple of years earlier. The two Dodge brothers, Horace and John, both died of pneumonia in 1920 within a few months of each other.

Mention has been made several times of Hudson's turning up on foreign soil: India, Paris for Eddie Rickenbacker, to name but two. Here's another—Montreal, where the Hudson Super Six was the official car used by the greatest tenor of his day, Enrico Caruso, for a Montreal singing engagement. First seen in 1916, the great Super Sixes were renowned for their sporting exploits and service reliability.

As can be imagined, early post-war years were difficult times in Germany. By 1920, Opel managed to produce an 8/25-PS six-seater. Torpedo styled, it was a conventional model in all ways, and (not surprisingly) was strongly reminiscent of prewar models. Gear lever and hand brake were outboard; with four speeds and reverse, it could do a modest 50 mph.

Peugeot Torpedo (F).

At least Peugeot could not be accused, as others were, of using American styling in their immediate postwar passenger cars. This slim-line, 10-hp torpedo type 163 was made from 1910 to 1924. It sported a modest 1,435-cc motor, four forward speeds and one that marched the other way (a free translation, from Peugeot's brochure, of the inimitable French description of reverse gear), and a maximum speed of 60 km/h (37 mph).

A short run (but not a very merry one) was the fate of the Leland Eight Speed Model, first seen in 1920 and aimed at the post-war luxury market. It housed a good-sized straight eight unit with single ohc, inclined valves and hemispherical combustion chambers. Other advanced features included a torsion bar, a starter incorporated in the transmission and automatic lubrication. Rear brakes only. Alas, only sixteen were made, although the car was later developed for racing.

A most untypical Lanchester was unveiled in 1919 (a very fast turnaround, after 4 years of making airplane engines). The 6-cylinder "Forty" can best be described as a stylist's example of the panel-beater's art. The two door coupe housed a single ohc engine of just over 6 liters, giving 90 bhp.

Some 18,000 Oldsmobile sixes were produced in 1920; this doesn't take into account a 4-cylinder model, and no less than 4 V-8 models, plus an "economy" truck. Oldsmobile completed a large expansion program that year, and William C. Durant left General Motors.

Renault Limousine, 1920 (F).

Pour les Grandes Boulevards, this great 24 CV 6-cylinder Renault of 1920 was based on an improved post-war design and was but one part of a wide range of vehicles from 10 to 40 hp, and *camions* (trucks) from 1,000 kilos to 7 tons, as well as agricultural tractors and industrial motors. By 1920, Louis Renault had built the largest manufacturing empire in France. The 24 CV was indeed, a luxury car, with a richly appointed interior—but why was that radiator still sticking out behind the engine, and why was the poor chauffeur still out in the cold?

The 30/98 (no one knows the reason for calling it this) was the Vauxhall car of the twenties. The first ones saw the light of day in 1913, although only thirteen were made before the war. After the war, it was another matter. Who could resist a car developed directly from the legendary Prince Henry—one with a 4½-liter, 4-cylinder engine which produced 100 bhp on the bench? The car leaped to fame in sporting circles in the early post-war years. In three seasons, it scored an astounding seventy-five racing wins and fifty-two second places, apart from numerous hill-climb victories. With the car came a guarantee that "with a single-seated body, the 30/98 Vauxhall will attain 100 mph on the track". In 1920 that was *really* sticking your neck out!

One more which sang a swan song in 1920—the 1,000-cc Stellite. Wolseley owned the parent company (and by 1920 it looked like a small Wolseley), but in that fateful year the market had caught up with the Stellite, and small cars, particularly of continental make, stole the bread from Stellite's table.

Vauxhall 'semi-racer', 1909. (GB)

A two-seater 2½-liter Star, 1909. (GB)

First of the Alfas, the 24-hp Torpedo of 1910.
The company was called Alfa Romeo after
World War I. (I)

Model T Ford, 1910.

Rolls-Royce Roi-des-Belges, 1910.

Renault two-seater, 1910.

Opel 10/18 hp Double Phaeton, 1909. (D)

1908 Hutton, built by Napier for racing. (GB)

The famous Renault 'Taxi de la Marne', first made in 1906. Six hundred were used to rush French troops to the front in 1914. (F)

Downtown Detroit, 1920

Downtown Detroit in 1920 looks almost empty, compared with the earlier picture of London in 1914. However, the same elements—buses, private cars, trucks, taxis, and even horse-drawn vehicles are present. By 1920, the car had indeed taken over, and the "Roaring Twenties" had arrived. There is one important difference between London in 1914 and Detroit in 1920—in the latter year, Detroit produced a total of 1,905,560 passenger vehicles!

One of those 1,905,560 appears in the other picture. After making what was reputedly the largest American production car, only Pierce-Arrow models 38 and 48 were offered by 1920, both with right-hand steering. (This was changed in 1921.) The car still didn't display its name, but the headlight placement (sort of erupting from the fenders) made it easily the most identifiable car in the USA.

Sunbeam's 24-hp model touring car was one of a range of refined, comfortable cars which bore, in 1920-1921, little relation to the Sunbeams participating in Grand Prix racing. In 1920, Sunbeam amalgamated—and became Sunbeam Talbot Durracq.

Note to male chauvinists: in 1921, a race called the "Grand Prix Gentlemen" and run at Brescia, Italy, was won by a 20/30 ES Sport Alfa-Romeo—driven by a lady. The Alfa-Romeo was powered by a 4-cylinder, 4,250-cc engine. Heaven only knows what powered the lady.

Pierce - Arrow, 1920 (USA).

97

The Open Road: 1920-1929

One of the companies often overlooked in the history of motoring is Autobianchi. Probably because of Bianchi's close association in later years with FIAT and Pirelli, (Autobianchi represented a change of name) the car doesn't seem to have made much impact. The company is one of the oldest in the industry, but Eduardo Bianchi went unspectacularly from bicycles to voiturettes and then to more ambitious vehicles of a steady, middle-of-the-road character. The car pictured is a 1,692-cc, two-seater tourer with a (remember them?) rumble seat.

Following the 1920 VB—the "fake Dodge", Marius Berliet produced his 16 CV VL in very much the same style, although this model represented a determined effort to recover from a severe reverse of his fortunes. The 16 CV VL was known as the Etoile Argent (Silver Star), and bore a 3,308-cc, side-valve engine under its hood. The product sold reasonably well, allowing the company a further lease on life—until 1939.

Autocarriers, formed in 1911 (preceded by Autocars and Accessories Limited in 1908) had produced the successful 10-hp A.C. before the war. Post-war, they updated with a 1½-liter, lightweight, wet-liner 4-cylinder Anzani engine or a choice of two sizes of 6-cylinder unit. The smaller A.C. was successful in reliability trials—so successful, in fact, that when six of them were entered in the London to Edinburgh run, all six won gold medals.

Autobianchi Tourer (I).

Buick, 1921 (USA)

This seven-passenger sedan Type 21-6-50 from Buick in Flint, Michigan housed a 6-cylinder, 242-cu in unit and had a reinforced pressed-steel frame—one of seven types listed in 1921, ranging from a three-passenger roadster to this luxury product, of which 7,292 were made.

It may look like a giant skateboard, but the Castle 3-wheeler shown was actually one of the less spindly cycle cars of the period. Some 350 of them were produced by the Castle Motor Company of Kidderminster, Worcestershire. The first dozen or so used Dorman-type 4KL engines; the rest were powered by Belgian Peters units. 4 cylinders, water cooled.

The Jordan cabriolet from the Cleveland company was typical of Edward Jordan's high standard. Powered by a 6-cylinder Continental unit rated at 25.5 hp, with three forward speeds and reverse, the model was also offered as a "Silhouette" five-or seven-passenger tourer, a brougham, sedan or "Playboy." Remembered as much for his advertising as for his cars, Jordan's *West of Laramie* ad was yet to appear and change the face of motor publicity in the USA.

FIAT made a leap at the upper bracket with a huge town-carriage style it called, appropriately enough, the Super FIAT. Its V-12 engine was the first and last 12-cylinder unit in the history of FIAT design. It produced a hefty 90 bhp, and top speed was around 75 mph. FIAT's leap fell far short, however—a total of only five were made—a comment on the venture and the times.

Castle-Three 3-Wheeler (GB).

Lancia Lambda, circa 1921 (I).

Two Italian approaches to racing cars in the early 1920's. The Lambda is generally considered to be Vincenzo Lancia's masterpiece. (The one shown is the prototype.) Of the car and the man, one of his engineers said at the time: "He intends to design a car that will carry the mechanical units without using the classical frame. The hull of a ship is quoted as a possible model. Sgr. Lancia also tells us of his idea of replacing the rigid front axle by a suspension in which the movements of the wheels would be independent of each other"—in other words, unitary (or monocoque) construction and independent front suspension.

The FIAT Corsa took a more convential approach. A new, post-war development, the 901-401 was first entered in the Parma-Poggio di Berceto event run on May 8, 1921. It finished first in the 3-liter class in its first effort, at an average speed of 81 mph. The power unit developed 112-bhp at 4,000 rpm. Top speed was around 100 mph.

The Essex was a plain, no-nonsense car built by Hudson for the lower-budget market. The 4-cylinder, 2.9-liter, 55-bhp model had, by 1921, became respected and enjoyed some sporting successes at Pikes Peak. As advertised, colors were "a rich dark Valentine blue, with hood and fenders in black." Sounds rather somber for a two-toned car, but they sold well.

FIAT Corsa, 1921 (I)

Ford Truck (USA).

Yes, it's a commercial vehicle—but this irresistible shot of a Model T at work fairly shrieks to be included! Ford brought out its first truck in 1917, rated at one ton; as can be seen, the front end was virtually a passenger car, but the frame was heavier and longer (heaven knows it needed to be!) and the rear suspension was stronger.

Citroën of France built something they called a B2 *Conduite Interieure.* (all that French meant was that the driver was inside with the passengers.) First to be introduced was the "Luxury Open Tourer" with a 1,452-cc, 4-cylinder side-valve engine rated (by the French Treasury, no less!) at 9-hp. Later forms of the B2, which was produced from 1921 to 1925, were the Clover Leaf, Caddy, which had some sports tendencies, Torpedo and a taxi with the well-known wickerwork body.

Laurin & Klement had established themselves as the largest automobile producer in the Austro-Hungarian Empire as early as 1914, but the post-war creation of the Czechoslovak Republic reduced its home market, and the political and financial instability of Europe stunted its export market, notably to Russia. During this period, L & K produced 4-cylinder cars based on the most successful of the pre-war range. Their Type S was revived at 2,402-cc, and a Knight side-valve engine was produced for the type MK (3,200-cc) and the MK6 (3,498-cc, 50-hp).

101

Locomobile, circa 1921 (USA).

Seen at a modern meet is the big Sportif Series B Locomobile out of Bridgeport, Connecticut. In 1908, this model, in the shape of the 90-hp Locomobile, driven by George Robertson, made its name by winning the Vanderbilt Cup in horrendous weather conditions. The Sportif shown here was an N.A.C.C.-rated 48.6-hp six, with bore and stroke of 4½ × 5½ inches. Surprisingly, it was classed as a four-seater, though it looks ample for six.

The German Daimler company had begun experiments with a super-charger (kompressor) as early as 1915 (presumably for military use) and the results were turned to account when the war ended. Two Mercedes models, the 6/25 and the 2,610-cc 10/40/65, were first fitted with super-charged engines as standard-optional equipment. Both used Roots-type blowers brought into use only when the accelerator pedal was almost fully depressed.

Pretty much of a flop was Peugeot's idea of a two-passenger car in early post-war years. It was called, for some unknown reason, a Quadrilette, and the seating was arranged in tandem—a layout, it would seem, much more suited to horses or bicycles. They realized their mistake, but the solution didn't do well, either. (The very narrow track of 30 inches was just wide enough to turn it into a pinched side-by-side.) Predictably, only 3,500 were made.

Maxwell went Henry Ford one better in color offering. You could have the Ford one way only—uncompromising black. Maxwell, in a wild burst of promotional fervor, proudly announced you could have theirs in blue-black also.

Rumpler, 1921 (D).

Engineer Edward Rumpler designed this early attempt at coupling aerodynamics with automobiles. Astonished Berliners got their first look at it at the 1921 Berlin Auto Show. Built on an aircraft-type hull supported on pressed-steel bulkheads with a rear engine and the driver up ahead at the 'midships wheel, the Rumpler car was unorthodox in every way. The engine itself was an extraordinary 2½-liter, W-formation, 6-cylinder unit. All in all, it looks like something in which Jacques Costeau might go searching for sunken Spanish galleons.

Sunbeam apparently got the idea that if you had great success with your racing cars—known as Talbot - Darracqs in some events—all you had to do was double the engine size for even greater success. In 1921, their smaller cars won just about everything in sight. So—they ballooned the engines, and it turned out to be a big, fat nothing. The big fellows were entered in both the French Grand Prix and the Indianapolis 500—and could do no better than fifth place in either.

The Renault taxicab made history during World War I—it became known as the "Taxi de la Marne", when thousands of French troops were hastily transported to the front by taxi to stem a German advance. Its post-war successor, a very basic 4-cylinder vehicle was produced in large numbers to serve the cities of France. The radiator-in-back-of-the-engine format was unaccountably retained until 1928, although Renault, as though realizing its obvious misplacement, made some abortive attempts to disguise it before that date.

Santler, circa 1921 (GB).

Thomas Santler is still something of a figure of mystery in the automotive world, claiming to have helped Benz in his early work and to have made a car in 1887, although little evidence of this has ever come to light. However, the Santler "Rushabout" in the photograph certainly existed and was made at the Malvern factory. Virtually a "Chinese copy" of the contemporary Morgan produced not 600 yards down the road, some twelve models were made. It was powered by a 10-hp M.A.B. engine.

The merger of Sunbeam, Clement-Talbot and Darracq produced a rather interesting result. Their 1½-liter cars won every race they entered in 1921 and 1922. As mentioned earlier, the 3-liter blowups fared poorly. But when the 1½-liter was offered to the public, it was offered with a choice of three radiators, with two or three different nameplates. Same car, but since the make was both French and English, you could have the car as a French or English product, dependent upon your national preferences!

Riley got into the post-war market with a long-stroke, 1½-liter, 10.8-hp car in 1919. By 1921, the 4-cylinder unit had inclined valves, detachable head and aluminum pistons.

By 1921 the Vulcan company had made a large range of cars and commercial vehicles on standard lines and were currently offering 12-, 16-, and 20/50-hp vehicles—all with 4-cylinder engines. Late in the year they announced a 3.6 "sports tourer."

Arrol-Johnson had to resort to desperate measures after the war. They designed, built, announced and sold a post-war car which they named "Victory". Trouble erupted when the Royal Family chose the "Victory" for a Royal tour of Britain's West Country and the cars kept breaking down. The embarrassed Scottish firm hurriedly updated their prewar 15.9-hp models, with the 4-cylinder side-valve, 2.9-liter, fixed ignition model shown. Then, in 1922 they brought out an even larger model.

Wolseley had been given the contract to produce Hispano-Suiza aircraft engines during World War I, and some of the technology had rubbed off on their post-war products, notably in their overhead camshaft power units—although they discovered that these esoterics did not appeal to some of the buying public. Apparently the post-war buyers (in the mass) were looking for meat and potatos—not rich desserts.

During the same year that the first car designed by Capt. W. O. Bentley of aero-engine repute was offered to the public (first seen at the 1919 Motor Show in London and on sale in 1921) a Bentley was raced. In 1922, a Bentley, modified for racing, was entered in the Indianapolis 500; it was not fast enough to keep up with the action, although it finished the race. The engine was a 4-cylinder, single-overhead camshaft, 3-liter unit.

Arrol-Johnson, circa 1921 (GB).

The Open Road: 1920-1929

To the British, Herbert Austin is as Henry Ford to the Americans—the man who put a nation on wheels. Although he built his first cars in 1896 while working for Wolseley and had manufactured cars under his own name since 1906, it is for the Austin Seven that most remember his—if only because this simple vehicle was the first transport of thousands of young English motorists.

A very light car, the Seven weighed just over 1,000 lbs, with an overall length of 8 feet, 9 inches and carried a 696-cc engine. (later enlarged slightly to 747-cc.) The car was the occasion for a great deal of amusement—jokes about "buying one for each foot" were standard fare in the British music halls. However, it rapidly took the place of the unloved cycle car and made large inroads on the motorcycle-and-sidecar brigade. It was built under license in four countries—Germany, France, Japan and the United States. Herbert Austin (later Lord Austin) is pictured in one of the very first Sevens.

In 1922 racing, Austro-Daimler had a banner year, winning forty-three races out of fifty-one starts. They called their four 1,100-cc cars "Saschas"-and all were designed by the company *generaldirektor*, Ferdinand Porsche. When Porsche got around to his later rear-engined designs, he was influenced rather strongly by another racing car of 1922—this one so streamlined it was called the Tropfennwagen (Teardrop). This one was designed by the same Edmund Rumpler who started Berlin buzzing with the strange-looking vehicle at the 1921 Berlin auto show. Teardrop's unorthodoxy was not confined to its shape—radiator, engine, floating rear axle and inboard brakes were all avant garde.

Austin Seven (GB).

BSA, 1921 (GB)

Two small cars that went after the postwar light-car boom. Burmingham Small Arms Company designed their two-seater with a 1,080-cc Hotchkiss V-twin unit which developed 18 HP.

The other pee-wee became far more famous. It was the lemon-yellow Citroën, two-seated, easy to run and highly maneuverable. It met with swift success and was one of the continental vehicles that put an end to the post-war cycle-car reign. Since the French world for "yellow" is *citron*, it was inevitably called the "Citron Citroën", and it was one of the first small cars to attract women buyers in large numbers. The Citroën Company followed it up with a three-seater version, which they named "Clover Leaf". Engine: 856-cc, 11-hp.

Winner at Indianapolis in the 500 was Jimmy Murphy, who had won the French Grand Prix the previous year. Murphy put a Miller engine into a racing Duesenberg chassis for the Indy and broke several records with the Duesenberg-Miller mating. The engine was a two-year-old design, a straight-8, 3-liter affair with mixed ancestry: Peugeot, Ballot and Duesenberg.

More on the peripatetic wanderings of the Hudson: they sold, of course, in quantity in half-a-dozen different forms all around the world. The company reported that they were replacing the bullock cart in India—and a Japanese hotel owner had taken delivery of forty-two Hudsons!

Citroën, 1922 (F).

ISOTTA FRASCHINI—1922

Mors SSS (F).

Three examples of continental luxury cars in the early 1920's: The old-established Milan company of Isotta-Fraschini made cars that were the stuff of dreams in the twenties and thirties. Luxurious and exotic, the Tipo 8 was made from 1919 to 1924. Its relaxed 6-liter engine was not designed to beat the Blue Train to Nice (as novels of the time had it) but it was a deluxe carriage of great elegance. The one shown has a sports body by Sala.

The Mors was large, luxurious and very French. Mors had gained its laurels in the early racing days, particularly in the tragic 1903 Paris-Madrid race. The car in the picture is the sports boat-tail SSS (Sans Soupapes Silencieuse) with a 3,500-cc, 4-cylinder power unit. The car appealed in vintage years to a select few—too few, unhappily—and the distinguished company ceased making cars in 1927, although its name lived until just after World War II as a manufacturer of scooters.

The legendary Lancia Lambda shocked the motoring public in 1922 when its monocoque (frameless) construction appeared on the scene. Over its life of eight years, the Lambda was constantly modified and improved. The final engine size was 2,570-cc and the power increased to 69 bhp. Nine versions and 13,000 Lambdas were eventually made.

Lancia Lambda (I).

Oldsmobile, 1923 (USA).

Oldsmobile called this one the Sportsman's Roadster. The rather square two-seater-plus-rumble was one of the last of the Oldsmobile fours. When the 6-cylinder Model 30 appeared on the market in 1923, the fours went into limbo—never to reappear. A close look will reveal something which would be frowned upon by the more discerning motorist of today—two different kinds of tread on the spare tires.

A bit of data about the Twin-Six Packard. The engine was a big V-12 (at 60 degrees) cast in two blocks of six, and was the first ever to be made for the commercial market. Its 7 liters developed about 88 bhp (N.A.C.C. rating 43.2) which took it up to some 83 mph maximum. First seen in 1915, it impressed the automotive world with its flexibility and smooth operation—moving from 4 to 30 mph in top in a vibrationless 12 seconds.

In 1922 Renault finally decided to try to hide the back-of-the-engine radiator under a flush-line hood, in the shape of an 8.3 Sports Tourer which was built until 1929. The radiator stayed put—they just hid it. This 3-seater design, by the way, was aimed head-on at Citroën's 5CV—the "Citron Citroën", even to the adoption of solid disc wheels. A number of innovations were included in the Renault, the most noteworthy of which was a removable cylinder head—the first used by Renault.

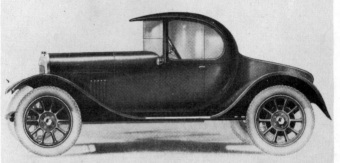

Standard two seater (GB)

A pair that went, so to speak, nowhere in particular. The Steyr was built by a former Austrian arms factory (one of the few automotive producers from that country) for the Italian Targo Florio, which at that time was run over 4 laps of Sicily's 286-mile "medium" circuit. Two French Ballots finished in front of it.

Why the 11.6 Standard from the Coventry company was built at all defies reason. It *looks* as though it might be an attempt at streamlining—except they appear to have gotten the whole thing backwards. That overhang in front of the windshield must have made the engine work twice as hard as it should have.

Sunbeam tried to match a 4-cylinder (four valves per cylinder) unit against the sixes and eights of FIAT, Bugatti, Ballot and Rolland-Pilain. Finding no success in the smaller engine, they went to the other extreme and put a monster V-12 aero-engine of 18.322 liters, developing 350 hp into a Sunbeam and this time—a world speed record of 133.75 mph, which probably made 1922 a year for Sunbeam to remember.

Every motoring aficionado knows the Stutz bearcat—but Stutz also had a couple of tourers; one a four- or five-passenger, the other held five or six, depending, it is supposed, on the squeezeability of the passengers. The big one developed 30.63 hp.

Steyr, 1922 (A).

Wills St. Clare Roadster (USA).

The 65 hp Model A68 Wills St. Clare Roadster housed a 4,350-cc V8 engine (designed by Childe Harold Wills after he left Ford in 1919), a unit that owed much to the wartime Hispano-Suiza aero-engine. Wills St. Clare had some initial success, but the highly sophisticated car (modestly priced) suffered when the American public came to the conclusion that it was too elaborate in design and too expensive to maintain.

A couple of 1½-liter racers that made some history: first, the Italian Type 13 Bugatti, which became known as the "Brescia" after a 1-2-3-4 finish there in 1921. It was the forerunner for most high-performance light sports cars that followed. The Bugatti was, and still is for that matter, one of the seven wonders of the automotive world—with steering, suspension, chassis design, transmission and engine mechanics far ahead of its time in sheer accuracy and operation.

The little 1½ liter Aston-Martin, in 1923, tore up the pea-patch in England at Brooklands track. The car took the standing half-mile record at 62.76 mph, the standing kilometer at 66.54, and the standing mile at 74.12. It also climbed the Brooklands test hill in 9.14 records, establishing another record. The car, nicknamed "Bunny", had also taken ten world records and twenty-two class records the previous year. All in all, these two (the Bugatti and the Aston-Martin) spread-eagled the field pretty well in their size. And wasn't the Aston-Martin the car James Bond drove in "Goldfinger?"

Chevrolet, 1923 (USA).

Successor to the popular "490" series, the Chevrolet Superior became the model line for ten years, to be interrupted only by the ill-fated "Copper Cooled" Chevrolet that was also seen in 1923—an air-cooled car designed by the famous Charles Kettering, but was discontinued after what must have been an all-time record low run for Chevrolet—just 759 were made. The Superior still used the 170-cu in, 4-cylinder engine and rode on wooden artillery wheels. Total emancipation from the pre-war look was not achieved until 1924.

Following the Type A, the 1½-liter B2 Citroën, built between 1921 and 1925, had a detachable cylinder head and engine-clutch-transmission unit. A multiplicity of bodies were offered in addition to the basic open tourer which had three seats and a boat-shaped back. A souped-up "Caddy Sport" with high-performance tendencies and a skiff-type body was popular with the young bucks—as was the dignified Coupe de Ville with their parents.

The Type GL 50/60 Delage made during the company's five-year involvement with racing, benefited greatly from the great French Company's sporting activities. The GL, which stood for Grande Luxe, used a sophisticated, 6-cylinder overhead-camshaft unit of 5.9 liters. It was in truth one of the finest French vehicles of its day.

Clyno Roadster (GB)

Two who fell by the wayside: Clyno had a background of motorcycle manufacture (they supplied the British Army from 1914 to 1918) before turning to cars in 1921. They hit the jackpot with an 11-hp light car of 1.4 liters—pleasant to handle, reliable, and from 1926, with four-wheel brakes as standard (unusual even then on light vehicles). Large-section tires were also an advance pioneered by the company. The powerful competition of the Morris finally put Clyno out of business.

Since the 1880's, de Dion Bouton had been making and selling cars successfully. But the great breed began to decline in the 1920s. Many reasons have been put forth—poor performance, technical stagnation and so on—but in fact the company failed in 1932 because their cars were not glamorous and exciting enough to attract buyers away from the other classic automobiles, and they were not cheap enough to compete with the Austins, Citroëns, Fords and the others at the other end of the market.

Early established in the production of engines, the British firm of Crossley first made cars in 1904. In October of 1923 the company announced its 20/70-hp with a high-lift camshaft jacking up the bhp so that 75 mph could be guaranteed. Recommended for "fast touring" by former British competition driver S. F. Edge, it also enjoyed numerous sporting wins at Brooklands and other events.

de Dion Bouton Tourer, 1923 (F).

Lincoln, circa 1923 (USA)

Ford had bought out the foundering Lincoln company in 1922. At the time of purchase, Lincoln had managed to produce just 3,407 cars. One of the first Ford-produced Lincolns was this four-passenger phaeton built on a 136-inch chassis with a 5.8 liter V-8 engine. It is reputed that this car, and the Hudson Super-Sixes of the period, were favored by the American gangsters of prohibition days. Since there were no posts supporting the tops, this provided a wide firing arc from automatic weapons (tommy-guns, for the most part) and a powerful engine for a fast getaway. If you think this far-fetched, listen to what one writer of the time said: "even the beer trucks had tail gunners!".

In contrast to the glamor of the racy-looking Lincoln, the British firm of Humber produced neat, sober, unspectacular vehicles during those years. One model, their 8-hp, had some claim to special notice—it used overhead inlet and side-valve exhaust disposition.

Also in Britain, at the Manchester works, Ford was building a Model T with right-hand drive. This was an out-and-out copy of the American Ford—the only change was in the steering wheel position. This was true of all the Fords from Manchester. In 1932, however, a new British Ford plant in the South began to manufacture a smaller car—the tiny Ford 8.

By 1923, four-wheel brakes, foot-controlled headlight dippers and powered windshield wipers were standard on a great number of American cars.

Maxwell, circa 1922 (USA).

The Good Maxwell appeared in 1921 when Walter Chrysler reorganized the Maxwell company, renamed the car and improved its quality. Maxwell sales increased, but the associate company, Chalmers, lost a bundle and the organization was terminated. By this time, the new Chrysler had begun to attract most of the available buyers.

Classed up in the rarified regions of the Rolls-Royce and the Napier, the Lanchester 40, a precisely made 6-cylinder car built to Edwardian standards and tastes, would travel, so they said, at a steady 90 mph and could use top gear from 3 to 90 mph. As more than one writer put it, "The Lanchester was designed and built to give its owner unfailing service forever".

The previous year, which saw a radical change in Renault's appearance, also saw four-wheel brakes on the larger cars from Billancourt. By 1923, they were standard on all but one of the smaller range.

Common practice in the early 20's was to offer a slightly tuned version of the family car for those more well-heeled and sportive than the ordinary buyer. Cecil Kimber ran Morris Garages (out of which the Morris empire grew) and he modified a Morris 11.9 Cowley unit to push-rod ohv, put it in a light chassis frame, used Morris parts exclusively—and called it an MG. Illustrated is the 1923 experimental car with Kimber at the wheel. Production began in 1925.

first MG, 1923 (GB).

Wolseley runabout (GB).

Economic factors and supply difficulties tended to suppress any too-ambitious venture in manufacture during the early years after the war. Wider demand had brought in a new section of buying public—the buyer whose purse was considerably lighter than that of the class who had bought automobiles in rosier Edwardian days. Thus, the modest 1.3 liter, 10-hp Wolseley pictured and its like, although Wolseley offered versions bodied in light alloy for the more sportif.

Three more British lilliputians, all after the workingman's hard-earned pound: the Rover, first seen in 1920: 8-hp with an air-cooled flat-twin engine originally of 998-cc (later enlarged to 1,130-cc) developing 14 hp. Through the years 1920-1925, 17,000 of these little cars were sold to owners who rarely failed to sing their praises.

The Austin Seven, one year after its debut, now with a 747-cc engine, a reduced price (cheaper than many motorcycle-side-car combinations), and the cozy name "Chummy", was the increasingly popular transport for the small family which had previously imagined owning a car well beyond its means.

Somewhat sportier in appearance was the A.B.C., which used an air-cooled, flat-twin engine of just over a liter. The noisy and somewhat fragile unit took the car up to some creditable speeds, however, assisted by the very light weight of the vehicle.

Three "Cs" and a "D" that didn't make it. During 1924 the car pictured was still available to the public, although the company had ceased production the previous year. Shown is the 6-cylinder over-head-valve, four-seater Pasadena model. Five other Dorris models were also available.

James Cunningham's company based at Rochester had built carriages since the 19th century and cars from 1907. By 1915 they made only cars—on a one-model policy. The Cunningham V-8 of 6 liters and 100 bhp was handsome and advanced and was offered for eighteen years. Owned by some famous names in entertainment and industry, the Cunningham was in a "price on application" bracket.

Balloon tires, and in some cases air suspension, were the platforms on which the Cole based its somewhat dubious claim to safety and comfort. The company offered 16 models in 1924, all of 39.2 hp—and all with fancy names like Aero Volante, Brouette and Royal Limousine.

The third defunct "C" isn't really defunct—they're still in their original business in Racine, Wisconsin, making farm machinery. Case got into automobiles in 1910, and on the strength of their reputation and reliable performance in the farm area, they did a respectable business for a number of years. Their conservatism finally defeated them, however, and the Case car disappeared after 1927.

Dorris, 1924 (USA).

Citroën, 1924 (F).

For twelve years—from 1914 to 1925—you could have your choice of any color you wanted in a Ford—if you wanted to paint it yourself. Ford sold it to you one way only—black. Even the brass radiator of the earlier models had long since given way to a black paint job, all in the (highly successful) cause of keeping the cost down. The car in the picture is the 1924 Fordor Sedan (with four doors, naturally) which followed the earlier Tudor (with *two* doors, of course!). Ford produced its 1-millionth car in 1924—and in that year, every seventh American owned an automobile.

The toy-like SCV Citroën hit the streets of Paris and the roads of France in 1922, and was an immediate success. By 1924, several body styles were available: a "doctor" coupe, a three-seater tourer, and the model shown, the two-seater "duck-back" tourer. Its 856-cc engine produced 11 bhp— enough to trundle along at 39 mph, and also enough to attract 80,000 buyers. It was copied by a number of European makers.

Mercedes' love affair with superchargers was going strong in 1924. They won 93 races with supercharged 1½-and 2-liter cars that year—and they had a real brute in their supercharged 24/100/140 6-cylinder tourer with an impressive 6.25-liters and 142 bhp under the hood.

Ford Fordor, 1924 (USA)

This is one of the cars which was inspired by the "duck-back" Citroën—and looked it. The 951-cc, 4/12 PS Opel two-seater was soon named "Laubfrosch" (tree-toad) for its color. It had immense popularity in a country that could not afford luxury models, post-war Germany being the financial cripple that it was. The "Laubfrosch" could travel at up to 45 mph, and by 1926 Opel was able to reduce the price considerably. Nearly 40,000 were sold by 1927.

Another price-cutter was Morris of Britain. From 1920 they dropped the price of the Morris Cowley year by year until in 1924, it could be bought quite inexpensively. How inexpensively? In 1924, the two seater was just under $1,000, the four-seater about $125 more, and what they called their "occasional four", went for £215, about $50 less than the four.

A group of Ford employees who thought they could do better got together in 1922 with ideas of their own about how a car should be made. The Gray taxi-tourer was the result. The company's problems arose when they found out that those "ideas of their own" had already been used by Ford. The Gray's engine specifications and chassis design were blood brother to the Ford, but the whole thing foundered in attempt to fulfill ambitious plans to flood the market with Gray products. They lasted until 1926, and disappeared into the automobile graveyard, sadder, but hopefully wiser.

Opel "Laubfrosch" (D).

The Open Road: 1920-1929

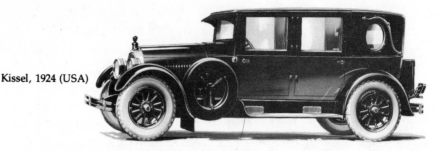

Kissel, 1924 (USA)

The model 55 Kissel was built in eight versions, from speedster to the luxurious Berline shown. This was a seven-passenger vehicle very similar to the company's brougham except for the dimensions of the rear compartment. Later in the 1924 model year Kissel offered 4-wheel Lockheed external contracting hydraulic brakes as optional equipment, and an alternative 8-cylinder engine.

Just sitting, with the grass trying to grow through its wheel spokes, is a long-goner, a McFarlan Town Car (2½ tons of it!) that first suffered under the name of a Kickerbocker Cabriolet. This one housed the large TV (Twin Valve), 6-cylinder engine with triple ignition and a total of 18 spark plugs, any one of which could foul, and most likely did.

After the long success of the Silver Ghost, Rolls-Royce abandoned its one-model policy in 1922 because of economic pressures. The chassis price of the new car—the 6-cylinder, 3.1-liter Twenty—was comparatively modest, and about 3,000 were made by 1929, when they upped the size to 20/25 hp—then upped it again in 1936 to 25/30. The car may have *looked* old-fashioned, but R-R never lagged behind in engineering improvements. Their only lag was in telling the world about it—most of their improvements went into their cars with no comment from the company at all.

McFarlan, 1924 (USA).

Produced from 1920 to 1924, the 12/40 PS, 3.2 liter Type II Steyr "Waffenauto" was manufactured in the (hold onto your teeth!) Oesterreichische Waffenfabriks-Gesellschaft at Steyr, Austria. It was the first passenger vehicle from this former arms company, which like others in eastern and central Europe, were forced to cast about for something other than guns to make. Designed by the ubiquitous Hans Ledwinka, the Waffenauto was the first of a sound line of cars from Steyr.

Hope-springs-eternal note: the 10-hp, four seater British Singer was introduced in 1923. In 1964, a letter from an owner in Vols, Greece, says volumes about the car and its owner, and is quoted verbatim: "Dear Sirs, I have purchased directly from you in 1924 a motor car; four seaters, four cylinder Engine S621. It is in perfect working condition and actually in use by me since I purchased it. I am informed by many motor car industries accept to give new car in exchange of the old one which is an evidence and proof and a sample of good workmanship. If you accept my proposition please let me know your conditions. Yrs. faithfully, G.A. Vafiades". Nice try, but his faith was misplaced.

The Rhode was made in Britain from 1921 to 1935. The most notable item about the car and the company was the fact that with the exception of the transmission, all the components were made in-house. It had some appeal, but as in so many cases during the period, its undoubted good qualities were largely overlooked by the buying public.

Steyr, circa 1924 (A).

Roamer, circa 1924 (USA).

No, it isn't another Rolls-Royce picture, even though it looks as though someone had sneaked R-R's front-end design. The Roamer has the appearance of a solid and well-finished model. It was, in fact, sold and merchandised by its parent company, Barley Motor Car Company of Kalamazoo, Michigan, as a less-costly American-type version of the Rolls. Its 6-cylinder, $3\frac{1}{4} \times 5\frac{1}{4}$ cu in engine was N.A.C.C.-rated at 25 hp, just about the equivalent of the British aristocrat after which it was patterned.

Not to be confused with the French company, which had connections with Darracq and Gladiator and even Léon Bollée, the British Talbot (the last "t" is sounded to distinguish it) company had been associated with the French Clement company and later with the Rootes Group, becoming Sunbeam-Talbot, with cars based on Hillmans and Humbers. Quite a family tree. In any event, in 1924 they were producing, among others, a 12/30-hp Talbot, a Coupe Cabriolet with a 6-cylinder, 1,609-cc ohv engine. It looked old-timey and staid, but it sold.

Sir Malcolm Campbell created nine World Land Speed records and four World Water Speed records during his lifetime. Two of the Land Records were in the same car—and what a car! 141.16 mph in 1924 in Wales—and a few months later up to 150.87 mph. The bomb he drove was a Sunbeam with a 350-hp, V-12, 18.322-liter aero-engine to haul it along. Ultra-streamlined (for 1924), of course.

122

This is the Bentley before Rolls-Royce took over in 1931. The 3-liter Red Label (short-chassis) is considered by many to be the archtypal vintage car. It made its name in sporting events: the 3-liter won both the 1924 and 1927 Le Mans 24 Hours race, although by 1927 it was somewhat dated. A large 6½-liter model was brought out in 1925, but the 3-liters remained in production until the company came under the R-R aegis. Four-cylinder, 2,996-cc, overhead valves by single overhead camshaft. If memory serves, the Bentley was another James Bond car—Ian Fleming put Bond into the 4½ liter model.

A car from Surrey, England, the A.C., had by this time gained a reputation for sportive action and performance, powered by the 1½-liter British Anzani engine that had been fitted after the war. From 1925 on the power unit was A.C.'s own product.

Duesenberg took the "Indy" in 1924, and in 1925 came right back and did it all over again with the redoubtable Pete de Paola at the wheel. In the latter race, Paola broke through the "ton" with a winning average of 101.13 mph in the event, run under the 122 cu in (c.i.) formula.

In the USA, the main mechanical trend was to the straight-8 power unit, and for the first time in automotive history more closed cars than open cars were sold in America—which bought its 25-millionth car that year.

Bentley, Circa 1925 (GB).

Doble E-series (USA).

This car was the last of the steamers to survive, and indeed, it deserved better than its fate. Abner Doble built his first steam car in 1906, while he was still a student. His first production car arrived in 1917. From the start it was recognized as an excellent product; much of its fame came from its Hollywood and European-nobility clientele. Read the numbers: the car in the photograph could get up steam in 80 seconds from switch-on and travel 1,500 miles on one tank of water. It could accelerate noiselessly (and gearlessly) to 85 mph or slip smoothly through crowded traffic. A 4-cylinder engine, located at the rear and connected to a flash boiler produced about 75 bhp. The luxury (and luxury look) plus speed and efficiency was not enough, unhappily, to persuade the American public to buy in numbers large enough to keep the company alive.

It's a little hard to believe, but a man who, more than almost any other single manufacturer (except for Henry Royce) impressed the automotive world with the mechanical perfection, performance and execution of his racing cars, produced fewer than 10,000 cars in his years of production. The man was Ettore Bugatti. His cars were the most consistently successful winners ever seen on the racing grid. He didn't just do racers—the racers were modified and sold as tourers—which is why the 10,000 figure seems so uncommonly low, in view of the world-wide esteem in which the Bugatti was held.

124

Hudson, 1925 (USA).

The seven-passenger Hudson phaeton in the picture was a key factor in Hudson's remarkable sales year of 1925—they actually sold twice as many cars in 1925 as in 1924—269,474 in all. They called it a phaeton, although the only difference between it and the tourer was in the way the doors opened. This year, Hudson announced the price of its Coach, "a high-grade commodious closed car of the best quality" at only a few dollars more than its open car.

One of the many versions of FIAT's first mass-produced model was the 509SM (Spinto Monza). Aimed at the cheaper market, the 2-seater runabout looked like a modified racer with its narrow streamlined body. The 990-cc engine had an overhead camshaft and produced 22 bhp at 3,400 rpm. More importantly, it could be purchased on the installment plan—and a year after its introduction it was, predictably, the most popular car in Italy. Variants included sedan, taxi and commercial models.

Why didn't the type of sports car described above ever become truly popular in the United States? While Europeans were tootling off by the thousands in these low-slung, narrow bombs from a dozen or more firms in Britain and the continent, Americans were content with boxy, prosaic, take-me-to-work-and-home-again cars. Perhaps an innate practicality, a hangover from America's pioneer days, was the answer. Those buzzing two-seaters had no tops, no trunks—nothing but wheels and an engine. Whatever the reasons, only Ford, with the early Thunderbird, and Chevrolet with the Corvette, ever made a run at the American market.

The Open Road: 1920-1929

Peerless Tourer (USA)

The Peerless was one of the three "P"'s of the American motoring world. (the other two were, of course, Packard and Pierce-Arrow) None of them stayed around—Packard was the last to give up. At the time the photograph was taken, Peerless had been in business for a quarter of a century, operating from its factory in Cleveland, Ohio. The tourer had a large V-8 unit of $3\frac{1}{4} \times 5$ in bore and stroke.

The two-seater Oakland was introduced in 1924 as a cheaper line than earlier cars from the company. A close look will reveal 4-wheel brakes. The car was painted in DuPont Duco cellulose, a significant advance, as this was a preparation that drastically reduced paint-drying time, thus eliminating (or rather, reducing) a delaying factor that had plagued many manufacturers in the past.

If you were rich and elegant, Renault had one for you in their Renault 45, a long-bodied, wooden-wheeled car called *Queen of the Road*. Although its 6-cylinder 9-liter engine did not even boast overhead valves (and lacked other post-Edwardian advances), the car was an essay into the enormous in the days of small, penny-pinching products from most other European motor manufacturers. So grandiose was this monster (which must have been a handful in Paris traffic) that it was the official car—hired—by various Presidents of the Republic of France for official receptions and journeys.

Oakland, circa 1925 (USA).

A page from a mail-order catalog of Gamages, the long-established London store, gives some idea of what British youngsters could expect in their Christmas stockings in 1925. Embedded in the small print will be found Citroën, Delauney-Belleville, Hotchkiss, Rochet-Snyder, Renault, Panhard, Delage and Voisin cars.

Alfa-Romeo, 1925 (I)

Almost the first true vintage Alfa-Romeo, the RL (Romeo Series L; 3-liter, 6-cylinder) was announced in 1921 and continued, in part, until 1927. This is the 22/90 hp RL SS (Super Sport) introduced in 1925, with an engine developing 83 bhp at 3,600 rpm and a top speed of 135 km/h (84 mph). It is shown in spider "Gran Premio" form.

Winston Churchill looks frustrated as he tries to start the Wolseley tourer of 1925, while a carload of politicians watch his efforts. Wolseley's war-time experience making large, V-8, overhead-valve Hispano-Sinza engines naturally influenced post-war production, and the single overhead camshafts of the 10-, 12-, and 15-horsepower cars were partly the result of lessons learned from the aero-engine experience. In 1925 the 15 was succeeded by a side-valve-engined car—the Wolseley 16/35.

This was an era of promotional stunts performed to obtain copy and pictures in the press. Chevrolet, looking for a gimmick, took their 2-millionth car to the State Capitol at Jackson, Mississippi and drove it up the front steps, presumably to the delight of the crowd of onlookers, which made a suitable background for pictures.

Wolseley, 1925 (GB).

Hispano-Suiza Alfonso, 1912; named after the King of Spain. (E)

Renault on land and in the air, 1913. Louis Renault
had made his first aero-engine in 1907. (F)

1911 Opel Torpedo; 4-cylinder, 1540 cc. (D)

Edwardian top brass. A 1912 N.A.G. raceabout. (D)

Chrysler, 1926 (USA).

Two years after introducing the car bearing his name, Walter Chrysler moved into the luxury-car market with the Imperial 80, guaranteed to do 80 mph. January of 1926 saw the first model, and the car soon became known for its low-gear "pull" and hill-climbing ability. The potent 92-bhp, 6-cylinder engine was the first Chrysler product to have light alloy pistons.

1919-1922 had been spent by Lionel Bamford and Robert Martin in experiment and racing, and only then did they offer an Aston-Martin production car (named after Aston Clinton, the British hill-climb location, and Lionel Martin). Their first engines were 1½-liter, side-valve units, intended for production cars, and several overhead-camshaft engines were made for racing. The original company lasted only until 1925, when the money ran out. Renwick and Bertelli picked up the pieces in 1926 with a new design.

A.C. cars had, by 1925, been collecting world records by the fistful as part of a strong promotional program instigated by S. F. Edge, who had earlier joined the Thames Ditton, Surrey, Company. The bigger 6-cylinder A. C. had put up a World 24-Hours speed record in 1925 at 82.58 mph, then a new 15,000 mile figure at just over 68 mph. The following year, the company highlighted its program with first place in the Monte Carlo Rally, thus becoming the first British car to win this event.

Citroën, 1926 (F)

Andre Citroën's B14 appeared in 1926, a development of the early "B" types, now with an engine of 1539-cc and an effective output of 22 bhp, plus an all-steel (*tout acier*) body and four-wheel servo-vacuum brakes on some versions. This is the famous wickerwork-sided landaulet taxi seen in every Paris street during this period and built just before the 1926 vehicle adopted the flat radiator.

The FIAT 509, this time as a milking machine. It was the smallest car FIAT had built to date (only 990-cc), and by 1926, it was immensely popular throughout Italy and the European continent. Another version of the 509, a tourer, had a back seat that, when removed through an opening tailgate, converted the vehicle into a light truck.

One of the pre-eminent British race drivers of the period was a Welshman—Parry Thomas. He had built several "Thomas Specials", both large and small, had broken world records, and had won uncountable races with them. His last car was nicknamed "Babs"—a Higham Special, modified by Thomas, powered by a 27-liter, Liberty V-12 aero-engine, chain-driven. It was a real monster. He had set one World Land Speed record in it before he made an attempt at another on Pendine Sands, a racing strip in Wales—and the monster slew him. The attempt ended in his death.

FIAT 509 (I).

Marmon, circa 1926 (USA).

Made for the overseas (British) market, the right-hand-drive Marmon Big Six sedan was a luxury vehicle in the best American tradition. With four-wheel brakes and balloon tires, it made a very handsome carriage, even, as shown, in antique England. The wire wheels were not standard on this model.

No four-wheel brakes on the Model T Ford. Throughout its long years of production, this was never offered on the American version—just another way of keeping the cost down. And so effective was the Ford program of economy that the Ford produced in Manchester, England in a four-seater version actually cost less than the Austin Seven Chummy, which Britishers looked upon as the near-ultimate in cheap. So rigid was Ford's policy that it wasn't until 1926, nine years after the Model T was introduced, that they put burnished metal plate on the radiator trim, replacing the grim Ford basic black.

One which went 180 degrees in the other direction was the British Lanchester. Their model 40 was a big 6-cylinder vehicle designed with an almost profligate disregard for expense. The company kept it in production through the difficult years of the mid-twenties. They did make some concession to the less well-endowed, however, with a smaller, lower-priced 3.1-liter car.

Pontiac, 1926 (USA).

This car was guilty of patricide—it killed its parent. The first Pontiac made its debut at the National Automobile Show in 1926. Produced by Oakland (General Motors), it was a cheaper car, intended to fill a market gap in Oakland production. The 3-liter, 6-cylinder Pontiac was so popular it knocked its progenitor out of the game, cutting the sales of Oakland by one-half in one year until, completely overshadowed by the younger make, Oakland gave up in 1931, after which only Pontiacs were built, and the company became the Pontiac Motor Company. The photograph shows a specially rigged Pontiac of 1926. It must have been specially rigged—unless Pontiac built a 13-passenger model!

One single basic model on which to hang various body styles was the production game plan of most American manufacturers after World War I. Oldsmobile pursued this for a time with their Model 30. A Landau Coupe was only one of no less than ten bodies available on the same chassis, using their 2.8-liter, 6-cylinder engine that was sold between 1924 and 1929.

As a final note before the Model T Ford sinks slowly into limbo in 1927, it was priced thusly in England: you could have the two-seater for just about $600 (based on a five-dollar pound). The Fordor "Saloon", top of the line, was just over $1,000 and a one-ton enclosed delivery truck went for about $950. Those days, it is feared, are forever gone.

Eddie Rickenbacker—war ace and famed racing-car driver. It was a natural move for him to secure financial backing and move into the automotive industry. By 1926, his company was making the smooth-running brougham pictured, a 58-hp six with two flywheels. By 1927, they were on the way out. Their final offering was a straight-8, 4.4-liter, which put out 107 bhp in sports tune.

The Morris picture was somewhat complicated at this time. At the low end was the Morris Cowley, with a "bull-nose" radiator which gave way to the flat-front in 1926. Moving up the scale only slightly, we came upon the Morris Oxford—only a touch larger and more expensive. And finally, the M.G. (Morris Garage) with just about the same degree of superiority over the Oxford as the Oxford enjoyed over the Cowley. To make matters even more confusing, there was a rather strong family resemblance among them.

Aster Engineering of Wembley, England, lasted from 1922 to 1930, producing comparatively large, well-made vehicles. But the company, like so many others producing quality machines during this period of rigid economy in Europe was forced to amalgamate. In 1927, they combined with Arrol-Johnson, but the merger only staved off the inevitable for both companies until 1930.

Rickenbacker, 1926 (USA).

Flint, circa 1926 (USA).

"The car", said the mechanic, "needs a wheel alignment." Perhaps that's why it's sitting dormant and dilapidated with its 1931 California plate. Flint was a product of Locomobile, employing a 6-cylinder Continental engine beefed up by a 7-bearing crankshaft. That year (1926) Flint was happily offering four body styles, with three size variations of that same 6-cylinder engine. The next year happiness went out the window, as Flint breathed its last.

From 1926 to 1928, British Hillman had only one engine on its production line: 14-hp, 4-cylinders, side valve. This was the period during which William and Reginald Rootes took over the firm.

Dodge finally made some styling changes in 1927, rounding off their roofline, fenders and window shapes—a rather timid step in the direction of streamlining. Additionally, they added a sun-visor over the windshield, typical of American cars of the period. In June of 1927, they brought out their Fast Four, with a 108-in wheelbase; the 40-hp engine gave it a comfortable top speed of a little over 60 mph. Much more important, however, was the addition of four-wheel brakes in the late fall. And completing the Dodge saga for 1927, they triumphantly announced the arrival of their first-ever 6-cylinder car.

It seems that just about everyone who ever owned a LaSalle remembers it fondly. (Weren't there *any* LaSalle lemons?) Introduced in 1927, the car was an instant success and sold some 60,000 units during the next three years. The engine was a V-8 and styles ranged from a roadster to a seven-passenger Imperial Sedan. Although the car was designed as Cadillac's representative in the medium-price field, it resembled the parent car in every way, including manufacturing standards. The exceptions were weight and size. Some of the LaSalle dimensions were slightly smaller than the Cadillac, and the LaSalle weight was slightly less. The picture is obviously posed, with the car motionless—with the windshield folded down, if that car had been moving, the pretty models would have been grabbing frantically for their hats!

Jowett, a British car designed strictly for utility, looked a bit rough but was reputed to be totally reliable and enduring. They used the same engine in Jowetts for approximately forty years—an 826-cc flat-twin unit. The reputation for longevity was such that the company claimed, in 1926-1927, that all Jowetts made were still running—a claim which, of course, had to be taken on faith!

1926 was the year in which the founding fathers got together. Daimler and Benz finally amalgamated, and from that date, all their cars were called Mercedes-Benz.

LaSalle, 1927 (USA).

The first car to exceed 200 mph—and it looks almost as though it could have exceeded 2,000! On March 29, 1927, Sir Henry Segrave reached a two-way run average of 203.79 mph at Daytona Beach, Florida. Some of the specifications are interesting; *two* 12-cylinder engines, each of 500 hp. *Three* radiators—one for the front engine, two for the rear. No one ever took the monster for a Sunday afternoon spin in the country—to feed those brutish engines, the gas tank held only 28 gallons! The car totaled twenty-three feet, six inches from stem to stern, and weighed three tons.

Coming down to earth, Hupmobile in 1927 offered a seven-passenger sedan on a long wheelbase of 125-in. (This was only a little over a foot less than the 1,000-hp Sunbeam.) There was a slight difference in horsepower, though—Hupmobile's was 28.8. Among the amenities offered as standard were balloon tires, ignition theft lock, stoplight, clock, dome light, sun visor and VV windshield with "automatic cleaner."

Oakland was going downhill by 1927, although it didn't worry the company a bit. The heady success of Pontiac, introduced the previous year, took away all of the sting. However, downhill or not, Oakland still was offered in seven different styles, including sedans, sports roadsters, phaetons and landaus. And to promote their "All-American Six", Miss America 1927 posed prettily for pictures.

Volvo, 1927 (S)

Over a restaurant meal, Assar Gabrielsson and Gustaf Larson decided to start a Swedish car industry and by 1927 had made the first Volvo (Latin for "I roll"). Nicknamed Jacob, the car had a sheet-metal body on a wood frame of ash and beech, and a 4-cylinder, 1,940-cc engine developing around 28 bhp, with an all-out speed of 60 mph. Strong even then (Volvos have been noted for their robust build ever since) it caught the Scandinavian imagination and sold well.

The London company that produced the Windsor was another which arrived, was briefly known and vanished. Windsor lasted just three years (1927 was the last one) even though the car was well-engineered and above-standard in finish. It had four-wheel brakes throughout its brief life, and its 1,353-cc power unit was highly efficient. Parts were made at the factory, the transmission was well-designed and the whole car was well-proportioned, What went wrong? It just cost too much money.

The Rolls-Royce Phantom succeeded the Silver Ghost in 1927, after the Ghost's record run of 19 years. The Phantom was a worthy successor, using an overhead-valve, 7.6-liter engine. This was one of the last styles in which the chauffeur got wet—and one of the first European cars to use white-wall tires.

Windsor, 1927 (GB).

Chandler, circa 1928 (USA).

This well-engineered car of the late twenties was another of the cars produced in Cleveland, Ohio. Chandler built quite a reputation for pioneering and technical advances. In 1928, they were one of the first to offer Westinghouse vacuum brakes, designed to reduce pedal pressure by two-thirds. Chandler was bought by Hupmobile in 1929.

On the subject of technical advances: Cadillac, in 1928, offered two. First in the industry with safety glass that year, they also (and more importantly) became the first to offer synchro-mesh transmission, which just about put a stop to gear-clashing. There was also a new engine—341-cu in (5.6-liter) V-8 of 90 bhp, used for both Cadillac and LaSalle. The LaSalle engine, in keeping with its lower price, was 5-liter.

Overseas, the most popular of all America's prestige cars in the middle and late twenties was the Buick, smaller and more maneuverable than some of the real giants from Detroit. With a 274-cu in, overhead-valve engine putting out some 77 bhp, Buick Models 47 to 58—all with the same general specifications—proved to be top sellers at home, too. In terms of financial turnover, Buick was among the highest earners.

Bentley didn't want to go to 6-cylinders, but they were being outclassed by multi-cylindered cars. They compromised by jumping the engine from 3-liters to 4½-liters, and got their good name back again with a win at LeMans.

Moon, 1928 (USA).

Poised at the top of an urban hill is a 1928 Moon, built in St. Louis, Missouri. Moon started in 1905 with high-wheel buggies and plodded along with conventional vehicles until after World War I, when they emerged as handsome, solidly constructed machines housing a Continental unit of 3.6 liters. The car in the photograph is the 5-seater Diana, with an sv, straight-8, 4-liter engine—and wooden wheels.

1928 saw the last of the German-owned Opels. Although in that year Opel was Germany's largest producer, they were having money problems and needed strong financial backing to face increasing international difficulties. General Motors moved in, and with their money and world-wide sales organization, took over and saved the company.

A word about Mercedes model initials. If you're wondering, S stands for Sport. SS is Super Sport. K is for *Kurz*, English translation, Short. L is *Leicht*, translating as Light. Now you know: SSKL is a short, light, Super Sport.

They couldn't have picked a worse time—but Chrysler brought out its first Plymouth in 1928, just in time for the stock market crash. It was supposed to compete with Chevrolet and Ford and replace the 4-cylinder Chryslers. Crash or no crash, 101,000 motorists thought it was a good buy.

Duesenberg, circa 1929 (USA).

Fred Duesenberg got to the U.S. in the 1880's. He had his first competitive car by 1903, and by 1929, his name was a synonym for high quality and performance. The Model J in the picture had an 8-cylinder power plant of nearly 7 liters, and could do 90 mph—in second gear! In high, it topped 110, which made it the fastest production car in America, along with a number of other superlatives.

Even closer to the stock market's debacle was the debut of another Chrysler product—the DeSoto, introduced at the New York Automobile Show in 1929. But Chrysler seemed to have a feel for the market. The DeSoto fitted into its price slot so neatly (aimed at Pontiac and Nash, among others) that 34,000 cars had been shipped to dealers before the end of 1928.

The first Auburn (from Auburn, Indiana) was built in 1900, but since 1924 the company had been part of the Cord Corporation, embracing Duesenberg and Lycoming Motors as well as Auburn. Auburn was a fast car (100 mph) that *looked* fast, and its low-profile design, coupled with a rigid frame and good suspension, gave better road adhesion than most large sports cars of the day.

Opel had a swat at rocket propulsion in May of 1928—a single-seat racer was fitted with twenty-four gunpowder rockets, fired in stages by a footpedal. They got it over 125 mph—and one year later they had it in a plane.

140

Ford, 1928 (USA)

It's hard to imagine two more dissimilar cars—but 1928 saw them both. The Ford Model "A"—the New Ford—was in full production and geared, it was hoped and anticipated, for the thirties. Americans had made full use of the Model T during the umpteen years of its production, but as standards were raised higher, the Model A filled the more sophisticated bill. Still only four cylinders—but the pesky planetary transmission was gone, replaced with a convention clutch and three-speed transmission. Believe it or not, orders for 400,000 Model As were taken before the car was ever seen by the public!

The regal Reinastella, built—and *really* built—by Renault from 1928 to 1934 was another example of the curious compulsion by Europe's bread-and-butter manufacturers to build castles-in-Spain luxury cars. In standard tune, this 8-cylinder landship of just over 7 liters would do just over 100 mph.

In 1929, Buick got together a smaller side-valve, 212-cu in, 6-cylinder product which they named the "Marquette." This was another attempt to inject a hypo into a market just starting to suffer before a slowly collapsing economic boom hit rock-bottom in October.

Sir Henry Seagrave pushed the World Land Speed record up another notch in 1929 at Daytona in "Golden Arrow"—powered with a colossal 930 bhp engine. His new record: 231.44 mph.

Renault, 1928 (F).

Chrysler Imperial, 1929 (USA)

The impending crash and ensuing world-wide depression didn't seem to faze Walter Chrysler. He devised the Imperial range in 1926 to break into the luxury-car market. By 1929, the Imperial enjoyed a high reputation. It had a 5-liter, 6-cylinder engine which developed 100 bhp, and a 136-in wheel base. The radiator grille had been slimmed in profile, fronting a hood that returned to the fluting of previous Imperials. The gentleman who always looked as though he needed a shave, and who seems to be milking the picture for all it's worth, is "the Champ"—Jack Dempsey, former heavyweight boxing champion of the world.

In spite of everything looming on the horizon, 1929 was an active year, world-wide, in the automotive industry. Skoda, in Czechoslovakia, put out a whole new range. Standard, in Britain, came along with a little four-seated tourer. Also in Britain, Star, one of the pioneers dating from 1898, introduced two new models, the Luna and Nestor—to go along with their earlier Diana, Athena, Cygnus, Flora, Cetus and Eclipse. (someone in the company had a classical education!) Humber, with a Weymann-bodied, 2.1-liter, 6-cylinder affair got into the act. So did MG—with their first small car. FIAT was another, with a racy-looking Spyder—the 514 Coppa del Alpi, successor to the FIAT 509. And finally, in the USA, Willys-Knight began delivering their Great Six '66'. Willys-Knight was part of a tangled web of companies that included Overland, Willys, Kaiser-Jeep, Crossley, and a half-dozen others.

142

Automobiles For All

The 1930's are often condemned both in Europe and the U.S. as the time when coachbuilt bodywork gave way to mass pressings, when hand-built machinery yielded to dull mass-made vehicles that were deliberately designed for the non-enthusiast and for obsolescence, when gimmickry took precedence over quality in the sales brochures.

All true, but the reasons behind the shift in emphasis were inevitable, as mass demand overtook the industry. The slow haul out of the Depression dictated that vehicles in Europe be smaller and cheaper and to some degree the same factor influenced the American market.

The Thirties were, despite the 'cooking' cars it engendered, the first years in which the ordinary family man in Europe could buy some modest mobility and take the kids for a Saturday trip to the green fields. The first two years of the period were not altogether happy ones for the U.S. auto industry; production figures of passenger cars had dropped from a peak of 4,587,400 in 1929 to a disastrous low of 1,135,491 in 1932 although five American makes showed 12-cylinder models this year, and a number of serious technical advances, contrasting with the fashionable gadgetry, were offered—automatic chokes (Oldsmobile, Packard), vacuum operated clutches (Buick, Cadillac, Chrysler, De Soto, Dodge, La Salle), rubber-mounted engine (Chrysler), hydraulic valve-lifters (Pierce-Arrow), and all-wheel drive. The years 1932-33 heralded the beginning of true aero-dynamic streamlining, the greatest milestone of which was perhaps Chrysler's and De Soto's Airflow model, Detroit's 'most successful failure' in that all its features were eventually accepted by a public who, in 1934, was not ready for them.

By 1935 U.S. production had climbed back to over 3 million units a year and was again on the upcurve. A noticeable trend to lower-priced cars was seen, made possible by cutting out some of the unnecessary features, and the production of larger numbers.

European family car sellers were going through a period of cynicism, selling the sizzle not the steak, as numbers of unimaginative cars were trundled out to the markets of Italy, Germany, France and Britain. What streamlining was done was carried out to seduce the eye rather than to increase the performance, and slab-sided bugs abounded. The new breed of motorist was a snob, too, and often turned down a real economy vehicle because it sported too little chromium plate, the exception being Ford's fully-equipped British 8 hp saloon priced at exactly 100 pounds, a car which appealed to the short-pursed.

Some of the great automotive names of America were in evidence during this period, a time incidentally when several of the country's finest cars were made—the fantastic Duesenbergs J and SJ, the Twin Six Packard, with its 7298 cc powerpack, the Franklin, Pierce Arrow and Lincoln top-line models, the V16's of Marmon and Cadillac. In Europe the great Auto Union and Mercedes-Benz Grand Prix racers, the V12 Lagondas, the spectacular Hispano Suiza Type 68, and of course, the Rolls-Royce Phantom III leavened the diet of the mass-made dullards. In France, Citroën stole much of the show in 1934 with the little 7 CV 'Traction Avant', the front-wheel drive car with unitary construction and independent suspension that set a design trend for many later products.

1930-1939

B.S.A. 3-Wheeler (GB).

As can be imagined, inexpensive-to-buy-and-run transportation was the order of the day on a world-wide basis in the very early thirties. The little number in the picture was one of a popular breed in Britain in those days—three-wheelers offered more comfort than the motorcycle-with-bathtub, their taxes were lower, and they cost only fractionally more to buy and run. The "Breeza", as the B.S.A. model shown was affectionately known, began when the motorcycle division of the Birmingham Small Arms Company acquired from Hotchkiss of Coventry the manufacturing rights of a 1-liter, V-twin, air-cooled engine. This drove the front wheels. The Breeza had car-type controls, an electric starter, a detachable hood and got up to 60 mph. Buyers could choose between light-blue or black.

Chrysler had a gimmick in 1930—their model 77, with a 4.3-liter, 93-bhp, 6-cylinder engine, was wired for an exciting new feature—radio. Bear in mind—it didn't *have* a radio—it was wired for one, in case you wanted to have one installed. Factory-styled sets were still several years in the future. However, the car was one of the first from a major manufacturer to adopt down-draft carburetion for better fuel distribution, and the gravity-flow vacuum tank was replaced by a cam-driven fuel pump.

1930—and Bugatti was at it again in the Grand Prix. At Monaco, his horseshoe-radiatored buzzer grabbed off first, second and third—with the winner averaging 53.5 mph.

144   Alfa Romeo (I).

Armstrong Siddeley, circa 1930 (GB).

Aberdeen, Scotland in the very early thirties. The car identifies itself as an Armstrong Siddeley by the V-shaped radiator, studded disc wheels and the Sphinx Mascot on the hood. A magnifying glass reveals that cigarettes (from the machine on the right) cost 6d, the attendant cranked oil into a quart container from the service stand (right center) and the lone gas pump, labeled "Multiple" on the glass dome, dispensed two grades of Shell, two grades of BP, benzol, and a mysterious something labeled "Pratt's #1".

They didn't make many of them—but what they did make was creme de la creme. The all-purpose Alfa-Romeo two-seat sports car was one of the great creations of designer Vittorio Jano and the ultimate development of a line that had begun in 1926 with a 1 ½-liter engine. The 1,750-cc model was offered in three forms: single-ohc, twin-ohc, and twin ohc-supercharged. The first gave 46 bhp and the last 84 bhp. The car won many races, including the Mille Miglia (thousand mile) in the hands of Scuderia Ferrari, who ran the Alfa factory team. After nearly 2,600 had been made, it was withdrawn in 1934.

Cord, circa 1930 (USA).

There were two tons of motor under that hood. The fabulous Cord was a real style-setter, with its long, low look and its transmission out in front to save space. It was the first American front-wheel drive car to win acclaim, with a 4.9-liter, straight-8 Lycoming engine developing 125 bhp. There were open and closed models and special 17-foot-long bodies, but the car was never a big seller: some 4,400 were delivered between 1929 and 1932, when production ended.

During the vintage period, the name Delage could be seen on the lists of sporting successes all over Europe; with 5- and 10-liter cars (the latter with 12 cylinders), the French Delage took many racing and hill-climbing laurels, and although manufacturers rarely match the successes of one field in another, Delage touring cars were of the highest quality and reputation.

Drivers of British Frazer Nash cars were nicknamed "the chain gang" because of the car's primitive chain drive. Practically everything Frazer Nash built was for competition on sand, roads, hill-climbing or sprinting. Whether by design or not, the Frazer Nash was Britain's reply to continental sports cars like Bugatti—and remained virtually unchanged for 15 years, except for replacing the Anzani engine with one made by Meadows.

Going down, up and around the steps of the Duomo di Urbino, the FIAT type 514 had a handbrake on all four wheels instead of the transmission. The car was on the heavy side and had a 26 mpg thirst. The spectators in the picture seem much more interested in the photographer than the car and its shenanigans, but the picture helped sell 27,000 such cars. Another FIAT, the 525, was a big, inexpensive car. In sedan form it could seat seven and was much used at the Vatican. Then, just to prove their versatility, the FIAT firm brought out an SS version. (not, obviously, designed with papal dignitaries in mind) This was a tuned, open two-seat sports body with wire wheels, twin-choke carburetion, and could do 85 mph. Also, it was the first FIAT with hydraulic rather than mechanical brakes.

Oldsmobile sold nearly 50,000 six-cylinder models in 1930, among them a sporty roadster with folding windshield, side-mounted spare tires and rumble seat. The classic styling of the roadster was to make it a collector's item in later years.

Also in 1930, Marquette was still Buick's cheapest range. Six models were offered, each on the same 114-in wheelbase. Another death notice: the name Marquette died in the depression later in the year.

FIAT 514 (I).

Stutz Black Hawk (USA).

This picture is calculated to bring back fond memories to all who owned or knew the car and its more famous sibling, the Stutz Bearcat. Made in Indianapolis, the Black Hawk Model M pictured had a 5.3-liter, straight 8 engine, which would work up a top speed of just about 100 mph. Like all the Stutz cars, it combined comfort and a racy beauty of line with its very high performance.

In Germany, the Wanderer WII had a 6-cylinder, 2.5-liter engine which gave 50 bhp; a seven-bearing crankshaft; and a low-geared, three-speed transmission. In 1931, they followed with a sports version at 3-liters. The car was also built under license by Martini in Switzerland, but the Swiss were not enthusiastic. In 1932, Wanderer joined the Auto Union combine, but its production ended in 1939, along with a number of German cars which stopped because of World War II.

A new kind of Chrysler Imperial arrived in 1931 with a long, low hood, sweeping fender lines and a new straight-8 engine. Various coach-work specialists also made bodies to order for the 154-in wheelbase. It was a lot of car, but a gallon of fuel carried it only eight miles, which made the Imperial not for the impecunious.

148

The station wagon was becoming popular during this period for its load-carrying capabilities (as it is today). The popular nickname for it in Britain, where *everything* has a nickname, was a "woody". The solid-looking timbering of the modestly priced Dodge shows why. It had a 6-cylinder, 3.5-liter engine giving 74 bhp. 1931 was the year that Dodge introduced the Rocky Mountain ram as a hood ornament—and kept it there for a quarter of a century.

The gasoline engine began to be put to some new uses in the late twenties and early thirties. For one thing, half-tracks appeared, a product of the French Citroën Company. They were called *Kegresse,* and in 1931-1932, fourteen of these vehicles carried forty men 7,500 miles across Asia, from Beirut in Lebanon to Peking, China, crossing the snow-clad heights of the Himalayas, and the hot sands of China's Gobi Desert. The trek was known as the Croisiere Jaune (Yellow Crossing), and the name passed on to the vehicles, which were also used in agriculture and the armed forces.

Britain's Austin Twelve-Six was an unexciting car, but not so unexciting that the rumors about it were true—it was alleged that the company found them so hard to sell they gave away large numbers to be used as prizes in competitions! Unexciting or not, the Six-Twelve stayed in the catalog until 1937, with the addition of a fourth gear and a more reliable engine.

Dodge Station Wagon, 1931 (USA).

Hillman Minx, 1931 (GB).

As soon as the prototype of Hillman's Minx left the factory in 1931, it was taken on the roughest roads of Europe by its maker, William (later, Lord) Rootes, who made a practice of trying out each new model personally. Escorted by a chauffeur and a tester, he drove the Minx through Belgium, France, Switzerland, Italy and North Africa. (The picture was taken in the South of France.) A modest family car, the Minx was typically middle class English, a compromise between the 8-hp "babies" and more luxurious models. Speed? 56 mph—and very, very popular.

One of those British "babies" was the Morris Minor— Nuffield's answer to Austin's Seven. Surprisingly, it could do 60 mph. The car was a mere 10 feet, 1 inch long by 4 feet, 2 inches wide. The gas tank held five gallons.

If you could use an automobile engine to power a half-track, (as FIAT did) why not take an engine built to propel a light tank and put it in a racing car? Or even one built for a seaplane? Invicta did the light tank trick and won some important races that way; Malcolm Campbell at Daytona in 1931 raised the World Land Speed Record to 246.09 mph in a monster designed by the famous Reid Railton and called Bluebird. Bluebird was powered by a Napier engine built for a Schneider Trophy seaplane. In 1932, Bluebird did it again, this time to 253.90 mph.

150

This was the ultimate one for "pot-hunters"—the car had 16 "pots"! The V-16 was Colonel Howard Marmon's masterpiece, and also his swan song, for the Indianapolis firm was wound up in 1933. The 9.1-liter, 200-bhp engine made much use of aluminum alloy, and the dashboard was genuine timber. The convertible coupe was capable of a spanking 105 mph.

August Horch, who began his career as a Benz engineer, started making his own cars in Cologne in 1899 and won himself a name for big, heavy, prestige motors. In the early thirties his Model 600 limousine was certainly big and heavy, as well as low-geared—but it carried a 6-liter, V-12 engine up front. As could be expected, it was expensive and only about 100 were sold. In 1932, Horch became part of Auto Union and built its racers.

In spite of the fact that Lincoln had been a part of the Ford stable for some nine years, the Lincoln name still represented opulence. For example: the Lincoln sport phaeton (with dual windshield) was over twelve feet long, with a 6.3-liter, V-8 engine delivering 120 bhp and churning it along effortlessly at a comfortable 85 mph. A new and additional feature: push-button freewheeling.

Marmon, circa 1932 (USA).

Oakland, 1931 (USA).

Last of the breed. The makers claimed the austere-looking Oakland was the latest in styling and performance, but only 12,417 buyers believed it. It had a 4-liter, V-8 engine, but it was headed for the boneyard. While Oakland was selling its 12,000-odd in 1931, upstart Pontiac moved six times as many, and the Oakland name was discontinued at the end of the year.

Pierce-Arrow was still a great prestige name in 1931, but demand and production were waning. Now under the control of Studebaker, the 8-cylinder model had a 6.3-liter engine which produced 132 bhp. It also offered servo-assisted brakes and synchromesh on the four-speed transmission. The one notable styling feature which everyone remembers about Pierce-Arrow—the way the headlights were streamlined into the fenders—was still very much in evidence.

France's Peugeot Berline was a workhouse, designed and sold as a simple family car with a small 4-cylinder engine that was popularly priced. They got around to independent front suspension in 1932, and synchromesh in 1934.

When German's Opel became a part of General Motors, the cars began to acquire Chevrolet styling and specifications. Introduced in 1931 was a disk-wheeled mini-limousine with a 1.8-liter, 6-cylinder, side-valve engine giving 32 bhp and a conservative speed in the low fifties.

152

Depression Dodge (USA)

At the lowest ebb of the depression, the American automotive industry just barely reached a year's production of one million units. Dodge held seventh position in that year—their 4.6-liter, 8-cylinder, 90 bhp car had "Floating Power" engine mountings and freewheeling as standard equipment and the new automatic clutch as an option.

"And first prize for elegance goes to the BMW." That announcement had just been made at a motor show in Baden Baden when the picture was snapped. BMW (Bavarian Motor Works) of Munich began by making engines for boats, trucks, motorcycles and aircraft. The car was another which was springboarded by Britain's Austin Seven—a baby sedan with a 790-cc, ohv, 4-cylinder engine delivering just 20 bhp.

Another Chrysler setback stemming from the depression occurred in February of 1932, when diminishing sales forced them to limit DeSoto production to 6-cylinder models only. Along with Dodge, they shared the new "Floating Power" rubber engine mounts, freewheeling and the vacuum-operated automatic clutch controlled by the accelerator pedal. Trumpet horns, projecting forward from just under the headlights, identified the deluxe models.

BMW, circa 1932 (D).

Rockne, 1932 (USA).

The Rockne Motor Corporation was formed in 1931 as a less expensive "back door" for Studebaker, and Rockne cars were just that: smaller models of Studebakers. The 6-cylinder, 3-liter cars sold well—better, in fact, than any other product built by Studebaker—but the grain of history was running against commercial success in most fields at this time, and the Rockne name disappeared after just two years. The car was named for Notre Dame's immortal football coach, Knute Rockne.

The Duesenberg was still the biggest, fastest, most sophisticated and most expensive car in America, with the comfort and prestige of a Rolls and the power and speed of a Bugatti. It should have been all those things, since it was custom-built. Duensenberg made only the chassis—bodies were made by a variety of coachbuilders. The number built is not nearly so impressive as the car—470 was the total. The Duesenberg era ended with the collapse of Errett Lobban Cord's empire in 1937.

The Seven wasn't the only string in Austin's bow in the depression years. They built (and sold) a large range of cars, including a modest four-door ten with a 1.1-liter, 4-cylinder, side-valve engine made at Longbridge, Birmingham, England from 1932 to 1947. One of its chief merits (and possibly the reason for its long run) was that it went 34 miles on a gallon of gas over 40 years before anyone heard of a fuel shortage.

154

The Alfa-Romeo P3 was also known as the "Monoposto", because it was the first successful single-seat racing car. Designed by Vittorio Jano, it used an 8-cylinder engine from the 1931 8C2300 racing two-seater bored out to 2.65-liters and double supercharged to give 190 bhp at 5,400 rpm. It won its first grande épreuve, the Italian Grand Prix of 1932, and was beaten only twice in its first season. In succeeding years the engine was progressively increased in capacity, to 2.9, then 3.2, and finally 3.8 liters.

In June 1932, a Peugeot 301C 4-cylinder, 1,467-cc sports car broke the Class F 24-hour record at Miramas, near Marseilles, between 7 PM on June 1 and 7 PM on June 2. The average for this little speedster was just over 68 mph. The driver was Andre Boillot, younger brother of Georges, the French Grand Prix winner of 1913. Andre was killed not long after while testing another car.

At this time there was a battle for top dog between conservative Renault and more adventurous Citroën. Citroën eventually won, but not before Renault pushed hard by stepping up production of small 4-cylinder cars. They were, for the most part, under-powered, but Renault made them with enough inside dimensions to justifiably advertise, "There's more room in a Renault."

Alfa-Romeo, 1932 (I).

Ford, circa 1931 (USA).

In 1932, competition pushed the Ford Motor Company into a major switch: bigger engines. The coupe shown began as a 50-bhp, 4-cylinder model, but from 1932 it was also available with the low-cost 70-bhp, V-8 of 3.6 liters, which gave it an exciting performance, and put another feather in the Ford cap: the first mass-produced V-8, years ahead of its rivals.

The 345C LaSalle sedan had the Cadillac engine, (V-8, 5.8-liter) but it was faster, lighter and cheaper than big brother. It sported a wheelbase of 136 inches, and a radiator grille which looked amazingly like the Mercedes.

"Balilla", which means "plucky little one", was the name given by FIAT to a small sedan of this period. With its 4-cylinder, 995-cc, 22 bhp, go-anywhere unit, it had pluck—and with a wheelbase of only 88 ½ inches, it was undeniably little. But it was tough, it handled well, and it could reach 70 mph. And most important of all, 113,000 were sold between 1932 and 1937.

Carrying the Balilla one more step: FIAT put a racing body on it, tuned the engine until it gave 48 bhp and did 75 mph, and it became a very advanced small car which managed to dominate 1,100-cc sports car racing.

Swallow Sidecars (SS) moved from the manufacture of motocycle sidecars to motor bodies and eventually grew into Britain's Jaguar firm of today. The SS1 pictured here was their version of a 16-hp Standard car. It used the Standard 6-cylinder, 2-liter engine untuned, as well as other Standard mechanical components, but it was given a long hood, a small coupe body, and helmet-style front fenders. Engine and chassis were lowered and this ''promenade sports car'' looked worth double its cost—a comment which was made frequently about the firm's subsequent offerings.

Even in the rarified air of Rolls-Royce, the depression was felt. R-R scaled down their Phantom to a 20/25 hp model, with a 3.7-liter, 6-cylinder engine. It was heavy and could reach only 75 mph, but they managed to sell 4,000 of them by 1936, when they scaled it back up to 25/30, 4.3-liter. In 1932, synchromesh became standard with R-R.

The German firm of Zundapp tried to move into automobiles from motorcycles with a car designed by Ferdinand Porsche. The result turned out to be something which looked like the grandfather of the Volkswagen ''Beetle'', with a genuine fastback and rear-wheel spats. The car had an air-cooled, 5-cylinder engine, but only a few prototypes were made. In fact, Zundapp didn't begin to produce cars until nearly twenty years later, and their venture lasted only two years—until 1958.

SS, circa 1932 (GB).

Citroën, 1933 (F)

The Citroën (Model 15CV) of 1933 was the company's first 6-cylinder car. The 15CV was, of course, a purely nominal rating, and the 2,650-cc engine developed 49 bhp, and gave effortless, restful, long-distance motoring comfort.

Vive la difference! A very different breed of cat was the racing car pictured. Citroën's "Petite Rosalie" was a special, based on an 8CV sedan with a 4-cylinder, 1,452-cc side-valve engine. It was one of a series of Rosalies which began in 1931. The Petite weighed more than a ton and had a top speed of 70 mph, but at Montlhéry a team of drivers ran it day and night for 133 days, covering 300,000 km (around 187,000 miles—more than seven times around the earth at the equator) at an average speed of 58 mph and establishing some 300 new and assorted records.

Cadillac, in 1933, came up with a Y-shaped radiator on its 7-passenger sedan, as well as a V-8 engine, swiveling ventilator windows at the rear, trumpet style horns, and the 1933 version of white wall tires.

Citroën, circa 1933 (F).

British Ford, circa 1933 (GB).

Ford had built cars in Britain since it began there with the Model T in 1911, but the car in the picture was the first Ford designed there and aimed specifically at the British market. Instead of a big, thirsty American power plant, it had an economical 4-cylinder, 993-cc engine which gave it 58 mph performance. A two-door four-seater just under twelve feet long, it offered more space than established British cars. It was christened "Popular", and it turned out to be just that.

Among the names virtually unknown in America was the German Framo, a firm controlled by DKW, but outside the Auto Union combine. The Framo Stromer was a 3-wheeler, with its two front wheels driven by a DKW engine. Very light—it weighed only 675 pounds—but it was a real car and could do 50 mph. Unusual features: rubber cord suspension and a tubular backbone frame which also served as an exhaust pipe!

In its Milan factory, Isotta-Fraschini produced a magnificently luxurious, 2-seater sports car with a straight-8 engine of 7.4 liters. Lightly tuned, it gave up to 150 bhp and could reach 100 mph. It was an arrow aimed straight at the American market—but the arrow was blunted by the depression. Only thirty were made, and Isotta went to aircraft and marine engines and commercial vehicles.

Zeppelin, circa 1933 (D).

William Maybach was a close associate of Gottlieb Daimler, but they parted company in 1907, when Maybach left to join Count Zeppelin in establishing a factory to make airship engines. Later, the factory began to make cars that were acclaimed as the Rolls-Royce of Germany. The name Zeppelin was a natural choice for a range of giant Maybach limousines in which the shortest wheelbase was twelve feet! The hood was seven feet long, the radiator three feet wide, the car weighed over three tons and there were *eight* forward speeds! The Zeppelin's power plant was an 8-liter, V-12 giving 200 bhp.

Elsewhere in Germany, Opel was going great guns in the thirties. Under the General Motors wing, it ranked #1 in European production. One of the reasons was an attractive, racy-looking two-seater with a 1,790-cc, 6-cylinder in-line engine under the hood.

Soon after the big 7-passenger KB Lincoln tourer was announced in 1932, Henry Leland died. He was the grand old man of the American car industry, and his last was a lot of car—it cruised easily at 80 mph and could be pushed to 100. A new V-grille, servo-assisted brakes and free wheeling (controlled by a dashboard lever) were added attractions.

Lincoln, 1932 (USA).

Opel Laubfrosch (Tree-toad), 1924. (D)

A Hooper-bodied Rolls-Royce '20' landaulette, 1926. (GB)

Fiat Mephistopheles, 1924. Born in 1908 as the SB4
the car was extensively modified in 1923-4. It broke
the world record in 1924. (I)

Citroën 5 CV Type C, 1922. (F)

1919 Standard 9.5 hp (GB)

1920 Aston Martin 2-4 seater with supercharged Anzani engine. (GB)

Peugeot 5 CV, 1924. (F)

Morris, circa 1933 (GB)

Hillman, circa 1933 (GB).

A couple of British wee ones. The Morris was the Ten-six, cheapest of the Morris sixes. The picture, showing the Ten-six sloshing around while fording a stream, had for its objective a demonstration of its rugged dependability and no doubt to draw attention to its ''Sunshine'' sliding roof, shown in open position. The roof was introduced in 1932.

The Hillman Aero Minx was a derivative of the 1,185-cc original Hillman Minx. The advanced, low-slung aerodynamic lines proved something less than popular with conservative Britishers, but it became the basis for Talbot and Sunbeam Tens when Rootes acquired that firm.

The Lancia Augusta was a rather ordinary-looking car with a 1.2-liter engine putting out a solid 35 bhp—and traveling 30 miles on a gallon of gasoline. Top speed was around 65 mph, but in spite of the fact that it was light-weight at 16 ½ cwt, it had good road-holding and hydraulic brakes and could drive quite briskly. Racing driver Tazio Nuvolari used one when he was not scorching around the European racing circuits.

Automobiles For All: 1930-1939

The French firm of Panhard & Levassor was one of motoring's oldest and most respected, and just about their entire model line was properly dignified and conservative. And yet, the 6CS2 shown had at least two unusual features. Instead of an oil-pressure ''idiot light'', it had a device that cut the ignition if the oil pump failed. More obviously, it had a so-called *''Panoramique''* windshield, an early version of the modern wrap-around windshield to improve vision.

1933-1934 was a good year for British Singer—or at least, for their 9-hp sports coupe. The Nine Sports, with a 972-cc engine giving 33-hp, ran in many reliability trials in those years, over such courses as London to Land's End and Edinburgh. The numbers were very, very good—578 cars collected 495 awards in trials.

Vauxhall, one of the early birds, was based in Luton, England. In 1925 it became another arm of the General Motors octopus, and by the early thirties some of their models were beginning to look like still another arm—the German Opel (which was beginning to look like the main arm—Chevrolet!). Brakes were still cable operated, but by 1935 the Vauxhall incorporated GM's ''knee action'' front suspension.

Panhard-Levassor, circa 1933 (F).

Terraplane, circa 1933 (USA).

The name Terraplane had replaced that of Essex on inexpensive Hudsons early in the thirties. The car was virtually the same as the Hudson in styling, with a 6-cylinder, 3.2-liter engine and three-speed transmission. However, despite the use of Amelia Earhart in pictures to promote the compact convertible shown, the Terraplane name failed to excite, and it was dropped in 1937.

It was not very rewarding to be a motoring enthusiast in Japan in the thirties. It has been estimated that there were only about 40,000 private cars (the overwhelming majority of American origin) when the decade began, and the poor-quality roads were far from crowded: motoring was just not available to the general public. One of Nippon's few makes was the Sumida, which looked suspiciously like the American LaSalle.

Few cars in Britain (in the medium-power class) were as esteemed as the Riley, and few were mourned more when Riley became lost in the giant Morris group in 1938. It was somehow an enthusiast's car, with a name for quality and performance, ride and road-holding. More than 20,000 of the Riley Nines had been made by 1934, using a 1,087-cc engine that could get it to 60 mph. It may be difficult to understand this loyalty to a medium-priced car with that modest top speed, but it was there, and the Riley Nine is fondly remembered.

William Lyon's Swallow Coachbuilding Company marketed cars under their own name, as the advertisement shows—but they didn't build them. They went to a manufacturer—almost any manufacturer—in the proper price range and bought everything but the body—then put their own body style and name on the hybrid. The two-seater runabout is Swallow's body on a chassis and mechanical components by British Wolseley.

The British Hurlock brothers, who ran A.C. Cars Limited, made custom-built cars. All their cars used a 6-cylinder, 2-liter engine that was introduced in 1919 and continued in production for half a century. Their cars were thoroughbreds and the engines spent twelve hours on a bench test before they ever turned wheels on a road. Any combination of body, color and engine tune could be selected, if you were prepared to wait one month for delivery.

The Wolseley Hornet was an inexpensive car with some sporting appeal. It was produced for a five-year period surrounding the middle thirties in a variety of body styles from open two-seater to four-seater sedan. Lengths varied from 10 ½ to 11 feet, and the 6-cylinder, 1.3-liter engine could do 75 mph, which, for a small, light car, was moving along rather nicely. An unusual feature—sliding windows.

The 4-cylinder, 1.4-liter Walter Bijou was the product of J. Walter of Jinonice, a town once in Austria, then, after national boundaries were shuffled around following World War I, in Czechoslovakia. The company began in 1908, and in 1933 offered the Bijou, the Junior (980-cc), and a 3-liter, 6-cylinder car.

Just as coachbuilders bought everything but the bodies (as illustrated by the Swallow), so some manufacturers *made* everything but the bodies—and bought *them*. Even the monster Austin empire went in for this sort of thing. Their famous Austin Seven, which continued until World War II brought things to a screeching halt, at one time during the thirties had a Swallow four-seater body grafted to it. The car was 9 feet, 10 inches long, and 4 feet, 1 inch wide, and plodded along at a top speed of 55 mph.

Another designer and coachbuilder emerged around this time—in Italy. The name of Pinin Farina was destined to have a large impression on automobile design. One of his models, for an Alfa-Romeo 2300B 6-cylinder effort, was far out in front in styling and line. Noteworthy was his fender and hood treatment (the rear fenders wore ground-skirting spats) and his elimination of the running board. The body was a cabriolet, and it was a stunner. Also in Italy, Jano was designing for Alfa-Romeo, too. His Gran Turismo was nearly as handsome as the Farina Cabriolet, but he kept the running boards.

Walter, 1933 (CS).

Humber, circa 1934 (GB).

Here's what happens when *haute couture* is welded to the automobile industry. Humber called in Captain Molyneux, the couturier, to advise on design, then went pell-mell after the women's market with advertising copy that read, "There was a rumor that all new body styles came from across the Atlantic—until Molyneux of Paris and London collaborated with Humber. Molyneux' flair for line and color and Humber's 35 years experience of chassis and body building have now produced the ideal sports car for those who want something out of the ordinary—a model of intriguing performance and unusual beauty of outline". It was called the Vogue sedan, and must have caused head-turning. Mechanically, it was a scaled-down Snipe (13 feet, 4 inches long) with a 4-cylinder, 1,669-cc engine.

BMW finally began to succeed in speed competition in 1934 with the successor to the 303—the type 315. The passenger-car version was a 2-seater tourer with the 6-cylinder engine increased to 1 ½ liters. The racing version had 3 carburetors compared to the standard two, and delivered 40 bhp as compared to the standard 34. It had a top speed of 125 mph in racing tune and after an auspicious debut in the 1934 Alpine Trial, Frazer Nash took over the concession in Britain.

World War II put a lot of cars out of business, including the small-car firm Hansa of Bremen, Germany. 1939—and farewell to Hansa.

Citroën, 1935 (F).

The 7CV was the first of Citroën's *"traction avant"* (front-wheel-drive) cars and the first mass-produced fwd model. Other innovations were unit construction, torsion-bar suspension, independent front suspension and removable cylinder liners. The car had a flat welded floor which gave good accommodation; it was strong, had 68-mph performance and handled well. Originally it had a 4-cylinder, 1.3-liter engine but in 1935 it became 1.6-liters. Apart from this, the car continued virtually unchanged until 1956, and 700,000 were made.

Encouraged by Adolph Hitler, the Horch, Audi, DKW and Wanderer companies combined to form Auto Union to seek prestige for Germany through motor racing. The first Auto Union racing car, designed by Ferdinand Porsche, (who seemed to be designing nearly every car in Germany) was revolutionary in that the engine was behind the driver. It took another quarter of a century for this engine position to become standard. The 4.3-liter, supercharged, V-16 engine gave 295 bhp at 4,500 rpm. Hans Stuck broke several records with it on the Avus track, averaging more than 134 mph, and then went on to win the German, Swiss and Czech Grand Prix.

The year contained a big day for Buick—the first Buick Special came off the line. No front bumper, but it did have "knee-action" independent front suspension, and synchromesh as standard.

Mercedes, circa 1935 (D)

How could you stop 'em, when they kept on producing dream cars that looked like the 2-seater sports job in the photo? The Mercedes-Benz 500K was a supercharged roadster. (In this case, the K stood for Kompressor, or supercharger.) It was a high-speed touring machine with an 8-cylinder, 5-liter engine that gave 160 bhp and 100 mph when blown. It also gulped fuel at the rate of one gallon for every 11 miles. Contrast this with the racer, where Mercedes went all-out. The picture shows it in action on the twisty Nurburgring, complete with front-mounted supercharger. Racing was under the 750-kg formula at this time—and the Mercedes 8-cylinder engine of 3.36 liters gave 354 bhp. By 1937, it had been increased to 5.66-liters and a howling 646 bhp.

In Britain, M. G. two-seat sports cars were deservedly popular with less-wealthy men who wanted the thrill of sports-car performance on a small budget. The M. G. Magnette N-type provided just that kind of experience for the young family man. The fact that it had a minimal amount of space for the kids pulled a bit away from its popularity with bachelors—they wanted the two-seater with just enough room for "a bloke and bird".

Mercedes racer, circa 1935 (D).

Lagonda, circa 1935 (GB).

The Lagonda Rapier was a small but expensive semi-sporting car with an 1,104-cc, twin ohc engine giving 46 bhp. It also had a rather heavy body which came in convertible or closed form, two-passenger sports models, and four-passenger tourers. Shown is an Abbott-bodied, four-seat tourer capable of 80 mph. In 1936 rights were passed to a small company set up for the purpose and called Rapier, and the car was additionally offered in supercharged form. Somehow, the car was never competitive and only about 300 of all types were made.

The fancied-up Humber was only one of their promotional efforts. A new, easy-change epicyclic gear system by de Normanville was introduced, called by Humber "Motoring's sixth sense." They put it into a 3 ½ liter Humber Snipe, attached a heavy caravan as a tow, and, with six passengers on board (a gross weight of over three tons) drove it across North Africa and the Sahara as a demonstration of reliability. The transmission worked, but the stunt didn't—de Normanville transmissions disappeared from Humbers in 1937.

At the age of twenty, "Wild Bill" Cummings won the "Indy" at a record-breaking 104.8 mph in a Miller—the first win by a 4-cylinder engine since 1920. Cummings' Miller was the ancestor of the Offenhauser units that were later to prove so successful in the 500. Miller engines took the race every year from 1930 to 1938.

Automobiles For All: 1930-1939

It isn't a very attractive picture, but the numbers involved made it attractive to Walter Chrysler. This was the one-millionth Plymouth, and the car rolled off the assembly line in August. When he produced the first one in 1928, he said the name Plymouth had been chosen "to symbolize the endurance, strength, rugged honesty, enterprise and determination . . . of the Pilgrim band who were the first American colonialists." Plymouth was the low-priced end of the Chrysler family, and only 4-cylinder units were used until 1933, but in 1934 they went to sixes—3.3 liters and 77 bhp. The would-be buyer could select from 258 different combinations of bodywork and color—all on the 107 3/4-inch wheelbase of the Six.

Racing oddments from 1934: Renault, with a 4.8-liter Nervasport fitted with a streamlined body, set a new 48-hour record (and nine others at the same time). The car traveled 5,000 miles in 48 hours at an average of 101.979 mph.

Riley won the Brooklands 500 with a 2-liter, 6-cylinder "aluminized" car. Speed, 104.8. And Panhard, with a narrow, knife-like speedster powered by a 8-liter straight-eight engine, set a new one-hour record at 133.01 mph. The car had set a new record twice before this last effort, and Panhard decided it had earned an honorable retirement.

Plymouth, 1934 (USA).

Morris Minor (GB).

The ubiquitous Morris. There was an embarrassingly large range of Morris Models at this time—built, at times, for obscure reasons. For example, the Family Minor was certainly a quality family sedan built on a lengthened Morris chassis—but the principal reason it came into existence at all was to utilize an overstock of 847-cc ohc engines!

Austin kept turning them out like sausages, also. They styled-up the Austin Seven, called it the Ruby, but it was just another 4-seater Seven with no fundamental change in engine or chassis.

Slightly higher in the social scale, Standard was a growing concern in the thirties. The deluxe model, with chrome-plated lights and leather-upholstery "extras", held a curious snob appeal for the British until the fifties.

Still in Britain, the Singer Airstream was an imitative tribute to Chrysler's Airflow models—like the Chrysler, the Singer had a full-width aerodynamic body. It did as badly as the Chrysler—only 750 Airstream Singers were built—apparently the British public was as suspicious of the Airstream as the American public was of the Airflow.

171

Brewster Town Car (USA).

The Brewster coachbuilding company of Springfield, Massachusetts, like Swallow in England, built cars under its own name, using components from manufacturers like Ford, Buick and others. The town car used a Ford chassis with the wheelbase extended to 10 feet, 7 inches. It conveyed well-heeled business leaders to board meetings, and, as a hearse, carried deceased of all classes to cemeteries. Other Brewster models included convertibles and limousines. Note the cow-catcher grille—behind it was a V-8 engine. Only about 300 Brewsters were made.

Ford produced its millionth V-8 in 1935. The Model 48, with a 3.8-liter engine was a twin of the British Ford Model 60, except for a more economical 2.2-liter engine. In both models, the engine had been moved forward to contain all the seating within the four-door, 112-inch wheelbase.

In Germany, among the most popular cars in 1935 were those of the DKW Schwebeklasse range of 1,054-cc, V-4 engined, rear-driven vehicles. This was the first DKW with synchromesh and hydraulic brakes. DKW had become part of Auto Union in 1932.

Packard took a crack at the lower-priced market at this time with a 120 touring sedan with a straight-8 engine, hydraulic brakes and independent front suspension.

172

Mercedes-Benz racers, 1935 (D).

When Hitler thundered "Here's the money—do it!", you did it—or you quietly disappeared from view. The state-subsidized Mercedes-Benz W25 Grand Prix car of 1935 was built without regard to expense—Germany was determined to be supreme in motor racing. The Mercedes debut as a team car was at Monaco, where they beat out the Italian Alfa-Romeos. The W25 went on to win nine out of the ten races for which it was entered, proving, if proof were needed, the importance of money in auto racing. The one race Mercedes didn't win (which quite likely caused some Hitlerian rug-chewing) was the German Grand Prix, in which Mercedes came in third. The car had a 4-liter unit delivering 430 bhp and was capable of nearly 200 mph.

Then, just to prove their versatility, Mercedes came up with an economy-class car. This one set a style in years to come with a rear-mounted, 6-cylinder, 1.7-liter engine which could do 68 mph. The Model 70 was the first Mercedes with independent wheel suspension and was highly successful in its home market—a mass seller until production ended in 1938.

And finally, they had a flop. Another rear-engined car, the oddly shaped 150S with a 4-cylinder, 1.5-liter engine developing 55-bhp. However, they somewhat shamefacedly claimed it was an experimental car, since only a few were made.

FIAT 1500 (I).

Heralding the shape of things to come, the FIAT 1500 was propelled by a 44-bhp, 6-cylinder, short-stroke engine. The one-ton aerodynamically styled car had a downward-curving hood to provide good forward vision. Headlights and door handles were recessed. Synchromesh, hydraulic brakes, and a headlight flasher were standard, and the speed was 70 mph. Nearly 24,000 were made in three seasons, but the 1500 was most important because the famous 500-cc Topolino (of which more later) was to be based on it.

The Frazer Nash Shelsley model was named for a famous British hill-climb course, where Frazer Nash scored numerous victories. The car was the ultimate in the FN range—one of those sporty two-seaters the British have always adored. Under the hood was either a Gough 1 ½-liter supercharged engine, or a more flexible 1.6-liter Blackburne power unit. Ironically, just as they got around to winning with the Shelsley, Frazer Nash decided to concentrate on the importation of BMWs from Germany.

The big number for Morris at this time was the Eight, an inexpensive family car with a 4-cylinder, 918-cc, side-valve engine. Quite a few were made with left-hand drive for the export market; others appeared as light panel trucks to be used by post office engineers.

The LaFayette name was revived by Nash in 1934 for use in their cheapest models, a decade after the original Milwaukee company ceased production. By 1935 there were eight body styles, among them the sleek coupe built around a 6-cylinder 3 ½-liter engine.

Besides their best-selling Eight, Morris had another current fast-selling number, the Ten-Four. A much-publicized feature of this car was a built-in jacking system. Considerably larger than the Eight, the Ten-Four weighed in at 2,100 pounds, with a 4-cylinder, 1,292-cc, side-valve engine, three-speed transmission and a maximum speed of 60-65 mph. Sedan and certain coupe bodies were available with two-tone paint finishes.

Reid Railton advertised "acceleration unequalled by anything on the road", for his 4-seater made in England by Noel Macklin, and built around a Hudson 8-cylinder, 4.1-liter engine delivering 124 bhp. The standard model took just over 13 seconds to reach 60 mph and got to the middle eighties at top speed. Modified by Railton, who built the Brookland Riley, it got to 60 mph in less than 9 seconds and could reach 107 mph.

A World War II casualty was Stoewer of Stettin—in business since the nineteenth century. In 1935, their 2-½-liter, V-8, front-wheel-drive model was a clean attempt at aerodynamics. They stopped making private cars in 1939, and the plant was destroyed during the war.

LaFayette, 1935 (USA).

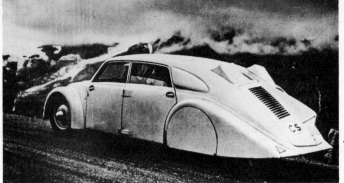

Tatra 77 (CS).

Made in Czechoslovakia, the big, smooth 90-mph Tatra 77 was designed by Hans Ledwinka. It had an air-cooled, V-8 unit of 2,970-cc over the back axle, giving 60 bhp, and the aerodynamic bodywork concealed two spare wheels under the front hood. The first ones produced had a central driving position, but later models had conventional front seating.

In Scandinavia, Volvo, the Gothenburg-based Swedish company, had already acquired a reputation for building solid sedans, but was not yet a major exporter. The PV36 Carioca was a kind of trendy fastback with recessed head-lights and rear-wheel spats. It also had an all-steel body (new to Volvo) and independent front suspension.

An illuminated radiator badge was the trademark of Britain's Wolseley Company; the power came from batteries under the front seats. The Ten had a 4-cylinder, 1,292-cc engine of 41 bhp in an 8-foot, 4-inch wheelbase. It didn't take an expert to notice its similarity to the 1935 Morris Ten. The company had been bought by William Morris in 1927.

The Auburn 852 didn't have much of a life. They introduced it in 1935—one year later, Cord-Duesenberg-Auburn was disbanded. It was a shame, too—every one of the 150-bhp boat-tailed cars had been test-driven at more than 100 mph before it was sold. That was the company's guarantee.

Auburn, 1935 (USA).

Chrysler, 1936 (USA).

"Detroit's most successful failure" was the unfortunate tag applied to the Chrysler Airflows. Six long years of study, experiment and wind-tunnel tests preceded the introduction of the Airflow range in 1934. The cars featured aerodynamically smooth, sweeping contours, a lower silhouette, improved weight distribution, and an integral body and chassis. The C9 sedan of 1936, with an 8-cylinder, 5.3 liter, 115-bhp engine, added a built-in luggage compartment, a front seat that adjusted up or down as well as back and forth, and Life Guard tires (a heavy-duty tube containing a second tube floating inside) as standard. In that every one of its features were accepted in time, the Airflow was a success. But in that a more gradual evolution was needed, it was a flop. The buying public just wasn't ready for the Airflow, and the range ended in 1937.

Down the Airflow road to disaster also went the De-Soto, which was the only Chrysler make devoted entirely to Airflows. Five thousand DeSoto Airflows were produced in 1936—but that was the end of the line, any way you care to read it. An interesting feature that year was a steel roof panel insert that was acoustically treated and electrically insulated to serve as a radio antenna.

One more quick obit: this was the final year of the British Alvis Silver Eagle range, first seen in 1929.

Topolino means "Little Mouse", and that was the nickname hung on this tiny FIAT. The Italian baby car caused a sensation, and was hailed as the greatest development in ultra-small cars since the Austin Seven. The two-seater was ideal for shopping and parking, being only 10 feet, 8 ½ inches long and 4 feet, 3 inches wide. It could U-turn in only 28 feet. It had a canvas roll-top roof, but it was a real car in miniature, with a 4-cylinder, 569-cc engine which could do 55 mph, and go the same number of miles on a gallon of fuel.

At the other end of the spectrum, the name of Lincoln still stood for American luxury travel: 6.9-liter, V-12 engines, 150 bhp and 95 mph. 23 gallons of gas in the tank. A new feature was the under-dash hand brake, plus new-pattern disk wheels. The luxury Lincolns of the period arrived at a time when the posh car market was dwindling. Later that year Lincoln introduced the more modest Zephyr range, with engine down to 4.4-liters.

Still further out on the spectrum, Rolls-Royce's Phantom III was the last prewar Rolls—and a vintage one. Engine: a V-12 of 7.3-liters, 165 bhp, 100 mph, although the stiff R-R upper lip did not permit vulgar shoutings about performance. More numbers: nearly 16 feet long and 6 ½ feet wide, 5,100 pounds heavy, 33 gallons of gas in the tank. Stunning fact: they drove one across the Sahara desert from London to Kano in Northern Nigeria without having to add any water!

The name Jaguar was used for the first time in 1936, although it was 1945 before the prefix SS was dropped. The SS Jaguar 100 was a shortened version of the standard 2,663-cc car joined in 1938 by a 3,485-cc model. The two-seaters performed well in sprints and rallies, although only about 300 had been made when production was shut down because of the war. Later they were much sought after by enthusiasts, particularly in the USA.

The Aero from Prague was derived from a series of small, two-stroke vehicles with origins in the twenties. By 1937 they had grown somewhat, yet they still retained their two-stroke units coupled with front-wheel drive. Smart in appearance, they had something of an English air about them.

Another Britisher who fancied the American Hudson engine was George Brough of Nottingham. He's best remembered as the maker of what became known as "the Rolls-Royce of motorcycles", but from 1933 to 1939, he also built cars, using the aforementioned Hudson engines.

Between 1936 and 1939, Germany's Wanderer had a very smart-looking supercharged, 2-liter, 6-cylinder two-seater with quite an advanced line. Top speed was well over 90 mph from its 83 bhp unit. That 1939 date marked the cut-off for European and British manufacturers—practically every one went on a war footing.

Jaguar, 1936 (GB).

During 1936, the 6-cylinder Type 135 Delahaye won just about every sports car race in sight and took second and third at LeMans, as well as winning a highly publicized sports-car race in England. One of the options on the 135 was the fingertip, clutchless, Cotal electric gear-change system which offered a selection of three or four gears—in either direction. History gives us no record of the opinion of drivers who may have chosen the 100 mph top gear—for reverse!

Mercedes-Benz W125 was the most powerful Grand Prix car to have been built. The 8-cylinder, supercharged engine of 1936 was enlarged in 1937 to 5.7-liters to give 640 bhp at 5,800 rpm and a speed of nearly 200 mph. The independent rear suspension was abandoned in favor of a return to the de Dion axle of the turn of the century. This consisted of jointed half-shafts to each wheel, with the wheels linked by a floating tube.

The Jensen brothers were clever body stylists. In 1937, they began a new line in Anglo-American hybrids, using a 3.6-liter Ford V-8 engine and a Columbia two-speed rear axle, giving, for practical purpose, six forward speeds. The 3,100-pound British Jensen had twin carburetors and over-drive and produced 120 bhp and 85 mph on the road.

Mercedes, 1937 (D).

Hotchkiss, circa 1937 (F).

A French 3 ½-liter car, the Hotchkiss 686 GS was based on the Hotchkiss that won the Monte Carlo rally in 1933 and 1934. It was austerely simple, but the Gran Sport model, the most powerful in the range, could accelerate from 0 to 50 in just over 11 seconds and go on to 93 mph. Later in 1937, the Hotchkiss firm, based at St. Denis near Paris, merged with Amilcar. The 686 range was reintroduced and developed further after the war, but the Hotchkiss name ended in 1955 after a merger with Delahaye.

The radiator was similar to that of the big Horch—but any resemblance ended there. The DKW convertible coupe from prewar Germany was another of the midgets from Berlin with a 2-cylinder engine giving a featherweight 20 bhp. It was part of the front-wheel-drive Meisterklasse range.

Model 812 marked the end of the Cord range. It had that Lycoming V-8 engine delivering nearly 200 bhp (with the optional supercharger) and 100 mph. It still retained the Cord front-wheel drive, but had a new, eye-catching feature: retractable headlights. The first sentence of this paragraph is perhaps best explained by the last: sales were small.

Nash (American Nash—not Frazer Nash of Britain) brought out the Ambassador 8 in 1936—biggest car in the Nash range. Its sales feature was its "weather eye" air conditioning, with heated air ducted to the windshield or the feet.

181

Panhard & Levassor, circa 1937 (F)

The 2½-liter Panhard "Dynamic" coupe was an extraordinary example of the stylist's art, with its curvaceous body, flared headlights and spatted wheels. The driver was required to occupy a central driving position, which necessitated the provision of three (count 'em!) wipers to sweep the panoramic windshield. For some reason or other, a number of manufacturers tried this untenable steering wheel position—and they all wound up doing what Panhard did—one year later, center was out—left or right was in, depending on where you drove. Engines of 2.7 or 3.8 liters were available as options.

Ferdinand Porsche had been working for years on the design of a small, economical "people's car". Of course, others were, too—and at the outset, more successfully—FIAT's Topolino, Austin's Seven, America's Ford, to name but a few. But in 1934, the German government gave him the backing to make it a reality. Thirty prototypes were built in 1937 by Daimler-Benz and in Porsche shops at Zuffenhausen. The final result of the *putsch* we all know, but one of those models forced the driver to look through the louvers covering the rear engine to see traffic approaching from the rear. It was not, needless to say, the final version.

The Triumph Gloria Continental of this period was a combination of coach work inspired by the SS Jaguar plus a Vitesse radiator—otherwise, it was a Dolomite model.

Auto Union racing car (D)

At the wheel of the Auto Union racing car is Bernd Rosemeyer, twenty-eight years old and the fastest racing driver of the day. Ferdinand Porsche, designer of the streamlined car, is apparently giving him instructions, prior to Rosemeyer's attacking two class B records on the Frankfort Autobahn. Tragedy followed shortly thereafter: a gust of wind caught the car when it was traveling at 260 mph; it crashed, killing Rosemeyer. Auto Union called it quits—no more record bids were made.

At the Horch plant in Zwickau, Auto Union racing cars were made, but in addition, the company produced a line of distinguished cars under its own name, some of them designed by Gottlieb Daimler's son, Paul. Among them was a large, solidly built V-8, 4,911-cc Type 853A Horch, giving 120 bhp at 3,400 rpm.

Surprisingly, the Austin Seven had a racing version during this period. They were single-seaters, designed by Murray Jamieson, and they looked like miniature Grand Prix cars with 16-inch-diameter wheels. Using a 4-cylinder engine, (some supercharged, some not) they could "rev up" to 9,000 rpm and do up to 125 mph. What's more, Austin had considerable success with them until the outbreak of the war and even afterwards, in hill-climbs and club races.

Horch, circa 1937 (D).

183

Lincoln Zephyr, circa 1937 (USA).

The Lincoln Zephyr, in spite of its aerodynamic lines and 100 bhp, was never a best seller. The 110 bhp, from the V-12 engine of 4.3 liters, was intended for prestige purposes—but the car was light and economical compared to other Lincolns. It can be supposed that a Lincoln purchaser didn't *want* light weight or economy—when you bought a Lincoln, you bought what the name implied—luxury—and hang the cost (and upkeep!).

The Sunbeam-Talbot-Darracq group dissolved in 1935. Then Major Anthony Lago took over the French factory and continued to race cars under the Talbot name. Lago Talbots dominated the French Grand Prix for sports cars at Montlhéry in 1937, finishing first, second and third. The car had a 4-liter engine developing 165 bhp, and the winner averaged 82.5 mph.

More small cars of the period: The Allard stemmed from a trial special evolved by England's Sidney Allard from a 1934 Ford V-8 engine and a Bugatti body. They built a dozen of them, some with the Lincoln Zephyr V-12 engine. It was made in a 2-seater body with flared fenders, a large slab gasoline tank and two spare wheels at the rear. With the pedal firmly on the floor, it could get into the nineties and was used for trials and sprints. This was another of those 2-seaters that the British couldn't seem to get enough of.

Something new for Peugeot—an aerodynamic body for the 402B limousine. Note the positioning of the headlights—behind the radiator grille and just in front of the radiator. (Would the headlights, therefore, throw a striped beam of light?) The engine was a 4-cylinder of 2,142-cc, giving 55 bhp. A dashboard gearshift operated the three-speed transmission, although a 4-speed transmission was available as an option.

Looking like a wheeled submarine, the three-ton Railton-Mobil special was designed by Reid Railton (who seemed to design *everything* in the superspeed area) for John Cobb to use in World Land Speed attempts. Cobb was housed in the nose of the car, which had a body that lifted off in one piece to give access to the engine room. *That* was occupied by a pair of 24-liter, 12-cylinder, supercharged Napier Lion engines, each of which developed 1,250 bhp and drove a pair of wheels—a drive system used to give maximum acceleration. At Bonneville Salt Flats in Utah in 1938, Cobb raised the record to 350.2 mph. Just under the gun of World War II, he advanced it to 369.7 mph and in 1947 he made it 394.2.

From 1935, Simca (Société Industrielle de Mécanique et Carrosserie Automobile) made FIATS in France under license. One of them was essentially a FIAT 5080—a 4-door sedan that could do 70 mph all-out.

Peugeot, circa 1938 (F).

Jaguar, circa 1938 (GB).

Another "Jag"—the 1½-liter SS. It was one of the best-looking cars on the roads of England in the pre-war period. As can be seen, the lines were modern and stylish, but dignified. The model in the picture was the smallest in the range. The largest was 3 ½-liters, with 125 bhp and 100 mph top speed. Over 5,000 of the big fellows were sold.

The 1938 Grand Prix Formula restricted supercharged engines to 3-liters. The Mercedes-Benz W154 produced for this formula had a V-12 engine giving 483 bhp at 7,800 rpm, which was a sizable increase in revs over previous models. Two superchargers, and the bodies were lower, wider and more streamlined. As usual, Mercedes did all right with the car—it won the Tripoli, German and Swiss Grand Prix.

Captain W. O. Bentley himself designed the 1938, 4-½-liter V-12 Lagonda (he had been chief designer for Lagonda since 1935). The unit was reputed to be one of his best. It developed 180 bhp and was smooth enough to take the car from a walking pace to 103 mph in top gear without discomfort.

The Volvo P 53/56, first seen in 1938, was one of the few European cars which continued production during the war. Sweden, of course, was a neutral, and unlike Norway, never suffered German occupation forces. The car was a Swedish version of an American medium-price car—and looked like one.

The Volkswagen (D).

This was the final realization of Dr. Porsche's dream, the Volkswagen 38 with a 704- or 984-cc, air-cooled engine and (unlike the prototype) a rear window. Officially, the car was known as a KdF *wagen*, KdF standing for *"Kraft durch Freude"* or "Strength through Joy" which was the name of the Nazi organization that sponsored the car. A vast amount of panoply surrounded the Volkswagen; a giant ceremony, full of the Nazi idea of Neo-Wagnerian grandeur, was held merely to celebrate the opening of a factory to put the car into mass production.

Dating from 1937, all Standard cars were designated Flying Standards; they carried a small Union Jack emblem on the hood. The grille was styled almost like a fencer's mask—and was referred to that way. In the late thirties a Standard best-seller was a Flying Twelve coupe, an attractive five-seater with a 4-cylinder, side-valve engine of 1,343-cc in an 8-foot, 4-inch wheelbase.

The W23, a 6-cylinder Wanderer convertible coupe, had a claimed 62 bhp and a *höchstgeschwindigkeit* (top speed) of 118 km/h (73 mph), and was a fairly breezy car for a long-distance trip on the autobahn, but without much else to recommend it.

Wanderer, 1938 (D).

Automobiles For All: 1930-1939

Another here today, gone tomorrow car. Developing 82 bhp from its 1,650-cc, 4-cylinder unit, the British Atalanta was an exclusive sports car with a number of options. A Gough engine of 1 ½ liters or 2 liters was offered at first (later the smaller was upgraded to the 1,650-cc unit). Later a Supercharger and Lincoln Zephyr engine were offered. It proved to be too exclusive for its own good—the make lasted for only two years because of its high cost.

The last pre-war Audi, the 920, had a rear-driven, 6-cylinder, 3,281-cc engine and was made under the same roof as Horch in the Auto Union organization. It was large and roomy, in the Wanderer pattern, and capable of 85 mph, but production only lasted six months. Auto Union's last great racer was a 12-cylinder, 2,990-cc model with Roots superchargers and capable of 185 mph. This car won the last prewar Grand Prix in Belgrade on the day war was declared, and as the Auto Union racing department was in what is now East Germany, racing was never resumed.

A new product of Ford's Lincoln division was introduced in 1938—the Mercury. It took dead aim at the medium-price field to compete with General Motors' Oldsmobile and Buick. A 3,917-cc version of the Ford V-8 engine gave 95 bhp and 90 mph. By 1941, when production stopped in the USA, Mercurys were rolling out at the rate of 90,000 a year.

Atalanta (GB).

Maserati, 1939-1940 (USA).

The double-dating on the caption means one thing—Wilbur Shaw, posing at the wheel, pulled off an Indianapolis 500 doubleheader, winning with the same car both years. His average time in 1940 was 1 mph slower than in '39—but it was good enough to win. The 8-cylinder, 3-liter, double-supercharged car was the last pre-war Maserati Grand Prix model. Oddly, the car was fast but unreliable in Europe, but it won on the bricks at Indy.

Just prior to the war, Chrysler brought out the New Yorker. Then, it was an aggressively styled Imperial model with a straight-8, 5.3 liter engine developing 130 bhp and able to rack up 90 mph. Dual overdrive was standard, as was a column gearshift. Wheelbase, 125 inches. The car also had "Superfinish", a process in which all major chassis components subject to wear were finished to a mirror-like surface. Other features new to Chrysler were push-button inside door locks and rotary-type door latches.

The range of Czechoslovakian Skoda models in 1939 included a small Popular—a novelty for the year. The engine was practically the same as previous Popular models, but was now mounted ahead of the front axle, with the radiator behind the engine, *a la* Renault. Larger models still had an ohv unit of 1,088-cc, developing only 32 bhp.

Cadillac 60 Special (USA).

The Cadillac 60 special had been introduced in 1938, and was a real trend-setter. It had a V-8 engine, four-seat bodywork, chrome radiator grilles, and column gearshift on a 10-foot, 7-inch wheelbase. Running boards had vanished. As a contemporary writer put it, "Every car now looks like a teardrop on a movie queen's face!"

Amédée Gordini, an Italian living in France, raced FIAT cars, but achieved more fame as a preparer of sports cars. He was nicknamed *"le sourcier"* (the wizard) because of his work on Simca cars, which were really FIATs made in France under license. In 1939, his Simca-Gordini extracted 65 bhp from an 1,100-cc engine, had a speed of 110 mph, and was a class winner at Le Mans.

As the thirties drew to a close, De Soto produced its longest wheelbase up to this time. The custom 57 was 122.5 inches and had a 6-cylinder, 3.7-liter, 100-bhp engine. Sealed-beam headlights became standard equipment on all Chrysler-combine cars at this time, while also new to De Soto was the optional all-weather air-control system with dual blower and heater units.

The Jeep And The Beetle

The 'Thirties had seen not only the introduction of mass motoring, but the building of roads for the new motor age. By 1939 Italy, first to perceive needs of the future had built hundreds of miles of autostrade partly to give employment to hungry workers, but primarily to accommodate the new age of long-distance road travel.

By 1937 some 800 miles of autobahn had also spidered throughout Germany, noticeably more thickly in regions where troops might one day need to be rapidly transported from place to place. Britain, as always, resisting change, built a number of 'by-passes' round major cities and drew grandiose plans for more. The U.S.A., traditionally the laggards in road-building, opened the first turnpike in 1940. Unaffected yet by the war in Europe, private car production still climbed, to 3,717,385 in 1940 and 3,779,682 in 1941 before the country turned its manufacturing energies to aircraft, tanks and other engines of war.

On February 9, 1942 all automobile companies in the United States ceased production of private cars. On May 3 a national speed limit was set at 40 mph, later reduced to 35 mph, and available gasoline was reduced by one half in 17 states on May 15. By the end of 1942 Ford were making combat cars, White were producing half-tracks and tank destroyers, Chrysler made tanks, Pontiac were working on anti-aircraft guns and General Motors on machine guns. By 1944 the gas ration for U.S. car owners was down to 2 gallons a week.

By the end of the war in 1945 most of the automobile-producing factories of Germany, Italy and even France were in ruins. Britain's car industry survived in part but the two automotive centres of Birmingham and Coventry had taken their share of the general devastation.

Just as the war had introduced the U.S. quarter-ton utility, the Jeep, to the fighting world, so the post-war gave the German-made Beetle to most countries of the world. Born in 1934 as three prototypes designed by Dr. Ferdinand Porsche, whose hand was seen in many vehicles of the time, then as 30 specimens made by Daimler-Benz in 1938, Hitler's 'Strength-through-Joy' car was ostensibly to be made so that the people of Germany could achieve mobility. However the Volkswagen was first made as a war vehicle. Not until both the British and the Americans had short-sightedly turned down the offer of the VW factory as reparations in 1945 as being 'of no commercial value' did the little air-cooled four-seater begin to take over the world's small car market finally overtaking (in 1972) the Ford Model T record production of over 15 million. By 1950 the French were trying to mount a similar operation with their tiny minimal equipment Citroën 2 CV, a car designed 'to get a farmer to market without breaking his eggs' and not much else. It caught on in a penurious post-war world as did the 500 cc Fiat derived from the pre-war Fiat Topolino.

Detroit producing swung back to civilian work quickly, producing some 65,000 cars before the end of 1945 in spite of wildcat strikes and a maximum price barrier. With 'dollar grins' and massive wrap-round everything, these immediately post-war vehicles were acknowledged by all to be the ugliest yet made in the country. There was, however, to be much improvement in the near future. . .

1940-1949

Oldsmobile Station Wagon (USA).

The Oldsmobile "Woody" station wagon was powered by a 6-cylinder engine—but the big item was an option: Hydra-Matic transmission—the two pedal version. Hydra-Matic was the first really efficient automatic transmission. Oldsmobile advertised it this way: "the most important engineering advancement since the self starter . . . no gears to shift; no clutch to press."

It was farewell to LaSalle in 1940. By the time they called it quits, the car (for example: the Model 52 sedan with 5.3-liter, V-8 engine) cost almost as much as the parent Cadillac, which outsold it by a considerable margin. So, LaSalle went to that big garage in the sky.

The last Chevrolet produced at the company's Buffalo plant was a special deluxe town sedan powered a 6-cylinder, valve-in-head engine. There was a full-width front bench seat with divided back, and running boards were shrinking to the vanishing point.

That year, Buick's cheapest car was the fastbacked 48 special sports coupe. Up front, the headlights were built-in, and under the hood was an 8-cylinder engine on a 120-inch wheelbase.

Aston Martin long-chassis tourer, 1933. (GB)

ERA, 1936; 2-liter supercharged. (GB)

1927 Renault Conduite Intérieure; 951 cc, 4-cylinder.
(F)

Mercedes-Benz, SSK 1927; 170 hp without supercharger,
225 with. (D)

Direct descendent of the Prince Henry, the 30/98 was
Vauxhall's great sports car of the Twenties. This is a 1927
car. (GB)

Mercedes-Benz promote the Nurburg, 1928. (D)

Bugatti 1927; 1496 cc supercharged. (F)

A 4½-liter Bentley won the 1928 Le Mans race.
This is a 1929 4½-liter (4398 cc) with blower. (GB)

A 1930 3.3-liter Talbot. (GB)

Alfa Romeo P3, also known as the Type B or Monoposto. The first successful racing single-seater. (I)

Packard 1929; at a recent meeting in Britain. (USA)

The Jeep (USA).

If ever there was a war baby, the Jeep was it. A major production item for the war years, this Willys-Overland product was actually a quarter-ton 4 × 4 truck. How did it get its name? It was originally designated GP (for General Purpose)—and Gee Pee became Jeep.

The first ones left the Toledo Factory in December, 1941; then Ford began building them to the Willys pattern. In all, 639,245 Jeeps were made by war's end.

The Jeeps used a 4-cylinder engine with six forward speeds and two reverse. With their alternative units of two, three and four liters, they served in every theater of war in every kind of role. Some were front-line ambulances, some were gun carriers, some were amphibians, some waltzed officers about, and some were actually fitted with flanged wheels and used as freight engines! Practically every army used them—including the Germans and Japanese—who undoubtedly captured quite a few!

La Salle, 1940 (USA).

Nash, 1942 (USA).

By 1942, the American automotive industry was following Europe's example: going to war. The last Nash came off the line on February 4 of 1942 and didn't surface again until 1945. The one shown is a unit-construction model with a 6-cylinder, 2.8-liter engine. It was an ancestor of the Rambler.

Interchangeable engines and extras were features of the Oldsmobile Dynamic Cruiser 76 sedan. The customary engine was a 6-cylinder, but an 8-cylinder could be supplied for little extra cost. Wheelbase was 125 inches, and they managed to make 89,000 of them before the war-time moratorium.

Chrysler, in the just-beofre-the-war period, built what they called an "idea car". It couldn't have been such a great idea—they only built six for exhibition and display. One of them served as the pace car for the 1941 Indy 500. The car was a 4-seater tourer, and its most striking feature was dual cockpits with separate folding windshields. The "idea car" also had a hydraulically controlled disappearing top and push-button door handles. Rear-wheel spats and a long, low look made it a strikingly handsome vehicle. The name was "Newport", built on the current Imperial chassis. Chrysler sent them around to trade shows and to selected dealers' showrooms, but they never built the first production model.

194

The old Triumph Company went into receivership in 1939 and was taken over by Standard in 1945, which at that time was still making the 1.8-liter, 4-cylinder engine for Jaguar. This unit was used to power the classic Triumph 1800 roadster, but by 1949 it had been replaced by the 2.1-liter Standard Vanguard Four. In spite of a peculiar right-hand gearshift, the aluminum content in the bodywork and its classic lines developed an enthusiastic response, and although ousted by the TR series, a good many have survived on both sides of the Atlantic.

Available with optional Hydramatic, (they had stopped hyphenating the name by this time) the 3,903-cc, 6-cylinder Oldsmobile Special shown in 1946 was basically the 1941 "Dynamic" and continued in production through the 1947 model year. For 1948, it received the "Futuramic" style treatment and by 1949, when the 4.9-liter "Rocket" was introduced, the old six had only two more years to run.

Mauri Rose won the last "Indy" before Pearl Harbor, then returned in 1946 with the Offenhauser-engined Blue Crown Special, going for a repeat. The post-war effort turned out badly: he had to pull out after colliding with a wall, suffering minor injuries. He was back in 1947, however, and brought the 4 ½-liter car home in front at an average speed of 116.34 mph.

Triumph, circa 1945 (GB).

Frazer, 1946 (USA).

A few "independents" managed to make it through the depression years in the USA, only to expire, like Cord and Pierce-Arrow, in the late thirties. Those that managed to hang on until the outbreak of war included Graham-Paige, and although their last offering—the Hollywood—would undoubtedly have bankrupted the company eventually, war contracts insured the survival of Joseph Frazer's empire. Joining forces with Liberty-ship builder Henry J. Kaiser in 1946, he produced the Frazer, an attractive car that became something of a style-setter, powered by the Graham-Paige version of the old pre-war Continental Red Seal 3.7 SV six.

The prestige car of the Ford stable, the Lincoln Continental, emerged in 1945 little changed from the 1941 models. Apart from a somewhat revamped frontal treatment, the last of Edsel Ford's Continentals was all '41. By 1949, with the introduction of the Cosmopolitan, Lincoln followed the common Ford engineering theme of "L"-head, V-8 engines, ladder frame and wishbone ifs, and entirely new bodywork.

Postwar from the now French government-controlled Renault works was the 760-cc, rear-engined 4CV developed secretly during the war. Snub-nosed, with an ohv engine producing 19 bhp and a top speed of 60 mph, it was an instant success. All-around independent suspension and hydraulic brakes helped, no doubt.

Lincoln Continental, 1945 (USA).

Holden, 1948 (AUS).

Bodybuilders even in the 1920s, Holden was a takeover by General Motors before the war. Under the GM aegis, Holden assembled both American and British GM vehicles for the Australian market. Basically a Buick, the "FX", introduced in 1948 as the first fully Australian Holden (it wasn't—there was a Holden built there in 1911) was a conventional GM offering, with unitary-construction body and a 6-cylinder, ohv, 2.2-liter engine. Unlike the previous "assembly" jobs, it was now 92% Australian, and over 7,000 were sold in 1949. Firmly established, Holden is now Australia's most popular carmaker.

British Standard's first post-war offering was the "humpty-back" Vanguard, introduced in 1947. It spearheaded a one-model policy that lasted until the "eight" in 1953. The 4-cylinder, 2,088-cc engine was virtually indestructible, but they had rust problems with the six-seater body.

Just like almost everyone else, Chevrolet's postwar cars were basically the 1942s. The Stylemaster, for example, didn't get a face-lift until 1949, when it was extensively revamped and re-named the Styleline. The old 3,548-cc six, however, continued in use; the fibreglass Corvette, introduced in 1953, employed a 160-bhp version of this unit.

197

Jaguar XK120, 1949 (GB).

Introduced at the 1948 Motor Show, production of the XK120 began in 1949, although few Britons saw it—the great majority went to the export market. The aerodynamic two-seater created a sensation, and, with a 6-cylinder, 3.4-liter, twin ohc engine, represented a remarkable value for the price. Capable of 120 mph in production form, the cars were successful in almost every sphere of motor sport, and Jaguar's showing at LeMans in 1951, 1953, 1955, 1956 and 1957 are now legendary.

In 1946, the Panhard "Dyna" range appeared and represented a complete change of direction for Panhard & Levassor. The specially streamlined sedan was not generally available, (it can be assumed that it was built as a sort of "come-on") the standard offering being a small four-door sedan with light alloy bodywork by Facel-Metallon. A Gregoire design, the car originally used an air-cooled, fwd, flat-twin engine of only 610-cc, four-speed transmission with dashboard change and independent front suspension.

Peugeot introduced a post-war successor to the 1,100-cc 202 model—the 203—in 1947. It proved to be a best-seller, using a 1.3-liter engine with a hemispherical head and wet liners driving through a four-speed transmission to a somewhat dated worm-drive back axle. Featured were unitary construction and all-around coil suspension with ifs.

Lea-Francis, 1948 (GB).

Another "good-bye" look. First introduced in 1938 during one of the Lea-Francis company's numerous reorganizations, the Hugh Rose-designed 14-hp, 4-cylinder engine continued in production after the war both in sedan versions and as a station wagon, in addition to the sports model shown. The push-rod-operated ohv arrangement with two high camshafts was similar to the smaller prewar Riley Nine unit, which Rose had also designed. The company had financial troubles, like other specialist independents in austere Britain. By 1952 production was down to 6 cars a week. Shortly afterwards, the company ceased production.

A rather ugly Lagonda coupe appeared at about this time—product of the David Brown organization, which had taken over Lagonda. Under the not-so-attractive exterior, however, was beauty—the last W. O. Bentley design—a beautifully engineered, 2.6-liter, 6-cylinder, twin-cam engine in an unconventional cruciform chassis with irs by torsion bar, in addition to coil and wishbone ifs. With column gearshift, it attracted few buyers. But some months later, the same engine, plus an Aston-Martin chassis, became the DB2—a vastly different story, aesthetically and financially.

Based on Vincenzo Lancia's last design, the little Ardea 4a first appeared just before the war. It came back in 1949, and was replaced in 1953 by the 1,100-cc Appia.

Lagonda (GB).

Packards, 1899 & 1949 (USA).

104,593 units produced in 1949—and Packard was going strong. The Clipper line—available as a 6 or an 8—still retained much of its former elegance. The chromium excesses of the late fifties were still in the future, and the company could not know that in less than ten years the great name of Packard would no longer exist. The older car is numero uno—1899 Model A.

Although made for export only in 1949 (left-hand drive), the Rolls-Royce Silver Dawn was significant in that it was the first "cooking" Rolls, i.e., it was supplied with a factory-built body. With a 6-cylinder engine (enlarged to 4.6 liters in 1952) and steering-column gearshift, the car was available cheaper with a Bentley radiator.

The availability of the Bentley radiator (which of course changed the name of the car to Bentley) was at one time explained by Rolls in one of their infrequent advertisements this way: "for those who are diffident about owning a Rolls-Royce". Who in his right mind would be diffident about owning a Rolls, except someone hiding from the tax collector?

The Chrome Age

After rationalizations, mergers and some fallings-by-the-wayside during the early Fifties reducing the choice of models to a more manageable number, technical progress was accelerated. American cars were built on much the same layouts as before; front engines with rear drive, using six cylinder power units on the standard, and V8s on the luxury models. Automatic transmission gave rise to a generation of drivers who thought the clutch was a back-seat pastime and a new mood began to filter into the motoring populace—that of non-aggressive driving, a principle which has sensibly been held to the present day in the U.S.

Motor sport in the Fifties added much to the technical advance of the road car, and engendered renewed interest, with the new system of Grandes Épreuves, Grand Prix races for which points were awarded towards the title of World Champion Driver. The first of the illustrious roll, Italian Dr. Guiseppe Farina, won the title in 1950 driving an Alfa Romeo 158.

The great Argentine driver Fangio won the following year and then another Italian, Alberto Ascari, took the title for two consecutive years in a Ferrari. Fangio scooped the next four years' championships (1954, 55, 56, 57) earning many historians' accolade as the best-ever racing driver. The year 1959 saw a change in design attitude and Australian Jack Brabham captured two years' titles in a rear-engined British Cooper-Climax.

In 1954 and 1955 Mercedes arrived, raced, and departed from the Formula 1 Grand Prix scene, taking just about every honor that the sport could offer. The silver 2.5 litre straight-8 Grand Prix cars were victorious in nine GP races over the two seasons in 300 SLR sports-care form, won the classic Italian road race, the Mille Miglia in 1955, and a number of other international events. At the end of the 1955 season Mercedes collected their silverware, and announced that they were withdrawing from Grand Prix racing. They had made their point, the advertising value of which lasted more than 20 years.

Genuine sporting machinery for the U.S. public was confined in the Fifties to the Chevrolet Corvette, seven years old at the end of the decade, and to the Thunderbird, which had been launched in 1954, a radical departure for Ford. The T-Bird was a car with a real promise of lively and safe performance—only to be reduced to a floundering luxury model as weight and seats were added. The Corvette however, more young-American in concept, was developing through sport and technological application into one of the outstanding cars of the time.

Sale of cars in the U.S. was now around 8 million every year, some of them smaller (the Falcon, Valiant, Corvair) than previously. The 'big three' milestones of 1958 were Ford's 50 millionth vehicle, Chrysler's 25 millionth, and the 50th anniversary of General Motors and, pointer to the future perhaps, GM demonstrated a car capable of steering itself over the road with a wire buried under the surface. Another pointer used the experience of the past—three companies in the United States announced that they would make electric vehicles.

1950-1959

The Chrome Age: 1950-1959

Jano's 1934 unsupercharged, 6-cylinder, twin-ohc, 2.3-liter car remained Alfa Romeo's staple offering until 1939 when, developed by Treviso, it became 2500 and remained in custom-made production until 1950. As a result of Alfa Romeo's "volte-face" in that year, the 1900 was introduced—a unitary-construction sedan based on mass-production lines—and since 1950 over 30,000 units have been sold.

Another "A"—the Aston-Martin DB2. This was the one originally designed for Lagonda by W. O. Bentley. The 2.6-liter, twin-ohc "six" finally achieved production installed in a chassis originally designed by Claud Hill for Gordon Sutherland's experimental post-war Atom. Sutherland sold out to David Brown in 1947, and by 1950, the cars had shown they could perform well at LeMans, and repeated in 1951.

And a third "A"—Austin A40 sports model. Introduced in 1950, it was more expensive than the Austin Saloon Devon, with which it shared a common basic specification, and it could not, in truth, be called a real sports car. Fitted with the 1200-cc, ohv engine and with ifs, the Sports was somewhat longer than the Devon. It was never a big seller, living in the shadow of the A90 sports models, and was given an exit in 1953.

Alfa Romeo, 1950 (I).

Chrysler Imperial, 1950 (USA).

Although it was the prestige car of the entire Chrysler line, the 1950 Imperial typifies the *malaise* which affected Chrysler postwar styling. Not only does the conservative "high-hipped" line date the car—the mechanics were also due for a face-lift. This came a year later when the old 5.3-liter "eight" was replaced by a 5,426-cc, ohv V-8, and not too soon, for the "eight" was basically a 1937 design.

Elsewhere in the Chrysler organization, Dodge had become rather submerged during the Forties, differing little from De Soto and deluxe Plymouths from the same stable. The 1950 Dodge Coronet still used the 3,769-cc "six" introduced in the early Forties on the D22 DeLuxe and Custom models. Dodge's president, Tex Colbert, spent approximately $90,000,000 on retooling and styling in 1949, and the resultant introduction of the "Red Ram" ohv, V-8 unit helped Dodge sales in 1952.

By contrast, clean and relatively unadorned lines characterized the 1950 Fords—most particularly the convertible. Automatic transmission became available during that year, and, together with the '49 line—longer and lower—and coil-spring ifs, brought plenty of customers—well over a million in 1950. Conclusion: good looks, good engine—good sales.

203

The Chrome Age: 1950-1959

Moskvitch, circa 1950 (SU).

Moskvitch—in Russian, "Son of Moscow". A more appropriate name would have been "Son of Opel". The prewar German Opel "Olympic" grew into a model called the "Kadett". Under the terms of reparations settlements after the war, the entire Kadett production lines were dismantled and shipped to Russia, where the car reappeared as the Moskvitch. With a 4-cylinder, 23-hp engine, the design was "dated" even in 1950, and no attempt was made to disguise its ancestry. The Russian government cared not a fig—the cars belonged to them—and if you wanted one, the government was the only game in town.

The Lancia Aurelia had a certain exterior affinity for earlier Lancias, but in 1950, the year of its introduction, the differences were interior. Overhead camshafts were "out", and push rods were "in", with an entirely new 1,754-cc V6 engine. The transmission, now located in the back axle, had synchromesh on the top three ratios, and in 1951 the car became available with an alternative 2-liter engine.

The "Cyclops" Rover 75—so-called because of its central headlight in the grille—was a completely re-styled version of the ifs, 2.1-liter six first introduced in 1948 with traditional bodywork. The P4 range—known affectionately as the "Aunty" Rover—was much beloved by British bank managers and other genteel folk, which probably accounts for the large number of good specimens still on the roads.

Cyclops Rover (GB).

Daimler, circa 1950-1951 (D).

After a war in which it built armored and scout cars, Daimler never quite recovered its position in the motor industry. Two limousine models were offered, a 4-liter six and a 5 ½-liter eight, the latter finding some favor with undertakers for hearse and funeral-car duties. This was perhaps a portent for the future, but in the immediate post-war period a number of the old carriage firms were still building custom-made bodies for those who could afford them. The Daimler Sedanca by Hooper is typical of the period.

Descended from the prewar 1100 S aerodynamic coupe, the FIAT 1100 ES was unveiled at the 1949 Geneva Salon and became available to the public in 1950. Although capable of 150 km/h (93 mph), it was never sold in large numbers and disappeared the following year.

The Hudson "Pacemaker"—an example of the revolutionary "step-down" series—was a brave, if unsuccessful attempt to fight off the "big three". Low-built, with a high-compression sv, in-line engine, unitary construction, coil springs ifs, and the rear wheels mounted inside the chassis frame, it deserved a better fate. But—no matter how chic the advertising, it was the car that brought the customers—and apparently the customers had stopped liking Hudsons. From a postwar high in 1950, Hudson sales plunged to 32,000 in 1954. The end was in sight.

205

Porsche 356 (D).

The first Porsche to be built in the Stuttgart factory, the Type 356 heralded series production after 50 prototypes had been built in Austria. Based on the Volkswagen, which Porsche had also designed, the 356 was propelled by a rear-mounted, VW-based, air-cooled, 4-cylinder unit of 1,086-cc, producing 40 bhp. As in the parent VW, this proved to be a successful formula, and the basic design survived with little outward change until 1964, by which time an enlarged engine of 1,966-cc was giving out 130 bhp.

Oldsmobile came out of World War II as the most innovative division of General Motors. They celebrated a half-centennial in 1948 (a little late) and introduced the "88" series the following year. Its ohv, "Rocket" V-8 engine was the first of its type (4.9 liters, over-square) and one year later, the old sixes had been completely phased out.

Staying with a basically pre-war design (the "L"-head six), the Plymouth Special deluxe ambled along for five years before the introduction of the over-square, ohv, V-8 heralded the coming of Chrysler's "Flight sweep" lines. Thereafter, Plymouth—the previously staid and respectable family car of the Chrysler stable—became the testing ground for new ideas.

Rover Turbine, 1950 (GB).

During the war, Rover had worked on gas turbines. They later drew on this experience to produce, in 1950, the world's first successful turbocar, JET 1. With a 200 bhp engine mounted in the rear of a standard "75" chassis, it recorded over 151 mph. It was followed by the T3 coupe which was exhibited in 1956, the T4 in 1962, and the Rover-B.R.M. which ran (unofficially) in the 1963 LeMans 24-hour race.

Introduced in 1946, the MK VI Bentley utilized the old 4,257-cc "six" first used for the 1937 season—an engine it shared with the Rolls-Royce "Silver Wraith" until it was replaced in 1960. The designation MK VI was dropped at the end of 1953, and thereafter the standard offerings were the Sports Saloon and Continental. The former was then dropped in favor of the "S" series in 1957.

1951—and British Ford introduced two models—the Zephyr, and the smaller Consul to replace the old V-8 Pilot. The Consul followed the fashion of the period with slab-sided styling. However, with a 1 ½-liter, ohv, 4-cylinder engine and ifs, it was a full five-seater and represented good value for the price. Convertible versions were later available and the car was not replaced by the MS2 Consul until 1956.

FIAT, 1951 (I).

Another variation on the wildly successful prewar "To-polino" theme, the FIAT Belvedere was introduced in 1951 and used the 569-cc, ovh engine which had first appeared in 1948. Producing 16.5 bhp at 4,400 rpm, the little Belvedere boasted an all-metal station wagon-type body beloved of parish priests, and with a maximum of 90 km/h (55 ½ mph) available even with four up, the model sold well.

In France, Simca, originally based on the FIAT 1100 built under license, popped up with a postwar car in the shape of a smart sports coupe with bodywork by Facel Metallon. They followed with a convertible—but by the time it was built the 1100 was replaced by a new 40-bhp, 1200-cc engine, and in 1951, producing 45-bhp, the same unit was used to power an entirely new car, the Aronde.

Based on *their* 1100 ohv model, the transient post-war Skoda 1101 was extracting 45 bhp from its 1,089-cc engine, which in 1939 had been giving only 32 hp; it was available in 2-seater and sedan versions, and was later developed into the Octavia range which continued in production until the introduction of the 1000 MB in 1964.

Skoda (CS).

Hillman Minx shipment, 1951 (GB).

It was still "export or die" in 1951 when Rootes chartered the 11,000-ton "Hoperidge" for this biggest shipment ever of cars and trucks to Australia. Differing little from the 1950 model apart from the chrome side flashes and spats, the Minx was the first really new post-war Hillman design, developed in 1949. Initially fitted with the prewar 1,185-cc, sv engine, the model shown here acquired a more powerful 1 ¼-liter engine in 1950, producing 37.5 bhp at 4,200 rpm and had full-width 5-6 seater bodywork.

Although the body lines of the Ford Custom represented a complete new style when introduced in 1949 (the old 1942 persisted for three years after the war), the engine was still the old sv, 3.9-liter V-8. This was supplemented in 1952 by a new "square" 3 ½ liter, ohv six, and in 1954 the V-8 was dropped. The Custom was also available with automatic transmission.

The first entirely new Jaguar saloon to appear after the war, the MK VII eschewed the push-rod engines of its predecessors and employed the 3.4-liter, twin-ohc unit. It was not replaced until 1957, when the MK VIII was introduced, won the Monte Carlo rally, and consolidated the Jaguar tradition of luxury and performance at a price others could not match.

Postwar Jaguar (GB).

Kaiser 2-door Sedan (USA).

Locating his plant in the Willow Run complex built by Ford for manufacture of the B-24 Liberator bomber, Henry J. Kaiser joined forces with Joseph Frazer of Graham-Paige in an attempt to repeat the success he had enjoyed with his Liberty ships by launching an entirely new make of car in 1946. The K-F combine started well, and at one stage built more cars than the established "independents" (including Studebaker, Hudson and Nash) but was never able to consolidate this lead. The Kaiser shown used an improved side-valve, 3.7-liter straight-6 of continental design.

The first completely new Lancia to appear postwar, the Aurelia was the result of the combined design talents of Jano (previously with Alfa Romeo) and Gianni Lancia (Vincenzo Lancia, founder of the firm, died in 1937) and was introduced in 1950. The production cars retained the shell and suspension of earlier models, but the engine was a new 1,754-cc, push-rod V-6 of 56 bhp.

The Mercedes-Benz 220 convertible, introduced in 1951 by Stuttgart, was still heavily influenced by prewar styling. Probably because they wanted to sell the 220s, no hint was given of the exciting new 300SL sports car they unveiled the following year. The 220 used a 2,195-cc engine, and was one of two sixes introduced by Mercedes in 1951. The other was the 300 of 2,996-cc capacity.

210

In addition to the Mini and its transverse engine derivatives, Alec Issigonis was also responsible for the ageless Morris ''Moggie'' Minor. First conceived as the ''Mosquito'' in 1948, the first production models appeared in 1949 as the MM series, but still powered by the prewar side-valve 918-cc engine. After the formation of the British Motor Corporation in 1952, the Austin A30 engine—an 803, ohv unit—was substituted in 1953, and by 1960 the car had grown up into the ''1000'', with a 1,098-cc power plant.

Following the same successful theme introduced by Ford in 1949, there was little to distinguish '51 Mercurys from the previous year's offerings. With hypoid back axle, coil-spring ifs, and a 4,185-cc V-8 engine, the pattern was continued until 1955, when customers had the option of two V-8 engines producing 188 and 198 bhp.

In spite of the faintly bloated ''new line'' that characterized Austins from 1948 on, the large 4-cylinder A90 Austin Atlantic power-top convertible was a fast car, and in a bid to attract transatlantic customers, a series of long-distance record attempts were made at Indianapolis. In spite of a good showing, sales were disappointing, although the engine—in Austin-Healey guise—gave the Triumph TR series a run for its money until 1956.

Morris, circa 1951 (GB).

BMW was one of the numerous German business firms which fell victim to the postwar partition of Germany. They lost their factory at Eisenach that they had acquired from Dixi in 1928. They began again in Munich in 1945 with motorcycles. Then in 1952, their first postwar car appeared—the 501 sedan pictured. Based on their last prewar designs, it utilized a 6-cylinder, 1,971-cc engine.

A very handsome 2-liter, 120-mph Continental by H. J. Mulliner represented one of the last individual Bentley designs at a time when Rolls-Royce and Bentley identities were being merged into a common manufacturing program. If nothing else, it showed that the coach builder's art was by no means dead. After acquiring a new 4.9-liter engine in 1956, the Continental was continued until 1966. Also in 1955, automatic transmissions, hitherto optional, became standard.

Post-war, Frazer Nash did very well for themselves. Their cars were a far cry from chain-driven models descended from the GN cycle car that established the reputation of the brand in the twenties and thirties. Powered by a 2-liter Bristol engine, the LeMans version, in the hands of Ken Wharton, notched up numerous competition successes. A Frazer Nash won the 12-hour Sebring race in 1952, and this gave rise to another model of the same name.

BMW, 1952 (D).

212

Agajanian Special, 1952 (USA)

In the last "dirt" car to win at Indianapolis, Troy Ruttman was never farther back than third. The race went like this: by the tenth lap, Ruttman was second to Vukovich. He stayed there, gradually closing in, and at the 200-mile mark he had passed and was leading by 34 seconds. He was forced into a pit stop, which cost him time, and when he came out of the pit he was second to Vukovich again. At lap 170, Ruttman was 31 seconds back, and it looked like Vukovich's race—until his steering gear collapsed and he hit the north wall. Ruttman went on to win at a new record average of 138.992 mph.

Here's how automobile manufacturers get grey hair—and throw money away. In 1952, Alfa Romeo came up with a very snazzy-looking 2-seater they called Disco Volante (Flying Saucer). Nine of them were built, employing a bored-out version of their "1900" engine, which was originally intended as a design study for a 3-liter sedan which was eventually abandoned. They tried four of the Disco Volantes in the 1953 Mille Miglia—one with a 4-cylinder, 2-liter engine and the others with a 6-cylinder unit. The larger versions also raced at LeMans, Spa and the Nurburgring, but without success. History does not record what happened to the other five. One hopes the Italian version of the Internal Revenue Service was lenient about the ensuing tax write-off.

Alfa Romeo, 1953, (I).

213

The Chrome Age: 1950-1959

DeSoto, 1952 (USA).

The 1952 DeSoto Firedome 8. Looking at this slab-sided monument to the mouth-organ grille from the hindsight of later years, it's surprising that DeSoto managed to unload 97,000 units in 1952. The car typified all that was wrong with Chrysler styling during this period. Although the 4-½-liter, 160-bhp, over-square V-8 introduced in 1952 boosted sales in 1953 to nearly 130,000, they never managed to repeat this, and even Chrysler's "Flight Sweep" line could do little to prevent DeSoto's decline throughout the fifties.

FIAT went way out of character at the Geneva Salon in 1952 with an effort to challenge the 2-seater "bombs" proliferating in England and the rest of the Continent. Theirs contained an ohv, 110-bhp, V-8 engine of 1,996-cc developed by Siata of Turin—well-known tuners of FIATs since before the war and builders of their own mainly FIAT-based cars. The engine gave the car a heady 120 mph, but it was unsuccessful in competition in the hands of various private owners. The effort, never produced in more than small numbers, was abandoned in 1954.

First introduced in 1948, the Vauxhall Velox was restyled in 1952, using a unitary construction in a standardized hull which it shared with the smaller Wyvern. Under the hood was a long-stroke, 6-cylinder, 2.3-liter engine delivering 54 bhp.

Vauxhall, 1952 (GB).

Packard, circa 1953 (USA).

Another case of trouble waiting in the wings—the Packard Patrician 400. A perfect example of the unfortunate post-war styling that dogged the company's products in its last years, the Patrician utilized the old straight-8 engine (eventually discontinued in 1954) and was not unlike, in outward appearance, the later Clippers. These, however, were only a pale shadow of the handsome 1941 Clipper line, and with the introduction of the Caribbean convertible, nemesis was virtually unavoidable. It was delayed only by a brief liaison with Studebaker.

Even though it, too, was afflicted with "chrome-itis", (a disease which was suffered by many American cars of the period) the Plymouth, restyled in 1949 and updated since, looked quite handsome compared to its competitors within the Chrysler stable. However, it was a sheep in wolf's clothing—the old 127-bhp, sv straight-8 continued to live under Pontiac hoods until 1955, when the 4.7-liter, ohv V-8 supplanted it on American-produced cars.

Basically the Morris Six, the 6/80 was the larger of two Wolseley models introduced when the factory moved to Cowley in 1949. The last vestiges of Wolseley independence disappeared in 1955 with the introduction of the Austin-engined 2.6-liter 6/90.

Pontiac, circa 1952 (USA).

Talbot, circa 1952 (F).

When the old Sunbeam-Talbot-Darracq combine finally folded in 1935, Major A. F. Lago took control of the Suresnes factory, while Rootes got the British end and combined Sunbeam and Talbot. The French factory had been known as Automobile Talbot since 1920, however, so when Lago produced the postwar 4 ½-liter sedan shown, the French called it a Talbot (this is a Talbot Lago Record Type T26) and the English called it a Darracq—all very confusing. What is quite clear is that despite racing successes (including the 1950 LeMans), postwar France was no place to be producing luxury cars with large engines, no matter how economical they might be, and taxation crippled the already financially weak company.

The ubiquitous 2CV Citroën (affectionately known as the *"deux chevaux"*) was designed by Pierre Boulanger, and 250 prototypes were tested during 1935 and 1939, but further development was prevented by the war. Making its debut at the Paris Salon in 1948, it quickly caught the imagination of the French in spite of its somewhat Spartan appearance. Like the larger *"traction avant"* (front-wheel drive) Citroëns, it had fwd and unitary construction. The 375-cc, ohv, flat-twin engine was enlarged to 425-cc in 1955. Andre Citroën, almost bankrupted by the 7CV in 1934, sold out to Michelin in 1935. The "traction avante" continued until 1957.

Citroën, circa 1953 (F).

Dodge Coronet, circa 1953 (USA).

Available also with the old 3.8-liter, side-valve six, the Dodge Coronet shown housed the ohv, "Red Ram", 3.8-liter unit introduced a year earlier. While it is doubtful that this model Dodge would, as John Steinback asserted, "go to hell and back on its belly", it was a tough car with a deserved reputation for longevity. After a period during which it was virtually indistinguishable from other lower-priced products in the Chrysler range, the Coronet once more gave Dodge an individuality of its own.

The post-war Allard was the only really successful Anglo-American produced after the war. The car evolved from prewar Ford V-8 trials specials of Sydney Allard. Whatever sold them, it wasn't their good looks. A popular poem of the period said "they ate Jaguars for breakfast and Bentleys for tea". Whatever the reason, the big type-M convertible wasn't responsible for any success overseas. It was the J2, introduced in 1950, with (for export) a 5.4-liter Cadillac V-8 engine (or similar units) which was responsible for Allards sending 75% of its production to the USA.

The 4-cylinder "1900" Alfa Romeo spawned a couple of successors, and marked a turning point in the company's history. Astral, somewhat curiously shaped (but very "Alfa" in appearance) was first shown in 1953, as was the Disco Volante, previously noted.

The Chrome Age: 1950-1959

Although the name "Rambler" was derived from the first cars built by the old Thos. B. Jeffery Co. from 1902-1913, there was nothing old-fashioned about the Rambler Custom. With its 2.8-liter, sv-six, unitary construction, short chassis and low weight, it was the first of the postwar "compacts" and was largely responsible for the survival of Nash (now American Motors) as the lone American "independent". Parentage of the Austin-produced Metropolitan is unmistakable in this photo.

The British Standard Ten first appeared late in 1953 in 803-cc, ohv guise, at a time when the Standard Company was building more tractors than cars. The 948-cc Ten followed shortly afterward and could be distinguished from its smaller brother by the chrome grill and more luxurious trim.

Whether or not it was the result of the British Government's exhortation to "export or die" in the immediate postwar years, a number of British makers slanted their products to the American market either in styling or nomenclature. The Austin Atlantic deserved a better reception than it received, but Hillman's Californian got the same cold shoulder, quite deservedly. However, the tried-and-true Rootes formula (take convential mechanics and put a pretty face on it) worked well enough in the home market.

Rambler, circa 1953 (USA).

One of the best-known American "independents" Hudson established its reputation in the 1920s with the Super Six and Essex Coach models. Although it managed to weather the difficult depression years, the 1930s were a trying time for the company. It staged a brief revival in the car-starved post-war years, and the Hornet, introduced in 1951, was the most successful of its postwar models. The car shown was one of the last Hornets produced by the company before its amalgamation with American Motors in 1954. Engine: 5-liter, 145-bhp, 6-cylinders.

In 1953, the smaller cars in the British Ford range were re-styled on lines similar to the Consul and Zephyr models, but were fitted with 1,172-cc engines. The exception was the Popular, which inherited the old pre-war "sit-up-and-beg" bodywork of the Anglia married to the 1172 unit. This antique design, renowned for its uncertain directional ability, was made until 1959.

The first Toyota cars appeared in 1937, built by an offshoot of a company making power looms and spinning machinery in Koromo. Spearheading its re-entry into the market after the war was a two-door sedan producing 27 bhp from its 4-cylinder engine. In 1953 a 4-door was added, and by 1955 some 700 cars a month were being produced, and a 48 bhp, 1453-cc model, The Crown, was introduced.

Hudson Hornet, 1953 (USA).

The Chrome Age: 1950-1959

Utilizing the versatile Standard Vanguard engine in 1,991-cc form, the triumph TR2 was an instant success when introduced in 1953. Like the Vanguard, the engine proved economical (even when coupled with performance in excess of 100 mph) and was renowned for its lack of temperament.

Joining the sedan and convertible Sunbeam-Talbot "90" models which had distinguished themselves in the Alpine Rally, the two-seater Sunbeam Alpine was introduced in March of 1953. Using a modified "90" engine of 2,267-cc, it, like the TR2, was capable of 100 mph. Rally driver Sheila Van Damm set up the Belgian and women's records in the 2-liter class at Jabbeke—120.135 mph. The car was a stripped version of the Alpine, with a high axle ratio.

First introduced by the Bristol Aeroplane Company as the type 400 in 1947, the Bristol was based on the prewar BMW 328. By 1953, the up-dated 403 was delivering a genuine 100 mph and developed 100 bhp at 5,000 rpm. The 404 Sports coupe was available with either 105- or 125-bhp engines, the more powerful being that used in the Cooper-Bristol Formula II racing cars. A team of experimental coupes based on the 404 won the 2-liter class and team prize at Le Mans in 1954.

Triumph, 1953 (GB).

FIAT turbine, circa 1954-1955 (I).

FIAT hitched on to the gas-turbine bandwagon in the mid-fifties with the FIAT Turbina. Quite a few companies played footsie with gas-turbine experimentation around this time—but apparently none of them found it economically practical, since to date, there has never been a production model anywhere. The futuristic FIAT coupe utilized the chassis of FIAT's limited production V-8 sports car, first introduced in 1952.

The 1300-cc Alfa Romeo Guiletta was introduced in 1954 as a companion for the 1900, from which it evolved. In spite of the reduced engine capacity, the classic twin-cam head was retained, and the power unit developed 80, 90 or 100 bhp, depending on whether you opted for the Sprint, Sprint Veloce, or Sprint Speciale. The Speciale was capable of 124 mph when fitted with twin Weber carburetors.

Of unitary construction, the "D"-type Jaguar was a development of the successful "C" type, which was a version of the twin-cam XK120. Jaguar's successes at Le Mans are now legendary, but it's worth noting that the company fielded 5 "D"'s for the 1957 event. They finished first, second, third, fourth and sixth! A few "C"'s and "D"'s were sold to the public, but the standard offering for non-racing customers was the XK140 (an improved 190-bhp XK120). In 1961, the "E"-type took over.

The Chrome Age: 1950-1959

Sometime, somewhere, someone probably needed a small truck, couldn't afford one, chopped off the back of his Model T Ford sedan, and presto! the pickup was born. This vehicle (called a "utility" in Britain and Australia) has been an essential vehicle ever since. The one in the picture is the Australian version. Continuing the frontal styling of the sedan Holden FX model which had received a minor face-lift with the introduction of the FJ series of 1954, this "ute" was a purpose-built version of a type of vehicle that has become synonymous with the way of life "down under".

The first Lancia Grand Prix car, designated the D50, was designed by Jano for the 1954 season and incorporated a number of new features. The V-8 engine formed part of the space frame and was mounted diagonally; suspension was by wishbones at the front, employing a very thin transverse leaf spring, and de Dion at the rear, also with transverse leaf spring and a complicated system of telescopic shock absorbers. The fuel tanks were slung on outriggers between the wheels. This promising design was handed over to Ferrari when Lancia sold out to FIAT in 1955.

Utilizing the same body shell as the prewar Kapitans, Opel reentered the market in 1948—and with some body modifications, kept the same 2,473-cc, 6-cylinder unit in the line until 1959.

Holden, circa 1954 (AUS).

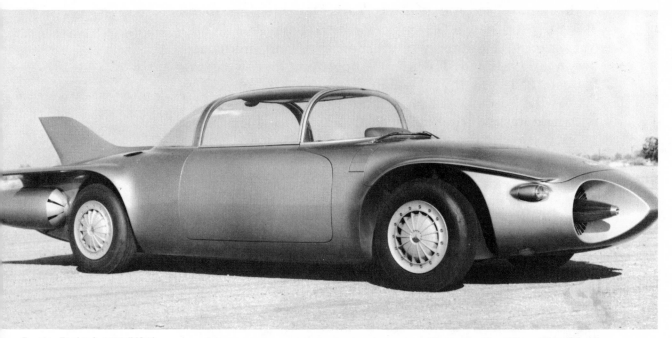

Pontiac Firebird, 1954 (USA).

No, you never saw one on the road. The Firebird "dream car" of 1954 was one of a number of such outbursts from designers who were indulged in their never-ceasing urge to design something different. This manifestation goes back to the early days, but the first earnest effort was one by Harvey Earl for Buick in 1938. The public never has had a chance to buy one, as the British say, "off the peg", but Buick models subsequent to Earl's creation incorporated more than a few engineering and body features inherited from it. Actually, so did the Firebird.

The Series II Morris Oxford differed little in outward appearance from the MO that it succeeded and which was introduced in 1949. Following the merger with Austin in 1952 and the formation of the British Motor Corporation, the Austin A50 unit was used in place of the 1,472-cc Morris. Unitary construction was introduced in 1955, and the model remained in production until the advent of the Farina-styled sedans in 1959.

Originally a product of Ford's factory at Poissy, the Simca Vedette in original form was powered by the old 2.2-liter V-8 engine. It continued in use until 1954, when a larger 3.9-liter unit was listed. Later in the year, Ford, not operating very successfully in France, sold out to Simca. The Chambord version of the Simca lingered on, and was still in production (under license) in Brazil as late as 1967.

223

The Chrome Age: 1950-1959

Introduced for the 1952 Le Mans, the Mercedes-Benz 300 SL used the 300S engine tuned to give 215 bhp (increased to 240 bhp in production cars) and production began in 1954. Fitted with fuel injection, they were the fastest road cars then available, giving 150 mph. The "gull-wing" doors were phased out in 1956, but the model remained in production until 1963.

1955 was the last year in which Austin-Healey used the 2.7-liter, ohv, 4-cylinder Austin A90 Engine. By this time, fitted with disk brakes and developing 132 bhp, the original 100 series had reached the limit of development, and in 1956 the 100-6 was introduced. Powered by Austin's 2.6-liter unit, this was in turn superseded in 1960 by the 3000 with a 2.9 liter six. Always popular with the "heavy brigade", the "big" Healeys did well in competition, but suffered from low ground clearance which hampered them in some events. Worthy competitors of Triumph's TR series, the "big" Healeys were discontinued in 1968.

The experimental 179 was a Volvo that never went into production. It was derived from the rugged PV444 (1,400-cc, 4-cylinder engine) although the body was considerably revamped. The final design was a prototype that didn't meet the standards of Volvo's severe test program. So—although it looked handsome, it wound up on the scrap heap.

Mercedes-Benz, circa 1955 (D).

Early post-war single-seater racer, a 2-liter Connaught, 1952. (GB)

Allard 30 hp, 1948. (GB)

Reliant Sabre 6 cresting a hill during the 1963 RAC Rally. (GB)

Plymouth Fury, 1961, and 1928 Plymouth. (USA)

Two Renaults of the emergent post war period. A 5 CV Dauphine of 1956, and Renault's attempt at a record-breaking turbine, the 270 CV *Etoile Filant* of the same date. (F)

Maserati 250F, 1955. Often called the most handsome racing car of all. (I)

Ford Anglia, 1953. (GB)

BMW 507 Touring Sport (3.2-liter V8), produced
1955-59. (D)

Alvis, 1955 (GB).

Developed by Alex Issigonis, during a brief sojourn at Alvis, from the earlier 2,993-cc, 90-bhp TA21, the Alvis TC 21/100 produced 100 bhp and carried a 100 mph guarantee. In 1955, when Graber designed new bodywork on this chassis, the shape of future Alvis production crystallized. Despite detail improvements, the TD and TE series followed the same handsome lines, but after the Rover takeover in 1965, all private-car production stopped in 1967.

By the time the Singer Special Saloon, a cheaper version of the Hunter, appeared, the sands of time were running out for the Singer Company. While capable of impressive performance when tuned (as in the postwar H.R.G.), the chain-driven, overhead-cam, 1 ½-liter engine was basically an updated 1920's design, and Singer couldn't afford the retooling necessary to rid itself of the slab-sided sedan first introduced in 1948. Rootes took over in 1956, and the first Gazelles used the old 1 ½-liter unit.

Sharing its, 1,500-cc power unit with the Morris Oxford, the Austin A50 Cambridge was also available initially with the 1,200-cc, A40 engine. It was still recognizably Austin, became known as the A55 in 1958, and in 1959, adopted Farina styling common to Morris, M.G., Wolseley and Riley.

225

Thunderbird, circa 1955 (USA).

Destined to become sought after by collectors as a postwar "classic", the Ford Thunderbird was introduced in 1954, and at that time was a genuine attempt by Ford to market a sports car. Ohv, V-8 engines of 4.8- or 5.1-liters were available, the larger of which would propel the car at 113 mph, but later T-birds lost their sports-car image and were never quite as popular with the true dyed-in-the-wool sports car *aficianado*.

In 1955, Chrysler developed the 300 (in both coupe and convertible) to compete with the Thunderbird. The car was very definitely influenced by Chrysler's "Flight Sweep" lines. The 4.9-liter, 188-bhp engines were enlarged to 6,423-cc by 1957, and developed more power than the competition. The car, however, did not have that sports-car look that the original T-bird enjoyed.

Financed by the wealthy MacAlpine building family, the British racing Connaught started life as a "special" with a much-modified Lea Francis 1750 engine. By 1954 the firm was building cars for resale, and their type B, using the 2 ½-liter twin-ohc Alta engine won the Syracuse Grand Prix in 1955, driven by Tony Brooks. Financial difficulties forced the closing of the firm in 1957.

Hillman had a quick success in 1955 with the "Husky", a short-wheelbase station wagon. The Husky shared the basic Minx 1265-cc power unit, somewhat smaller than the Californian and enlarged Minx units of 1,295-cc. Hillman allowed the Husky to lag behind until it was discontinued in 1967.

When Citroën at last supplemented the prewar *"Traction Avante"* models with a new car, it created almost as much impact as its predecessor in 1934. A foretaste of things to come had been the introduction of hydropneumatic suspension on the old "six" in 1954, but when the DS 19 was introduced, its only affinity with the old order was fwd and the old long-stroke, 4-cylinder engine, now producing 65 bhp. Lines that still look advanced today were combined with self-leveling suspension and power assistance for brakes, steering and gearshift.

Designed by the versatile Spaniard, Wilfredo Ricart, the Pegaso in it original form was introduced in 1951 by the Spanish E.N.A.S.A. firm in Barcelona. The factory was located in part of the old Hispano-Suiza plant, and despite E.N.A.S.A.'s reputation as primarily commercial vehicle manufacturers, this gave rise to hopes of great things to come. However, only about 125 Pegasos were built, three or four of which were Z103s fitted with the firm's own push-rod-operated V-8, available in 4-, 4 ½-, or 4.7-liter form.

Only a year of independence remained to the Salmson Company when their "2300" was produced in 1955—Renault took over in 1956. Developed from the 2.2-liter Randonnée model introduced in 1951, the 2300 used a tuned version of the twin-camshaft, light-alloy engine, producing 105 bhp and speeds in excess of 100 mph. The end was in sight, even though Renault tried a long-wheelbase version in 1957. No more Salmsons appeared thereafter.

Citroën DS 19, circa 1955 (F).

MG, 1956 (GB).

The M.G.A. was the first fully streamlined production MG, and was introduced in 1956 as a successor to the traditional TF. With an Austin-designed, 68-bhp, 1½-liter engine, it proved to be faster and more economical than its predecessor and was publicized by some very convincing record-breaking activity. A twin-cam engine briefly introduced as an option proved to be very fast indeed, at the expense of a prodigious thirst for oil and an uncertain temperament, but the 1,600-cc, push-rod, ohv, 78-bhp engine that subsequently replaced it as standard proved almost as fast and totally dependable.

Introduced in 1955 as a companion to the popular but aging 203, the 1½ liter Peugeot 403 was another winner that quickly established a high reputation. Fitted with all-synchromesh transmission, it was available with two-pedal control in 1958, and, for those who wanted one, an Indenor diesel engine was offered in 1959.

The Mercedes-Benz 300 SLR was an outstandingly successful sports/racing car. It was developed from the W196 Formula I car, with a straight-8, 3-liter, fuel-injection engine. Not only did it provide Fangio, in 2½-liter form, with the car in which he won the World Championship in 1954 and 1955, but it also enabled Stirling Moss to win the 1955 Mille Miglia—the first time a British driver had ever done it since the race was first run in 1927.

228

Wolseley, 1956 (GB).

Fitted with bell and central aerial, the Wolseley Six-Ninety was the car no British motorist wanted to see in his rearview mirror, for ever since Scotland Yard adapted the 18-hp model in 1937, Wolseley sixes have been synonymous with the police force. The model pictured employed the Austin 2.6-liter engine and shared its body shell with Riley's Pathfinder. In 1956 it was available with overdrive or automatic transmission.

Interest in alternative methods of propulsion became rather widespread during the early and mid-fifties, possibly spring-boarded by the work done by Rover on their "Jet 2", T3 and T4 models. Certainly Chrysler was running a gas turbine in 1954. Among the hopefuls to appear about this time was Renault's *"L'Etoile Filante"*, which achieved some success in establishing turbine records. "L'Etoile Filante" was an elaborately streamlined, rear-finned vehicle, with the driver placed midship. At one time or another, FIAT, Austin, Ford and General Motors have also had a whack at gas turbine-propelled cars, but none have gotten past the prototype stage.

By 1956, American Motors was really "thinking small". They introduced the Rambler in 1950 (it was Nash-Kelvinator at that time), and it became their biggest asset. They dumped the large Nash and Hudson lines in 1957, and the 2.8-liter sv "six" saved the day—all 2,576 pounds of it. When compact fever hit the USA in the late fifties, Rambler was ready. They sold 400,000 Ramblers in 1959, and by 1960 pushed Chrysler out of third place in the production tables.

Chevrolet, 1956 (USA)

Renault, 1956 (F).

The Belair Chevrolet represented the largest group in the Chevrolet range. The engine was now a 4.3-liter, V-8—up from the 3,858-cc, 6-cylinder of the previous year. In that previous year, Chevrolet sold more than one-half of all private cars in the United States.

Also introduced in 1956, the 845-cc Dauphine continued Renault's policy of rear-engined small cars and proved to be an even greater success that the 4CV. Over 2 million were sold, and this might have been more. With a 30-bhp engine, the car was developed further during Amédée Gordini's tenure with Renault, and this resulted in the 38-bhp Dauphine Gordini and, in 1959, the Florida Sports coupe. Dauphines were finally discontinued in 1968.

Derived from BMW's 502 and 503, themselves a continuation of the postwar prestige theme that began in 1951 with the 501, the 507 Sportswagen employed a 3.8-liter version of the sedan's V-8 engine. It looked very much like the contemporary Mercedes, and this two-seater was no mean performer in its own right. From a standstill, it could reach 70 mph in just over 10 seconds—and with the pedal on the floor, 130 mph was top speed.

The Lotus MK XI won a remarkable total of 156 races during 1956, including the 1,100-cc class record at Monza.

Performance was the watchword at Pontiac during the late fifties. A year-by-year step-up on power and size began in 1956 with the introduction of the Star Chief with a 5,189-cc, V-8 engine. In 1957, it was increased to 5,687-cc; in 1958, to 6,063-cc; and when Pontiac went to their wide-track chassis in 1959, a 6.4-liter unit with output ranging up to 345 bhp was available.

By the time the 1956 Allard Palm Beach MK II was produced, with its Jaguar "C" engine, Sidney Allard was building cars to special order only. With a tubular frame, torsion bar, wishbone ifs, and a rigid axle, the car had been available earlier with the 3.6-liter, sv, Ford V-8 unit, but the firm's heyday (during which they won the 1952 Monte Carlo Rally with their P-type sedan) was now over. No cars were built after 1960.

When the Volvo PV444 was finally pensioned off in 1965, its engine had increased in size to 1.8-liters, but the limited-production 70 bhp Sports Roadster introduced in 1956 used the original 1.4-liter engine. Coinciding with the introduction of the Model 122 with completely new four-door sedan bodywork married to the 444 engine, the Sports lasted barely two seasons, despite the novelty of a 5-speed transmission.

Buick, after a good year in 1955, developed problems in the braking system in 1957 and 1958—and this brought on a major engineering overhaul for Buick.

Pontiac, 1957 (USA).

Mercury, 1957 (USA).

Originally introduced in 1938 to fill the gap in the Ford program, by 1957 Mercury was offering this stylish convertible with a 5.1-liter, V-8 engine producing 255 bhp. This was augmented by the option of a de-tuned Lincoln unit. To avoid an overlap with the unfortunate Edsel, 1958 and 1959 Mercs became larger and more expensive, fielding a 6.3-liter, V-8 in addition to the existing engine. With the Edsel's demise, Mercury could afford to come down a peg, and 1961 saw the introduction of their 2.4-liter Comet.

The Lotus MK 7 of 1957 followed the same stark functional layout of the earlier cars, but adopted the frame of the larger MK 11 sports car. The two-seater was normally fitted with the Ford 100E engine, but a Super Seven with Coventry Climax engine and disk brakes was also available. The car was more successful with the Ford engine.

Heralding the re-entry of the now-nationalized Czechoslovakian Tatra company into private-car production after a three-year hiatus, the 603 appeared in 1957 and reverted to the rear engine principle that had dominated their products during the thirties. Once again, an air-cooled V-8 was employed—this time of 2,472-cc—and this continued until 1972, by which time the model was designated the T3-603, and boasted the following refinements: twin carburetors, servo-assisted brakes and power steering.

232

Posed with members of the East Sussex Constabulary, the 2 ½-liter Riley Pathfinder was a remarkable car in that its 2,443-cc engine survived not only the rationalization of the Nuffield take-over of the old Riley Company in 1939 (it has been introduced as the 85-bhp "Big Four" in 1937) but also that of the B.M.C. merger in 1952, in postwar form developing first 90- and then 100-bhp. By 1954 the handsome fabric-topped Riley bodywork had been exchanged for Wolseley's 6/90 body well; 1957 saw the last of the old Riley 2 ½-liter engines, and in 1958 they were replaced by Austin's 2.6-liter ohv six.

When British Air Vice-Marshall ("Pathfinder") Bennett introduced his first Fairthorpe—an unprepossessing 650-cc minicar—in 1954, its chances of survival seemed slim. No hint was given of the exciting and successful little sports car that was to emerge (and is still emerging) from the same stable. The Fairthorpe Electron Minor with Standard 10 engine/transmission and running gear in a conventional ladder chassis was the cheaper running mate to the 1,098-cc, Coventry-Climax-engined Electron. The EM3, fitted with a Triumph Spitfire engine, was still selling well nine years later and in 1972 was being offered with the Triumph 1300 engine.

The name Auto Union was resurrected in 1958 for some of the D.K.W. cars which continued in production until 1962.

Riley, circa 1957 (GB).

The Chrome Age: 1950-1959

The Edsel (USA).

Unquestionably the biggest, most expensive flop in automotive history. The Edsel was not a bad automobile—in actuality, what killed it was something that could be referred to as "lag time". A full and expensive market research program told Ford that there was room for a full-size car to fill a gap betwen the Ford and the Mercury. By the time the research had been implemented by a $250,000,000 tooling-up, compacts had caught the public fancy—and the Edsel caught it in the neck.

After three seasons of hard sell, the Edsel had sold barely one-third of what was projected for *annual* sales. 300,000 units was the annual projection, so Ford had moved only a little better than 10% of what they had planned for.

With a choice of two engines—V-8s, either 5.9-liters or 6.7-liters—the Edsel had its virtues, and, ironically, the car has become something of a cult. The distinctive grille—sometimes likened to a horse collar by unfriendly critics—set the car apart, but didn't do anything for sales. It all ended dismally in 1960.

Another name that disappeared in 1960 was British Armstrong-Siddeley, but not for the same reason as Edsel. The parent company was heavily in aviation and merged with still another aircraft outfit. They tried to make a go of it with an independent company, but 1960 saw Armstrong-Siddeley disappear from the Buyer's Guides.

Armstrong-Siddeley, circa 1956 (GB).

Ferrari, 1958 (I).

After winning the Manufacturers' Championship with the improved Lancia/Ferraris he had inherited from Gianni Lancia in 1956, Enzo Ferrari embarked on the development of a new G.P. car with a V-6 engine of his own design. Designated the Dino, after his son who had just died, this new 2 ½-liter Ferrari was outstandingly successful, giving Mike Hawthorn his 1958 World Championship and coming within a whisker of once again winning the Manufacturers' Championship for Ferrari.

Introduced in prototype as the Nash NX1 by American Motors in 1950, production Austin Metropolitans first appeared in 1954 as the result of a transatlantic deal with the British Motor Corporation whereby the cars were built in Austin's plant in England. In reality Nash Airflytes in miniature, there were some who said that the transition was an unhappy one. Nevertheless, little change was made in the styling of either the convertible or coupe models during their seven-year life span. Powered at first by the Austin 1,200-cc, A40 engine, they later inherited the A50 Cambridge unit.

Back in 1953, the Italian Ardea was replaced by the Appia, with a 1,100-cc, 38-bhp engine. Small, but it moved Appia along at up to 75 mph. Money was the problem, however. Appia was hopelessly high-priced in comparison with other 1,100-cc cars. In 1964, it was replaced by the Fulvia, based on the Fessia-designed Flavia.

The Chrome Age: 1950-1959

Van Doorne's Automobielfabrik, known as D.A.F. (fortunately, as otherwise there wouldn't have been room on the car for the name), introduced their first car in 1958, and production began in 1959. Despite their angular lines and eccentric specification, they rapidly gained acceptance—particularly with women drivers and those for whom conventional gear-changing held unknown terrors. Publicized as "the cheapest automatic", the D.A.F. employed a unique vee-belt drive with centrifugal clutch and limited-slip differential and was powered by a 600-cc, front-mounted, ohv, air-cooled, flat-twin engine.

Restyled for the last time in 1959, the Standard Vanguard model represented the final development of the old 2,088-cc "four" Vanguard unit. By the time this model appeared, wearing Triumph's "world" badge, the basic formula was somewhat out of date, although still popular in Australia, where the name survived a little longer than in England. The company joined the ranks of "lost causes" in 1963, partly because by that time the word "standard" had come to mean something less than best quality in our debased advertising language:

Introduced in 1959, the Triumph Herald went to a separate chassis and was the first British small sedan to be equipped with all-around independent suspension. It must have proved a fairly redoubtable seller, since it wasn't until 1971 that it was replaced by the Toledo two-door sedan.

Triumph, 1959 (GB).

Vespa, 1959 (F).

Designed by the Italian Piaggio aircraft company, and bearing the same name as their successful scooter, the Vespa was built in France by A.C.M.A. Enjoying some popularity in the economy-minded days following the Suez crisis, it boasted unitary construction and a rear-mounted, air-cooled, vertical-twin two-stroke. It was pushed to one side by the BMC Mini which made its appearance in 1960. The last Vespas were made in 1961.

After the Volkswagen factories were returned to German administration in 1949, only the sedan version of the Beetle was made by the company, but alternative bodywork was offered by a variety of coachbuilders. Karmann, an old-established German company, offered a four-seater convertible, and eventually the Karmann-Ghia coupe and convertible two-seat versions that evolved became generally available and were adopted as factory alternatives. Employing the well-known and tested VW formula of rear-mounted, air-cooled, 1,131-cc (1,192-cc from 1954), horizontally opposed engines, the Karmann-Ghia proved popular, and updated versions were still being offered in 1973.

Normally offered as a hardtop coupe, the XK140 version of the original Jaguar XK120 theme was extended in 1959, and the resultant XK150 model was available with 2.4-, 3.4-, and 3.8-liter engines (the latter producing up to 250 bhp) and disk brakes all around.

237

The Motor Boom And The Orient

The decade started, in Europe at least, with the introduction of a new word in automotive language—the Mini. A tiny unitary constructed transverse-engined car to accommodate four adults, the British Mini was gobbled up as fast as it could be turned out of the factory at Longbridge. Good handling and adaptable performance soon had them on the racing circuits and winning contests of the calibre of the Monte Carlo Rally. The new car wiped away the then current bubble productions like the Heinkel, Messerschmitt, Frisky, Scootacar, that had been cornering the mini-car market, and gave a dozen other major manufacturers a good reason for copying the new trend—which they did as fast as they could re-tool. The period was perhaps Britain's automotive engineering heyday, with the Jaguar E-type, Aston Martin, MGA and later B, supported by specialists and exotica like Lotus, Jensen, A.C., Gilbern, Morgan.

But during the 'Sixties the choice again began to diminish. Sales methods, in line with American precedents (and so much of European industry was now part-owned by U.S. concerns) began to persuade motorists—logically enough—that an automobile was a washing machine, was a freezer, was a vacuum cleaner—was a consumer product essential to daily life and to be regularly and frequently replaced when worn. Some of the light went out of European motoring as cars became distinguishable in some cases only by the packaging, and as the vast jams built up.

Another factor dangerous to home production in both American and Europe raised its head. Small artifacts such as cameras and motorcycles and ingenious electronics had been coming out of Japan for some time; now small cars were infiltrating the markets, and their engines were beginning to grow. Only the German Volkswagen (over half a million had been imported into the U.S.A. by 1960) the Mini, the smaller Fiats and French cars could compete in the new sub-compact market. The effect was less in the United States than in Europe where gas prices and taxation had governed the size of the private car for some time, allowing these oriental models to compete on an equal footing.

In spite of Nadar's 'Unsafe at Any Speed' the American driver had tired of smaller, slower cars, and in 1964 Ford came up with the Mustang, a close-coupled compact with a good turn of speed and handling ... which sold a million in 30 months. The rise of the Mustang coincided with the awareness of a pollution problem, perhaps high-lighted more than normally by the fact that political capital was to be made out of it. It marked the start of a series of emission regulations that were to become more and more severe over the following years.

Speed on another front became an American preserve during the 'Sixties—the World Land Speed Record. Since the 'Jet Set' entered the field in 1963 the conventional record-breaking car, in which the power drove through the road wheels, was on its way out. Jet cars of Craig Breedlove and Art Arfons jousted with each other to push up the world record from 434.20 mph in 1964 to 622.41 mph in 1970, where it rests today.

1960-1969

The Mini, 1960 (GB).

Equally at home outside a flat in Chelsea or at Buckingham Palace for a Garden Party, the ubiquitous Mini, designed by Alex Issigonis and introduced in 1960, revolutionized small-car motoring for millions. Ousting the many nasty "bubble" and post-Suez economy cars that abounded in the late fifties in much the same way as its illustrious namesake, the Austin Seven (both of them are in the picture) had killed the cycle car, the Mini fairly bristled with innovation. Its 848-cc, ohv, 4-cylinder engine was mounted transversely and drove the front wheels. The sump contained not only the oil, but the four-speed transmission, and all four wheels had independent suspension by rubber in torsion. Not only did it pave the way for the larger 1100, 1300 and 1800 models with similar layout, but it distinguished itself in numerous competitions, frequently beating the "heavy brigade". The Morris and Austin versions, differing in detail only, lost their separate identity, and the car survives as a "make" in its own right as the "Mini".

Coinciding with the introduction of the V-8, ohv engine in 1960, and the discontinuance of the old "six", a very handsome Park Ward convertible on the Bentley S2 Continental chassis graced the Bentley stand at the 1960 Motor Show. In spite of its bulk, the use of lighweight steel and alloy in the body construction ensured brisk, comfortable performance when allied to the new V-8, the output of which was stated (very characteristically) by the makers as "adequate".

The Motor Boom & The Orient: 1960-1969

Looking for all the world like the purposeful cockpit of its World War II namesake—the ME 109 fighter plane—the Messerschmidt Tiger was one of the better minicars. A four-wheeler, it was powered by a 500-cc Sachs engine and was developed from the earlier three-wheelers built to Fend design from 1953. The three-wheelers, using 175-cc and 200-cc engines (the latter introduced in 1955) continued to be made in the aircraft company's factory until 1962.

Moving to a new factory in 1959, Colin Chapman formed Lotus Cars Limited, and one of the first fruits of the upheaval was the Lotus Elite. A coupe built almost entirely of plastic materials, with a 1,216-cc Coventry-Climax engine, the car employed coil and wishbone ifs, suspension at the rear being taken care of by a unique system whereby the coil-spring struts protruded into the passenger compartment. This latter innovation caused some headaches (literally) through the hammering of the struts on their stops. In spite of an early reputation for unreliability, almost a thousand were built before production stopped in 1963.

The Rolls-Royce Phantom V was a phantom in name only—it remained in production for ten full years, before it was replaced in 1970 by the Phantom VI. The Park Ward Phantom limousine had a 12-foot wheelbase—plenty of leg-room even when the rear occasional seats were in use.

Messerschmidt, 1960 (D).

240

Wartburg, circa 1960 (D).

Following the same mechanical design as the Model F9 previously built at the old Audi plant in Zwickau and later at Eisenach, the Wartburg (reviving a name last used in 1904 for the products of Fahrzeugfabrik Eisenach) was basically a prewar D.K.W. of a type that never went into production. After the partition of Germany in 1945, East Germany nationalized its motor industry and revived the design. With front-mounted, 889-cc (later 991-cc) 3-cylinder, two-stroke engine and front wheel drive, the format was familiar, although cloaked in the not-unattractive Wartburg bodywork. The Sport model pictured used the same engine with the standard bhp increased from 40 to 50.

Retaining the Bentley-designed twin-cam engine (by now with alloy head) the 3.7-liter Aston Martin DB4 was probably one of the fastest sports cars of its day. The G.T. version developed 302 bhp, and in coupe form, 240 bhp was sufficient to propel it from 0 to 100 mph in 26 seconds.

Although Buicks of the late fifties made their mark with flamboyant delta tails and extravagant fins, the 1961 "Invicta" displayed quite restrained clean lines, although the distinctive Buick "portholes" were retained. In spite of the industry-wide swing away from larger cars to compacts (catered to by Buick's "Special"), the Invicta sported a 6,570-cc, V-8 engine, which it shared with the top-of-the-line Electra 225 series.

The Motor Boom & The Orient:
1960-1969

DeSoto, 1961 (USA).

Last of the breed. The end came to DeSoto with the 1961 models, introduced late in 1960. The Chrysler Corporation had managed to unload only about 19,000 in 1960, well below the break-even point. The outrageous Buick-inspired fins did nothing to bolster sagging sales. Available with 5,907-cc V-8 or 3,686-cc "Slant Six" engines, very few '61 models reached the public before production shut down for good.

The Monte Carlo Rally has attracted some unusual entries in the years since it was first held by the Sporting Club of Monaco in 1911, but probably none so bizarre as the Austin taxi entered for the 1961 event. An almost standard FX3 model, differing little outwardly from the first models introduced in 1948, it had already been superseded by the FX4 at the time of the rally, in which it was entered by the BBC. Predictably, its performance was no match for the prevailing conditions. Good promo for BBC, though.

Another company which ran out of gas in 1961 was that of Carl Borgward. He was perhaps the last of the original breed of car manufacturers and he clung to absolute ownership and control of his company until the end. At that time, his 2.3-liter Grosse limousine had been in production for only a few months. It had a 6-cylinder engine with an output of 100 bhp—and it was a good, stable car. But by 1961, the company—always short of capital—was unable to survive in the highly-competitive passenger-car market.

Borgward, 1961 (D).

Formula 1 Coopers, 1961 (GB).

By 1961 when this trio of Formula 1 Coopers (driven by Brabham, McLaren and Surtees) were built, the company's highly successful era of the late fifties—culminating in the World Championship in 1959—was past its peak, and a period of slow decline was setting in. Having set the pattern with their rear-engined designs, Coopers were placed in the unpleasant position of watching the competition adopt their principles, catch up, and eventually overtake them. With the introduction of the new 1 ½-liter formula in 1961 which precluded the continued use of the 2,462-cc, Coventry-Climax engine, Coopers found themselves without a suitable engine with which to compete with Ferrari, and the V-8, 1 ½-liter introduced in 1962 came too late for them.

Money alone can't do it. This was rather expensively demonstrated by Lance Reventlow, son of Woolworth heiress Barbara Hutton. Apparently bitten by the racing bug, he began building Scarab sports cars in 1957. A Formula 1 G.P. Scarab, begun in 1959, failed to make any kind of mark during the 1960 season, in spite of a lot of money spent on development. A 3-liter model, built for the 1961 Intercontinental Formula, was another expensive mistake. No more success was attended a Buick-engined, rear-engined car built in 1962. Thereafter Reventlow closed down his factory and no more Scarabs were built.

243

The Motor Boom & The Orient: 1960-1969

Oldsmobile F85, 1961 (USA).

The F85 Cutlass sports coupe represented a complete breakaway from the traditional Oldsmobile image. Featuring an aluminum V-8 Rockette engine of only 5,325-cc, it could, nevertheless, push out 185 bhp and represented Oldsmobile's entry into the low-price field in 1961, when the "compact" fever was at its height. The standard F85 compact used the same engine, but with a lower output of 155 bhp, and the V-8 unit was replaced by General Motors' V-6 unit (shared by Buick) in 1964.

A ten-year production run for one model Renault ended in 1961. The Fregate, hardly the best-looking Renault to come from Billancourt, nevertheless was one of the company's very good sellers. Its even more successful smaller sister, the Dauphine, used a rear-engine layout, but Fregate originally appeared in 1951 with a front-engine of 1,996-cc. By the time of its withdrawal in 1961, the engine was up to 2,141-cc—but that was the end of the road for Fregate, now with a hopelessly out-dated shape.

Introduced in 1962, the B.M.W. 3200 CS represented the final development of the Munich-built range of prestige cars which began with the 501 in 1952. Its V-8 engine of 3,168-cc produced 160 bhp; the car was available only in two-door coupe form, but by 1962 B.M.W. had decided to re-enter the medium-price market, and for some years concentrated mainly on their 4-cylinder 1500.

BMW, 1962 (D).

244

Alfa Romeo, 1962 (I).

Derived from the 1300-cc Giuletta, the Alfa Romeo Sprint first appeared in 2600 form in 1962. With a 6-cylinder, twin-camshaft, aluminum engine of 2,584-cc, it was also available as the Berlina and the Spider. With this model Alfa introduced disk brakes as standard, and with a five-speed transmission, the car offered luxury coupled with superlative performance.

It might be supposed that the diminutive 105E Anglia introduced by Ford of Dagenham in 1960 was an unlikely contender for laurels in the grueling conditions of winter rallies. However, Lloyd Howell and Bill Silvera brought their Anglia home first-equal in the 1961 Canadian Winter Rally out of 190 starters, and in the '61 Monte Carlo Sutcliffe and Crabtree, they turned in a creditable performance. In spite of its unconventional rear sloping window, the 997-cc sedan—first Anglia ever to employ a four-speed transmission—proved to be a best-seller.

The Lotus MK25 made its first appearance in the Dutch Grand Prix in 1962, featuring monocoque construction for the first time, with a stressed skin and a rear-mounted, 1-½-liter, Coventry-Climax, V-8 engine. Designer Colin Chapman must have been flattered, because the "25" set a pattern that was copied by virtually all contenders in Formula 1 racing. Jim Clark drove the car successfully through its first season, and both he and Lotus finished 1962 as runners-up in their respective Championships.

245

The Motor Boom & The Orient:
1960-1969

Pontiac Tempest, 1962 (USA).

In the early Sixties it was compacts all the way. Pontiac got into the act with Tempest in 1961, sold 116,000 of them, and continued the successful formula in 1962. Following the normal General Motors recipe of unitary construction, the car was unusual in having its three-speed transmission located in the back axle, power being provided by a 3.2-liter, ohv, 4-cylinder engine. With a wheelbase of 9 feet, 4 inches, its overall length was over 2 feet shorter than its big sisters (Bonneville and Star Chief), but this was apparently what the public wanted, and Pontiac moved into third place in the U.S. sales race.

Introduced at the 1962 Olympia Motor Show, Reliant's Sabre represented a complete departure for the Tamworth company, which had previously concentrated on economy three-wheelers, a field in which they still excel. In an unusual intermarriage, it was developed in conjunction with Sabra of Haifa and was marketed in Israel as the Sabra. Powered by a Ford Consul engine of 1,703-cc, it sported front-disk brakes and coil-spring ifs. Its somewhat unappealing fiberglass styling was later replaced by the handsome Scimitar on the British versions, and the model evolved into the Cortina-powered Sussita in Israel.

Studebaker made a last-ditch attempt to stem lagging sales with their Lark Daytona in 1963, but with sales of only 68,000, even the revolutionary fiberglass Avanti couldn't do the trick. Three years later, Studebaker breathed its last.

Reliant (Sabra), 1962 (GB).

Triumph, 1962 (GB).

Although the headlight placement gave it the appearance of a slant-eyed squint, the Triumph Vitesse was nevertheless able to show a clean pair of heels to most other traffic when the need arose. Derived from the Alick Dick-designed Herald and introduced in 1962, it squeezed a 1,596-cc, 6-cylinder engine into the space previously occupied by the Herald's 1,147-cc unit. Later versions utilized the 2-liter engine introduced in the 1964 Triumph 2000 sedan, and in this 90-bhp form, the Vitesse found favor with those who wished to combine sporting proclivities with sedan-car comfort.

The 1963 Ferrari 250 Pininfarina coupe was one of a line of 12-cylinder, luxury G.T. cars first introduced in the early fifties by the Modena-based company, which was to continue until the end of the sixties, when flat sixes and flat twelves were adopted. A relatively small engine of 2,953-cc powered the car which, with an overall length of 15 feet, 5 inches, was of reasonably modest proportions, but few could affort the price required for one in England.

Two more wins for Mercedes Benz: the first in a 220SE, the second in a 230SL. Both were in the Spa-Sofia-Liege Rally—1962 and 1963. Engine: 6-cylinders, 2,306-cc. In the 1963 version of this grueling marathon, only 22 finished out of 129 starters—and the event was the 230SL's maiden effort.

Mercedes-Benz, 1963 (D).

Lotus Elan, 1962 (GB).

Employing the successful Mundy/Ansdale-designed, twin-ohc version of the Ford Classic 116E engine first used in the rear-engined Mark 25 racing car, the Mark 26 Lotus Elan was introduced in 1962. A front-engine car, it had a backbone chassis of box-section sheet steel, coupled with the Chapman rear-strut suspension which had been well tried on the racing models. The bodywork featured vacuum-operated, retractable headlights (echoing the Buehrig-designed Cord 812) and the Elan earned for itself an enviable reputation for roadholding. Standard models offered a 105-bhp, 1,558-cc engine.

Basically a badge-engineered version of the Wolseley 1500, the 1962 Riley 1.5 was capable of considerable re-development. Little larger than BMC's Morris Minor, the 1,489-cc, 4-cylinder engine gave it a good power-to-weight ratio, and this, coupled with its close-ratio, four-speed transmission, prompted some owners to fit high-lift cam conversions for competition. In this form, the car was able to acquit itself quite well, but even in standard trim it was a rapid compact sedan.

Originally introduced in 1961, the Mini-Cooper "S" used a standard Mini engine bored out to 997-cc and fitted with twin U.S. carburetors. It was later upped to 1,293-cc, and in the hands of a number of well-known drivers, notched up a number of rally successes, including the European Rally Championship.

Champion rally driver Eric Carlsson drove a Type 93 Saab in the 1963 Rally of the Midnight Sun. The Saabs of this period were staunchly adherent to the fwd, two-stroke formula pioneered by D.K.W., using a 3-cylinder, 748-cc engine producing 38-bhp. Carlsson managed a second in the Midnight Sun, but he and the type 93 dominated other Rally events in the early sixties.

The Mercedes 220SE was becoming somewhat dated by 1963, even though it had won the Spa-Sofia-Liego rally in the previous year. The 2,195-cc, 6-cylinder engine (basically the same unit as the parent 220) was still capable of doing well in competition, although it was primarily intended as a luxury sedan. 220SE had at least one last hurrah left, however; in the hands of Ewy Rosquist at the 1963 Monte Carlo Rally, the car (and, of course, the lady driving) won the Coupe des Dames.

Four generations of Rover turbines are seen in the unusual photograph below: JET 2, the P4-based car built in 1950; the T3 exhibited at the 1956 Earl's Court Motor Show; the T4 of 1962, a 140-bhp with front-wheel drive, which, although it did not achieve series production, provided the prototype for the later and successful "2000" introduced in 1964 (its shape is readily identifiable); and the Rover-B.R.M. The latter car is being driven by Graham Hill, who, with partner completed the 1963 LeMans race at an average of 107.84 mph, the first gas-turbine car ever to complete the race.

Rover Turbines, 1963 (GB).

The Motor Boom & The Orient: 1960-1969

Mercer-Cobra, 1964 (USA).

Whatever design exercise Virgil Exner undertakes, the end product is bound to be unusual, and frequently bizarre. No exception was the Mercer-Cobra exhibited at the Paris Motor Show in 1964. Bodied by Sibona-Bassano of Turin to Exner's design, the car used a modified A.C. Cobra chassis and Ford engine and appeared on the French Ford stand. Nicknamed the "Copper Car", it was apparently designed for the express purpose of demonstrating the colorful warmth and beauty of copper and brass in car design; it boasted a copper radiator, brass-trimmed swiveling headlights, brass wheel embellishments and a copper exhaust cover.

A badge-engineered BMC "110", the 1963 M.G. continued BMC's somewhat unfortunate policy of sticking the M.G. octagon on smaller sedans in the company's range. Sharing its 1,098-cc, 4-cylinder with Austin and Morris, it followed the transverse engine layout and front-wheel drive pioneered in the Issigonis-designed Mini, later inheriting the 1,275-cc "1300" unit. The model was dropped after the formation of British Leyland.

In reality a D.K.W., the 1964 Auto Union 1000 was the only model in the D.K.W. range to adopt the old prewar corporate name. In spite of fins and other attempts at updating, the car followed the time-honored D.K.W. formula—front wheel drive and two-stroke engine—in this case, 3-cylinders and 981-cc. The model was dropped at the end of 1964.

Auto Union, 1964 (D).

Austin-Healey, 1964 (GB).

Representing the final development of the "big" Austin-Healey, the 3000 MK III employed a 2,912-cc version of the Austin Westminster engine. 3000s performed consistently well in international rallies, winning, among others, the G.T. class in the 1964 Tulip Rally. The model was discontinued in 1968, and the Austin-Healey name was dropped from the British Leyland range when Donald Healey joined the Jensen organization to produce the Jensen-Healey.

The result of a marriage of ideas by American Carol Shelby and the old-established Thames Ditton firm of A.C., the Cobra was based on the Tojeiro-designed, tubular-framed Ace which had already been in production for nine years with a variety of engines. Shelby's suggestion that A.C. should drop a 330-bhp, 4.7-liter Ford V-8 unit into this chassis produced a potent contender for the 1964 LeMans, in which the Cobra finished fourth. It also paved the way for a line of Ford-engined cars, marketed by Shelby in the U.S.A. as Cobras until 1968, and culminating in the 7-liter A.C. 428.

An independent company set up by M. Redele in 1955, Alpine's development has always been closely allied to Renault, on whose components they have depended heavily. Since 1969, when Renault withdrew from competition, they have been the unofficial competition arm of Renault. By 1964, when the Berlinette was produced, the little cars were capable of over 100 mph, a speed which helped them to a class win in the 1964 Tour de France.

Ford G.T. 40 (GB).

Built by the Advanced Vehicle Division of the British Ford Company, and partly based on Eric Broadleigh's Lola G.T., the Ford GT40, put together by Roy Lunn's design team at Slough, was the British end of a determined effort by Henry Ford II to commit his company—on both sides of the Atlantic—to a racing program.

In America, this took the form of assaults on the Indianapolis 500, but for Europe, Ford had his eye on the Le Mans 24 Hour Race. The first prototype, a semi-monocoque construction mid-engined coupe, was completed in April of 1964. After initial problems of rear-end instability, a single car was entered in the 1,000-km (620-mile) Race at Nurburgring, driven by Hill and McLaren. Although it retired with suspension failure, the car's potential was amply demonstrated, and a team of three cars was entered for the 1964 Le Mans. This time, all three were retired—two with transmission failure, and the Atwood/Schlesser car catching fire—but not before estimated speeds of almost 200 mph had been reached.

The late fifties and early sixties saw the emergence of a new luxury G.T. class with American engine, but produced in Europe. The Iso Grifo, a coupe, was powered by a 5,359-cc, V-8 Chevrolet engine mounted in a chassis of Bizzarini design. By the time the 1966 Grifo was produced, the engine was propelling the car at 142 mph. Iso, who began car production in the fifties with the miniature Isetta "bubble car", had come a long way.

Oldsmobile Toronado, 1966 (USA).

After the War, Oldsmobile tended to become the proving ground for General Motors' innovations, and thus the division spawned a number of advanced features, some of which were taken up throughout the group. The front-wheel-drive Toronado introduced in 1966 caused something of a sensation. A six-passenger, hard-top coupe with fwd allowing a flat floor, it was spacious and, fitted with the 6,965-cc Toronado V-8 engine driving through the Turbo-Hydramatic transmission, it was fast. The model was still in production seven years later, although after a spree with 7 ½-liter engines producing 360-bhp-plus in 1968, power plants became more modest in size, and by 1972 output was down to 265-bhp.

Looking very unlike its predecessor, the wartime "vehicle-general purpose", the 1966 Kaiser Jeep Wagoneer was nevertheless a rugged, hell-for-leather multi-purpose vehicle. The station wagon was powered by a 5,359-cc, V-8, Rambler engine (a case of one independent supporting another) and anticipating the merger with American Motors in 1970. A bewildering variety of drives (2- or 4-wheel) and engine sizes were available.

"Car of the Year" in 1965, the Renault 16 was full of innovations. A full four-door sedan, it featured front-wheel drive and a 1,470-cc, 4-cylinder engine with removable wet liners and ohv. Like other Renaults, the 16 continued the practice of sealing the coolant, something pioneered by the firm. Suspension was independent all around, and front disk brakes were fitted as standard.

Renault, 1965 (F).

253

Rolls-Royce Silver Shadow (GB)

Introduced at the 1965 Motor Show, the Rolls-Royce Silver Shadow represented an entirely new concept from Crewe. Lower lines combined with the traditional "Greek Temple" radiator and unitary construction to disguise the vintage of the engine (the V-8, 6,230-cc unit introduced for the 1960 season). Although the larger separate-chassis Phantoms were continued, the bulk of production activity was concentrated on the Shadow and its Bentley equivalent, and there can be no doubt that the popularity of the model was largely responsible for the survival of the motor-car division when the parent aviation company went bankrupt in 1971.

At first closely following the styling of the prewar and highly successful B.M.W. 328, Bristol styling went through a slab-sided period of the doldrums during the middle sixties, and the type 408 of early 1966 was typical. Bristol had switched to American engines in 1962, and the 408 used a 5,130-cc, ohv, Chrysler V-8 (enlarged to 5,211-cc on the 409 introduced later in 1966) and adopted Torque-flight automatic transmission.

The 1965 Cadillac Calais was a big one—almost 19 feet long, with a massive 7,030-cc, V-8 engine (later enlarged to 7,736-cc!). The Calais (and the even larger Fleetwood and Eldorado) were available with such refinements as air conditioning, a variable power steering, and a six-position steering wheel.

Bristol, 1966 (GB).

254

Isuzu, 1966 (J).

The rising sun finally arose when Isuzu, better known for their commercial vehicles, began postwar series production of motor cars with a license to build the Rootes Hillman Minx. In 1961 the Minx gave way to a wholly Japanese design—the 2-liter Bellel—and in 1966 this was supplemented by the Bellett 1500, powered by a 1,491-cc, 4-cylinder engine. In G.T. form, and fitted with twin carburetors, the Bellett was imported into England, primarily, so it is said, to challenge the supremacy of the Ford Lotus-Cortina in sedan-car racing. Producing 90 bhp, the car was capable of a genuine 100 mph, while the "cooking" version produced 75 bhp, but, while road-holding was enhanced by independent suspension—front and rear—general finish and the transmission came in for criticism.

Eric Broadley's Lola Company adopted monocoque construction for its Formula 1 cars in 1965 and continued in close association with Ford (which had resulted in Broadley's work on the Ford G.T. 40 cars) employing Ford V-8 engines mounted behind the driver. 1966 was a very good year for them. Graham Hill won the fiftieth Indianapolis 500 in the V-8 engined Type 90 with very little difficulty, and no real opposition from the Offenhauser-engined contingent. Jackie Stewart managed sixth place in another Lola-Ford.

The 1967 4X4 version of B.M.C.'s Mini, called the Moke, was a spartan development of the Issigonis theme. Simplicity and easy maintenance were the keynotes, and they proliferated at Autocross events, as dune-buggies, and as heralds of "flower-power".

Audi, 1967 (D).

Two years after the Audi name was revived by the Auto Union combine at Ingolstadt in 1965, the original offering of a 1,696-cc, medium-sized sedan had been augmented by the "Variant" station wagon. Employing the same inclined 4-cylinder engine, the car followed the front-wheel-drive formula of its predecessor, the D.K.W., but there the similarity ended. The fwd layout permitted a beam back axle, and disk brakes on the front wheels and ifs had been standardized on the first 1965 models.

As a sort of cherry atop the whipped cream, General Motors took the Toronado front wheel drive and added it to the massive 1967 Cadillac Fleetwood Eldorado. And by 1970, the engine was up to a whopping 8.2 liters.

British Ford started a four-year fling with electrics in 1967, no doubt as a result of the pollution and energy crises rapidly developing. They called their tiny car (4 feet high, just over 6 feet long) "Comuta". They gave up on the project in 1971.

Following a period after the war when they built Austin A40s and A50s under license, the giant Japanese Nissan concern introduced the first Cedric model in 1960. By 1967, this had evolved into the Cedric Special Six, fitted with a 1,998-cc, 6-cylinder engine, although a smaller version with a 1,982-cc, 95-bhp, 4-cylinder ohv unit was also available.

Toyota Corona Mkl, 1968. (J)

Ubiquitous Mini. (GB)

An Alpine A110 coupé brakes into a control in the 1970
Monte Carlo Rally. (F)

The greatest invention
since the wheel.

Lincoln luxury. A 1974 Continental. (USA)

Popular American: Ford Mustang, 1974. (USA)

Under the enthusiastic and capable management of Kjell Qvale, the Jensen company has grown from strength to strength and the Interceptor Mk III introduced in 1967 represents the better features of Anglo-American cooperation in car construction. Returning to steel bodywork after using fiberglass, the Mk III was designed by Vignale and used a husky 6,276-cc, Chrysler V-8 engine producing 330 bhp. Also available was the revolutionary FF (Ferguson Formula) which used the same body and engine but which also employed four-wheel drive and anti-lock braking. The FF was discontinued in 1972, but Interceptors are still selling steadily.

Introduced in 1963 as a sports derivative of the Triumph Herald, the Spitfire followed Herald practice with its forward-opening hood which encompassed the front fenders, headlights and grille, affording excellent accessibility. The Mark III, by 1967, was fitted with an enlarged 1,296-cc version of the 4-cylinder, 1,147-cc Herald engine and appealed to younger enthusiasts who couldn't afford the more sophisticated 2 ½-liter TR5.

Buick's contribution to the sporting idiom for 1967 was the Buick Wildcat. Wielding a hefty 7,048-cc, V-8 engine—largest in the Buick range—the Wildcat followed a more dashing trend introduced the previous year, but, with an overall length of 18 feet, 4 inches, was still a large car. Engine sizes went up by 1970, but Ralph Nader-inspired alarm bells went off, and thereafter, things were reduced to more manageable proportions.

Jensen, 1967 (GB).

Jaguar 240, 1968 (GB).

Representing remarkable value in the United Kingdom in 1968, the 2.4-liter Jaguar 240 still looked good, in spite of the fact that the design was by then thirteen years old. Unveiled at Earl's Court in the autumn of 1955, the model was nearing the end of its long life, but by 1968, over 200,000 had been sold. Another ageless Jaguar design, the immortal "E" type originally derived from the "C"- and "D"-type racing cars was available in 1969 in 2 plus 2 Series Two guise, employing the 4.2-liter version of the famous overhead twin-cam engine. Customers for the 2 plus 2 also had the option of automatic transmission—an innovation missing from Jaguar's sporting range since the demise of the XK150 in 1960.

Like Ford, General Motors also dabbled continuously with pollution and energy conservation problems, and this lineup of experimental vehicles shows that (at the time, at least) they were keeping an open mind about the solution. Designed to provide short-range personal transport, their top speed was limited—in the range of 30-45 mph—and it was agreed that special roads would have to be built to accomodate them, since it would be unsafe to mix them with conventional traffic. Left to right in the picture: the 511 gasoline-engined three-wheeler, the 512 gasoline-electric, the 512 electric, and the 512 gasoline-engined four-wheeler. All of them could park simultaneously in space little larger than that required for a conventional car.

GM experimentals, 1968-1969 (US

Volkswagen (D).

Variations on a theme; Volkswagen's Beetle has changed little in outward appearance since Porsche produced the first prototypes at Stuttgart in 1936, and the Karmann Ghia derivatives are virtually identical to those first introduced in the early fifties. The VW has, however, been constantly improved technically and by 1973 was offering a "1600" version of the same theme.

The FIAT Giardiniera station wagon of 1968 provided real miniature motoring, but with a surprising amount of space. It was powered by an overhead-valve, twin-cylinder, air-cooled engine mounted horizontally under the floor at the rear to provide for a large, single rear-opening door. Producing 22 bhp, the 499-cc (originally 479-cc) unit was also used in the Bianchina, which had heralded Bianchi's post-war return to private car manufacture.

Employing the 3,995-cc, 6-cylinder engine first introduced in the DB5 in 1964, the Aston Martin DB6 Mark II was announced late in 1969 for the 1970 season. Featuring a five-speed transmission and power steering, this model also gave customers the option of fuel injection. The 6-cylinder, twin-ohc engine was, however, destined to be replaced by a 5.4-liter V-8 of Aston Martin design derived from a racing engine intended for Lola. First announced in 1966, this eventually materialized in 1972, when Aston Martin was sold by the David Brown Group and the 6-cylinder engines were finally abandoned.

AMX, 1968 (USA).

1968 was the first year that no American Motors car bore the Rambler name. The AMX introduced in 1968 utilized the same 290-cu in, V-8 engine as the larger Javelin and was a two-seater sports coupe with bucket seats and a dual exhaust system. Intended to compete with the Chevrolet Camaro and Ford's Mustang, the Javelin and the AMX were introduced during a somewhat rocky period in the company's fortunes, and sales between 1967 and 1969 continued to fall. The AMX was finally discontinued in 1971.

During this period, the Wankel engine was attracting a great deal of attention. In 1969, Mercedes-Benz showed a research-and-development car, the C III, using a three-chamber version of the Wankel. With a displacement of 36.6 cu in, the C III was comparable to a normal 3.6-liter engine. Mounted amidships and fed by means of direct injection via a mechanical 3-plunger pump, the unconventional power plant was capable of 330 bhp at 7,000 rpm and drove the vehicle from 0 to 62 mph in 5 seconds, with a top speed of 162 mph. Bodywork of fiberglass-reinforced synthetic material was bonded and riveted to a frame floor. By 1970, it had acquired a four-chamber engine producing 350 bhp and 190 mph, but as yet, no production car has been offered.

Now: The Seventies

Already the products of the Seventies show an awareness of the changing needs—automobile manufacturers have conformed with most antipollution controls, and with speed and other safety measures that have become necessary with increasingly powerful vehicles and with increased numbers of cars on the roads. Design and construction bend toward safety today as never before (only ten years ago, whoever thought of putting the baby in a safety seat at the back of a car?), and antipollution measures have been taken by oil companies and automotive design engineers in response to new legal requirements, some of which are so stringent that some exhaust emissions are said to be cleaner than the air taken into the engine.

Other advances, more on the positive engineering side, have been made—the rotary engine, long tested in Germany and Japan, has overcome its initial sealing troubles.

Since the early Fifties, engine life has doubled, as lubricants and metals have been subjected to intense scrutiny and development. Tires, today so often radial, and with so much bigger surface, cling to the road twice as efficiently and last twice as long as they did ten years ago.

The experimenters and advocates of other methods of propulsion, their energies stimulated by the world oil shortage, have been busy. GM has long pioneered the re-emergence of steam, and their Pontiac steam-powered car is a good example of serious application, although as yet the clutchless, gearless, silent, nonpolluting 100-mph performance is offset by its bulky size and heavy thirst.

With the long search for a convenient form of electric power, one could be forgiven for expecting something more in this area, but the problems remain the heavy weight of batteries, the short range on a single charge, and slow speed—although commuter city cars may be a viable proposition.

The methane or LPG (liquid petroleum gas) engine has long been in limited use, and conversion kits are available in some countries, but the cost is still high, and storage difficulties arise. The Stirling engine, a hoary old system invented in 1816, that does not burn the fuel inside the cylinder but employs heated air to do the job, may, if made considerably more efficient, prove a marginal contestant to the internal-combustion engine.

However, the "nasty explosion engine" with the inefficient reciprocating pistons that shake and shudder, using a fuel that burns and smells, to say nothing of wasting most of its energy through the water and exhaust systems, is likely to remain for a while. Well, until the earth's depleted supply of oil runs out.

1970-1979

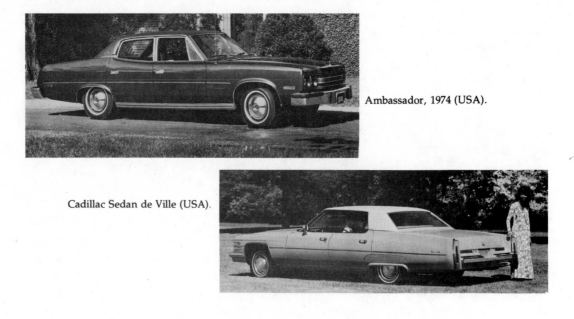

Ambassador, 1974 (USA).

Cadillac Sedan de Ville (USA).

The largest and most deluxe car on American Motors (known for its smaller car leanings) 1974 list was the aristocratic 195-bhp Ambassador sedan. Restyled for looks and greater safety, the engine had no less than six emission-control features.

The Cadillac Sedan de Ville incorporated a new feature: telescopic rear-bumper-ends which retreat into the fender ends under impact. The V-8, 205-bhp engine stayed put, but deep pile carpeting, two-tone velour, quality floor pads, etc, were diversions to move the buyer's eye from speed performance to leisurely luxury.

The Chrysler New Yorker was completely redesigned for 1974, using the 440-cu in, 4-barrel, V-8 engine.

Introduced in 1966 and restyled in 1972, the Anadol was first designed by Reliant of Britain for the Turkish market. It's now produced by Otosan Sanaytii AS at Istanbul. About 10,000 a year are made, still with Reliant's technical collaboration. Also made by Reliant is the Bond Bug—a three wheeler with an ancestry that dates back to the 1950s. With a single front steerable wheel (the engine turns with the wheel), it employs a system used by Cugnot on the very first road vehicle in 1769! The Bug has a 700-cc, 4-cylinder engine and coil-spring suspension—and is taxed as a motorcycle in Britain.

One of the top-drawer British products is the Aston Martin V-8, built to the same basic principles as the original in 1913—*to produce quality cars of good performance and appearance for discerning owner-driver with fast touring in mind.* The body line of the car has been determined by many factors. Racing experience, wind-tunnel statistics, safety data and design principles relating to comfort and driving ease have all influenced the contours and interior of the V-8. Its power unit of 5,340-cc employs four overhead camshafts and four Weber carburetors and can take the car from rest to 60 in a rapid 6 seconds.

The Audi 100 Coupe 5, smartest of the Ingolstadt line, is a 4- 5-seater fastback powered by a 1,871-cc unit developing 115-bhp and 0-60 acceleration of 9.7 seconds. As usual with Audi, the quoted top and cruising speeds are the same—115 mph.

The 1974 version of the 411 from British Bristol Motor Company housed a 6,556-cc engine and was claimed to be "the fastest true four-seater car." Only a handful are made each week, and a high proportion are USA-bound. In accordance with American regulations, they use low-grade gasoline.

Aston Martin V-8 (GB).

BMW 520i (D).

A faster and more powerful version of the BMW 2-liter sports sedan is the 520i with a fuel-injection, 1,990-cc, 130-bhp engine giving a top speed of 115 mph and acceleration from 0-60 in less than 11 seconds. Lessons learned from racing have been incorporated—cool air ducted onto the front disks, airflow panel under the car helps hold down the front wheels at high speed, and the hood has a built-in "weak spot" for bending in case of frontal impact. And as BMW so aptly put it, the car is "larger inside than outside".

Chrysler U.K.'s 2-liter model, with the accent on automatics and European travel, is the larger of two models made in France and distributed in Britain by Chrysler U.K. at a competitive price. With 90-mph cruising speed from its 4-cylinder, ohc, 100-bhp unit, it is a comfortable, fast ride, has a spacious interior and a number of standard items that are usually optional extras, including a tachometer.

The 4-cylinder, 602-cc Citroën Ami 8, typical of a modern utility car, has a folding back seat in the current style, more than doubling its luggage capacity to 16 cu ft. Its all-around independent hydropneumatic suspension and anti-roll bars front and rear give it a stable ride over almost every type of terrain.

Citroën Ami (F).

Corvette (USA).

The legendary Corvette is called the "only sports car in America" with some justification. After twenty-two years on the highway and in motor sport, it has become a car typical of its country—fast-moving, sophisticated, highly tuned, incisive. Passing through some fifty different forms, including experimental cars, the Chevrolet Corvette has stayed true to its original concept—a two-seater with the most advanced drive-lines and chassis possible using high-volume production components. Engine: 7,500-cc V-8, developing 275 bhp (optional).

Corvette showed two experimental cars in 1974. One of them, called the Four-Rotor, was equipped with gull-wing doors for easy entry. Low-line architecture (5 inches lower than the then current production model) reduced drag without bringing on unmanageable lift. The car was equipped with a computerized digital readout system for all working dashboard information.

The latest from Holland in 1974 was the DAF Marathon, with a 1,289-cc unit producing 63 bhp and employing the unique DAF Variomatic automatic gearing with an infinite number of ratios between 14.22 to 1 and 3.60 to 1. Maximum cruising and top speed—145 km/h (90 mph).

The 1974 British Daimler Double-Six sedan displayed a V-12 unit of 5.3-liters—identical to the Jaguar's XJ12 engine, and externally looked very much like the Jaguar, except for the traditional Daimler fluting on the radiator.

Experimental Corvette (USA).

Ferrari Daytona (I).

New to the prancing horse stable in 1974 was the Ferrari Berlinetta Boxer (or just "BB") with a V-12, 4,930 rear-mid engine developing a beguiling 380-bhp at 7,700 rpm, which, as the very few who have had the experience will confirm, conveys one at some 188 mph when the road is available. A slightly older Ferrari, first seen in 1972, was the Ferrari 365 GTB Daytona, with a 4.4-liter, V-12 engine of great flexibility and energy; breathing is by six Webers, and power output is a nearly top-of-the-track 352-bhp. Top speed is slightly under that of the "BB", but it does 180 mph and goes 0-60 in a breathtaking 5.4 seconds. It was dropped in Britain in 1973 because of emission-control regulations, but manufacture in Italy continued.

Datsun of Japan brought its 6-cylinder, 2.6-liter version of the extremely sporting 240Z to Britain (it was introduced in Tokyo in 1973), calling it the 260Z. With a power-output of 162-bhp, 0-60 is reached in a bolting 7 seconds, and one has only to look at the rally results to judge its overall performance. An outright win in the East African Safari Rally in 1973 proves the point.

In 1974, FIAT listed some twenty-six different models or variants, from the 600-cc 126 to the 3 ¼-liter 130. The middle range included the 1.5-liter 124 Special, developing 75-bhp; the 124 sedan (1,197-cc and 65-bhp); and the 124 coupe with a 1,756-cc twin-cam engine producing 118-bhp.

Mustang, 1974 (USA)

The 1974 Mustang was shorter by 19 inches than the previous year's model—a change in the right direction—and seven inches shorter than the original car of 1964. A claimed 20 mpg in normal city and suburban use was made, and Ford produced two versions, a notchback and the increasingly popular hatchback. A choice of a 4-cylinder, 2.3-liter and a 2.8-liter engine was available.

The front-wheel drive Honda Civic was elected No. 3 in the "Car of the Year" choice by journalists in 1973, the year of its introduction. A water-cooled, twin-choked, 4-cylinder, 1,169-cc engine performs well, and conforming to the policy of most Japanese companies, the Civic has a number of standard fittings that would not be expected in a small car.

The development of the 16-valve, single-overhead-camshaft engine was another chapter in Triumph's history of technical innovation—and is the most important feature of the Dolomite Sprint. Capacity: 1,998-cc, with a surprisingly high output of 127 bhp—an increase of 40 percent.

An old name brought back from a new design, the Lancia Beta was Vincenzo Lancia's first production car—and the company's latest in 1972. This one gives a choice of three (transverse) engines, all of them FIAT twin-cam derivatives. The stylish five-seater model has a five-speed transmission, high flexibility and sure-footed handling.

Honda Civic (J).

267

Lamborghini Espada (I).

Now building some of the most expensive and advanced cars in the world, Italian Ferruccio Lamborghini started to tune FIATS after the last war, graduating to building his own vehicles from war-surplus parts. The Espada 400GT Mk3 is an exciting car. The comparatively small (3,929-cc) front-located engine gives 350-bhp from its 12 cylinders in V formation and a top speed of considerably more than any normal driver can use.

The Jaguar E-type Series Three, introduced in 1971, continued virtually unchanged into 1974, with the 60-degree, V-12 engine of 5,343-cc, developed from Jaguar's original V-12 which was designed and built as a racing unit. The first E-type was seen in 1961, with a 3.8-liter engine; all-around independent suspension and all-around disk brakes have been featured since those days, while anti-dive front suspension and lucas transistorized ignition are later developments.

British Fords (GB).

This flight of sporting Fords at Britain's Brands Hatch racing circuit during a sedan-car championship illustrates how the small Ford takes a large part in the United Kingdom. The Escort in its various forms (all nineteen of them!) is second only to the Ford Consul in number on the roads of Britain, from the modest 1,098-cc sedan to the extremely sporting Mexico and the 2-liter Escort RS2000.

Another from AMC at this time was the new-look Gremlin, a sub-compact that helped set a trend toward smaller personal vehicles in the USA—although with its 6-cylinder, 4,200-cc engine, it would be classed as a large car in Europe. Its upswept rear end was a bold departure from the norm, heartily liked—or disliked—by all who saw it.

The Hillman Hunter, Grand Luxe version, carried under its hood a lively, 5-bearing, 1,725-cc, 4-cylinder unit with alloy head and high-lift camshaft plus twin-outlet exhaust manifold. Just in case you were expecting walnut veneer—it had it.

The twin-rotor engine designed by Wankel is the power unit for the German NSU Ro80, first seen in 1967. Front-wheel drive and selective automatic transmission give a light, positive steering and deep range of performance. Equivalent to a 2-liter, the unit puts out 113-bhp at 5,500 rpm, but has a fairly high gasoline consumption.

Now—The Seventies: 1970-1979

Lincoln two-door (USA)

The two pictures might well be entitled "beauty and the beast". "Understated elegance" is the term used in the brochure, and a new sporting rear appearance is also emphasized by the Lincoln. The brand has close links with the office of President, and has also been classed as one of the largest production cars ever made. Its grandeur is undeniable, and its ultra-smooth, 7,537-cc, V-8 engine continues to complete the atmosphere of elegance, although perhaps not all that understated.

The legendary Mini still attracts worldwide attention. Not really a beast, but the top of the Mini range is the high-performance 1,275 GT. The transverse-engined Minis come in a dozen guises, from the modest 850-cc to the car pictured, and after 14 years of development it has been brought to a high level of reliability. Its road-holding and handling have long set the standard by which others are judged. Well over 3 million had been made by 1974.

The Mercury Cougar XR-7, redesigned in 1973, entered the middle-sized luxury market with more styling than previously. As is becoming traditional in automotive advertising throughout the world, more emphasis is placed on comfort, safety, and in-car entertainment than ever before, to the exclusion of eulogistic essays on speed and high performance. Engine: 5,752-cc, V-8.

The Morris-Marina Range was introduced in 1971—and sold some 300,000 within its first two years. It remains one of the top-selling cars in Britain.

Mini 1275GT (GB).

Maserati (I).

Now under the Citroën flag, Maserati first produced the Bora in 1972. The car was offered with a 4,719-cc unit with the astonishing performance figures that would be expected from this make—0 to 60 mph in 6.5 seconds and top speed of 160 mph. As could be anticipated, it proved a pretty good guzzler—12 mpg.

The British Morgan Motor Company has done the almost-impossible—kept going under its own power since 1910, in the face of overwhelming competition. Its products are directed to an exclusive band of motorists who want to own a somewhat spartan, if high-performance, car that makes few concessions to modern styling. For example: the Morgan Plus 8, a 3 ½-liter, 8-cylinder, twin-carburetored, very open, low-slung sports car with a cruising speed of 125 mph and a zero to 70 mph time of 7.5 seconds—a performance not given to many vehicles.

Shown first in London during 1973, the British MGB GT V-8 housed a 5-bearing, 3.5-liter unit (as an option to the established 1.8-liter B-series 4-cylinder version) producing 137 bhp at 5,000 rpm. For many years the make has strongly appealed to a small cross-section of enthusiasts (in addition to selling well in and out of its country of origin) who enjoy what could be termed nostalgic driving; it was the make owned by those fortunate enough to be able to buy a medium-priced sports car between the wars.

271

Mercedes-Benz, 1973 (D)

The 4½-liter Mercedes-Benz 450 was voted "Car of the Year" at the end of 1973 by a panel of forty-five European motoring journalists. The 4.5 range of four cars was unveiled at Geneva in 1973 and all had automatic transmission as standard. The "new engine", observed the company modestly of its V-8, 225-bhp unit, "does not significantly raise the top speed beyond the 131 mph level, but has greater effect in terms of strong acceleration throughout the speed range." The one in the picture is the long-wheelbase 450 SEL.

The stylish Mazda Rx4, also introduced in 1973, was the largest rotary-engined car produced to date by this company, and coincided with their half-millionth production rotary power unit. Claimed as the first rotary-engined car in the world to be fitted with automatic transmission, Rx4's two-rotor unit developed 130-bhp and is equivalent to a conventional 2½-liter engine—although 30 percent lighter and with 30 percent fewer moving parts.

The Lotus Elite, also from the early seventies, carried a 2-liter, twin-ohc, 4-cylinder engine producing 155-bhp with a top speed of around 128 mph. A wedge-shaped four-seater, it was built to take advantage of the high cruising speed allowed on Europe's auto routes. At the same time, it complies with all European and American design and safety regulations.

Mazda, 1973 (J).

272

Toyota Celica (J).

The Toyota Automatic Loom Works made its first, somewhat experimental, Chevrolet-based car in 1935, after Kiichiro, son of the family, had visited British motor manufacturers during 1930, and in 1937 the Toyota Motor Co. was formed. Now, about 40 years later, the Toyota range is one of the most sophisticated in the middle-market. The Celica 1600 ST (Sports Tourer) was first put on the road in 1972 and continues to increase in popularity in Europe and the USA. A choice of four- or five-speed transmissions gives the car a sporty and flexible character, and its 105-mph top speed is enough for most conditions.

Established Swedish safety pioneers, Saab have made their ''99'' one of the most advanced models of the Seventies—right down to the headlight wipers. Front-wheel driven, the 99 has a safety body consisting of cage plus welded steel beams with reinforced side and front pillars and impact-absorbing bumpers. Its 2-liter unit puts out some 95-bhp.

A favorite in Britain and America as a sporting vehicle is the Triumph TR6, last of a line of lively TRs (the TR2 was first produced in 1953 from the Coventry factory). Its 2-½-liter, 6-cylinder, fuel-injection power unit gives a top speed of 112 mph and an 0-60 time of 10.1 seconds.

Plymouth's full-size wheelbase was extended to 121.5 inches in 1974, with the 400-cu in, V-8, 2-barrel carburetor as standard on the Fury.

Rolls-Royce Corniche (GB).

Evocative of the sunny South of France, the Rolls-Royce Corniche was first produced in March of 1971 and sold in addition to the Silver Shadow. The *dernier cri* in luxury, the distinguished vehicle has long lost the town-carriage-and-dignity image and can show most other vehicles a clean pair of back wheels without apparent effort. The 6,750-cc, V-8 engine, independent suspension, disk brakes all around, height control, and numerous other refinements combine to offer a car of unsurpassed comfort, smoothness and silence—at any speed. Also, it is expensive enough for an Arab oil potentate—or a member of the New York Yankees. It is not, however, quite the top of Rolls-Royce's line. That distinction goes to the R-R Camargue—designed by Pininfarina of Italy.

From the outrageously expensive to the sensibly inexpensive. One of the least expensive cars available in Britain, the Czechoslovakian Skoda is small, and typical of Eastern European productions, firmly based on economy of running costs. Using low-grade gasoline, its 1,107-cc engine develops 53-bhp and will take the car from 0-60 in an unspectacular 19 seconds. However, this is no pared-down "utility" vehicle—with four doors, forward-tilting rear seats, wall-to-wall carpets, twin-circuit braking systems, front disks, four-speed wipers, etc., the car is well equipped for the price.

In 1974 the Rover 2200 replaced the 10-year-old 2000, with a bored-out engine giving 10 percent more capacity. With other refinements, it was a much-needed uplift.

Pontiac Firebird (USA)

From Pontiac, the V-8, 7 ½-liter, 250-bhp Firebird Transam showed the current fashion in front-end styling. Most powerful of the Firebirds from this stable, the Transam was extensively restyled, although keeping some of its distinctive features, such as the twin ports. The two scoops under the front bumpers were new.

The 1974 version of many a motorists dream car was the 1974 Porsche Type 911. Introduced in 1964, when it appeared with a new body, the 911 is still going strong, grown now from 2-liters to a 6-cylinder, 2,687-cc, and still one of the fastest and safest cars in the normal driving range. The one in the picture is the 2-liter car.

Another car from Eastern Europe—the 991-cc Wartburg Knight from the German Democratic Republic is a two-stroke with a performance above the expected at a maximum of 87 mph. Rugged in construction, it shares some of the spartan qualities of other European small cars—the Citroën Dyane, the small Renaults and the Russian Moskvitch.

The 1974 Volvo offered a four-stage safety steering column, a heated driving seat (!), and for the 164E, an electrically-controlled fuel-injection system and 175-bhp from a 3-liter engine.

Porsche, 1974 (D).

VW Scirocco (D).

The Scirocco is another attempt by Volkswagen to widen the range and break free, at least in part, from the eternal Beetle. Scirocco has its 1,471-cc, 4-cylinder engine installed laterally, unlike a similar model, the Passat, which is conventionally fitted. Three versions of Scirocco are built, including a 50-hp "economy" 1,093-cc car and a high-compression 1.5-liter TS developing 80-bhp. The one in the photograph is the 70-bhp standard model.

A luxury variation on a theme by Austin and Morris, the Wolseley is by now merely badge-engineered. However, the Wolseley Six has the east-west mounted 2-¼-liter, 6-cylinder overhead-camshaft (108-bhp) unit with a decidedly "torquey" character, and a smooth, easy-holding ride with a considerable degree of interior comfort.

The Audi 80, a smaller version of the 100, was given a 1,558-cc unit for 1976, with the exception of the basic model, which retained the 1,296-cc engine. Developing 85-bhp and running on low-octane fuel, the 80 is an economy car of the middle (European) range that brings with it the quality of the famous Audi NSU combine.

The 1.6- and 1.8-liter Alfettas from the Milan stable were joined in 1975 by the GT version. Housing a 118-bhp 1.8 unit with a rear-mounted 5-speed transmission, it is a handsome small car with distinct sporting tendencies in the classic Alfa Romeo manner.

276

Cadillac Seville, 1975 (USA)

A completely new, smaller Cadillac was announced in 1975 by Cadillac Motor Car Division, GM's top-of-the-tree luxury USA car makers. The Seville, with an overall length of 17 feet, is 27 inches shorter than the full-size Sedan de Ville, 8 inches narrower and 900 pounds lighter—common-sense designing for the late seventies. Powered by a healthy 5.7-liter V-8 with electronic fuel injection, and developing 180 net bhp, this latest addition to the classic Cadillac line still represents the ultimate in American luxury and style.

In the current fashion of being either an "Easter egg" or a "wedge", the new Austin/Minor 18/22 range Princess is designed as the latter—an aerodynamic wedge that you either like or hate. However, British Leyland, now state-owned, describe the range as the biggest event since the previous biggest event in automotive matters, the Mini. With transverse engine, front-wheel drive, and hydragas suspension, the Princess owes much to the Mini tradition. Two engines are offered: a 1,798-cc, 4-cylinder and a 2,227-cc six. The car has a number of refinements, including dual-circuit, power-assisted brakes, and a surprisingly high standard of luxury trim for a medium-priced vehicle.

In its first year in the Buick line the subcompact Skyhawk gave a good account of itself, taking more than eight percent of total Buick sales for the year. The key feature is the Buick V-6 engine which combines economy, performance and reliability. During 1976, in line with the fuel economy pattern, a 5-speed overdrive manual transmission was offered.

Austin/Morris Princess (GB).

277

Now—The Seventies: 1970-1979

A genuine Chrysler Europe venture is the 1976 Alpine. A transverse front-mounted engine of either 1,294- or 1,442-cc supplies front-wheel power for a 5-door hatchback in the current style. Aimed at upper-middle European market and sold in both France and Britain, the car is fast becoming a best seller. Forty-seven expert judges from 15 countries in Europe voted the Chrysler Alpine (or its French equivalent, the Simca 1307/8) Car of the Year for 1976.

Even more multi-national in scope, General Motors' T-car saga began way back in the sixties when Opel of Germany set out to develop a replacement for its 1-liter Kadett. It rapidly grew into an international GM project. Now as Brazil's, Chevrolet's, and Vauxhall's Chevette, Opel's Kadett, Japan's and Holden's Isuzu Gemini, the stubby minicar (engine sizes vary from 1-liter to 1.8-liters) has proved a sound GM move and a popular buy in much of the world's market.

A venture into the smaller-car bracket was Chevrolet's Monza Towne Coupe with a 4.3 V-8 unit. The model has handsome, clear lines with a sensible minimum of metal-work.

Chrysler Alpine, 1976 (GB, F).

Dodge Aspen, 1976 (USA).

The 1976 Dodge Aspen represents current thinking—directing major sales efforts to buyers forced by the economic climate to buy smaller cars. It has a 225-cu in standard power plant, with larger units optional. A combination of aerodynamics, body design, and an all-new isolated transverse-torsion-bar front-suspension system makes the Aspen one of the smoothest and quietest riding cars ever produced by Chrysler, yet the handling is considerably more positive than past Dodge compacts.

A proven sporting success—winning the East African Rally is no sinecure—Mitsubishi Colt Gallant has recently invaded import markets in several areas. In 1600-cc and 2-liter form this compact car produced 100- and 115-bhp at just over 6,000 rpm respectively—and in its newly offered GTO Sports Coupe form it puts out a full 125-bhp. The Gallant 1600 is the car adopted by Chrysler U.S. for their American small-car operation in place of the British Avenger.

Top of the Citroën tree, the CX2200 appeared as the 1976 leader for the company. In its 2000 form, it was voted car of the year in 1975. In line with Citroën policy, the CX design is advanced, although not so radically different from the ID and DS as they were from their predecessors in the mid-fifties.

Ford covered their market with a total of 8 car lines and 32 models in 1976, among them the Thunderbird. The original T-Bird was a genuine attempt to produce what Ford called a "personalized car"—in effect, a sports car—and it became a collector's item shortly after its demise. The 1976 model is not a direct descendant, although the name may suggest it. Standard power is a 460-cu in engine, now recalibrated for improved fuel economy, coupled with automatic transmission.

Cobra II, the sporting version of the Mustang, is a name evocative of high performance and famous road-circuit races ever since Carol Shelby mounted a Ford V-8 engine in a British sports car. Racing versions of that Cobra swept to the World Manufacturing GT Championship of 1965. The Cobra II has a standard unit of 2.3-liters with 4-speed manual transmission, but 2.8 V-6 and 302-cu in V-8 engines are optional.

For 1976, Peugeot produced a car at the top end of its range—the 604, aimed at the luxury market and challenging Mercedes-Benz and Jaguar. Designed at the official French "ministerial" car, the 2.7-liter, twin-cam engine powers a vehicle resplendent with *comfort sensuel* for a nation otherwise known for its somewhat Spartan approach to transportation.

Thunderbird, 1976 (USA).

280

Chrsyler Cordoba, 1976 (USA).

The classically styled Cordoba, Chrysler's intermediate 2-door hard top, nearly trebled its sales forecast during 1975, its introductory year. Not much changed for 1976 except for its rather weighty grille, changed instrument cluster, and a new high-efficiency catalytic converter. It may be comforting to know that all 1976 Chrysler-Plymouth cars are designed to roll over a full 360 degrees without any fuel leakage!

The solidly conventional good looks of the Gemini from General Motors of Australia cloak a lively performance from the lightweight, 1,584-cc unit made specifically for the Gemini. This small car is heavily corrosion-protected, thoroughly ventilated for its climate, and offers full air conditioning. Three models—the sedan, the SL and a coupe complete the range. The coupe offers power-boosted disk brakes, fully reclining bucket seats with integral headrests, and a sleek and sportive appearance.

Ford of Britain's new Escort range was joined in 1976 by the Mexico. Powered by a 1,600-cc, single ohc engine, it is a high-performance sedan. The rest of the vehicle—suspension, transmission and body shell—is identical to the Escort RS 1800s that were driven to the first two places in Britain's RAC International Rally in 1975. This light, sporting model has special competition seats, additional instruments, and the fashionable ''beard'' air dam under the front end to prevent front lift at speed. Maximum speed is around 106 mph.

Lotus Esprit (GB).

Exciting, mid-engined and aerodynamically near-perfect, the new Lotus Esprit is a 2-liter 2-seater with Italian styling. Successor to the Europa twin-cam, its 156-bhp twin-ohc unit is reputed to give a 0-60 acceleration figure of 6-8 seconds, which puts the car among the world's most fleet-footed. Set in a backbone and space-frame skeleton, the engine, which has passed USA emission tests, drives through a Maserati (Citroën) transmission.

The 1976 Fiat 128 3P joins the line of rear-opening cars that so many manufacturers have opted for in the mid-seventies. A successor to the 128 Coupe, this little model from Turin is usefully short at 12 feet, 6 inches; its 1,290-cc engine has a light thirst and a remarkably high 73-bhp. Disk brakes, 4-speed transmission, an "indeformable" passenger compartment, and sophisticated suspension come with the package.

The long awaited successor to the Jaguar E-type arrived during 1976. The XJ-S, the most exclusive and expensive Jaguar ever produced, sets new standards of engineering and comfort for the up-market purchaser. Its 5.3-liter fuel-injection V-12 power pack can take the coupe from 0 to 60 mph in just 6.8 seconds, and the sleek aerodynamic styling helps return a figure of 15-18 mpg. Aimed primarily at the North American market, the XJ-S is claimed to be the ultimate in luxury motoring for the really discerning driver.

The Bobcat was introduced in March of 1975, and has proved to be a popular move for Lincoln-Mercury. Offered as the Runabout—a 3-door hatchback—or the Villager station wagon, the Bobcat has as its standard power pack a 2,300-cc 4-cylinder unit and 4-speed manual transmission. The car in the photograph is the "MPG", an economical version.

Lincoln-Mercury said of its 1976 lineup: "No changes have been made for the sake of change this year. All expertise and effort has gone into refining the product lineup". In evidence of this, Mercury Monarch has just one addition to its range—the Grand Monarch Ghia. A luxury version, it features 4-wheeled disks, aluminum-spoked wheels, power winders and steering, and an optional-to-standard 250-IV 6-cylinder engine.

As to the flagship of the line, the Continental also offered nothing radical for 1976, but a "search" stereo radio is available as is a quadrisonic tape player. Or, would you care for a Cartier-signed digital clock? America's "Car of State" has them for the asking.

The most sportive model of an Italian range that now includes sedan coupe and spider (open sports 2-seater), the 2-liter Lancia Beta Monte Carlo has a transverse mid-engine rear-wheel drive layout similar to the World-Championship-winning Stratos.

Bobcat, 1976 (USA).

Oldsmobile Starfire, 1976 (USA).

Oldsmobile made a number of fuel-economy improvements in all their 34-model lineup for 1976, mainly through higher efficiency of the 260 cu in V-8 power unit, a lighter axle, a manual 5-speed overdrive transmission, and a 2.41 to 1 axle ratio. Highlights of the 4-seater sports coupe pictured are the soft plastic front-end panel, energy-absorbing front bumper and rear hatchback. A GT option, introduced in 1975, is equipped with tachometer, rally wheels and special trim.

Mercedes-Benz continues their sporting image with the 350SL. A 2-seater with a reputation for speed plus safety, this once could be called the antithesis of the extreme sports car in its sophistication and silence. However, its performance is certainly in the upper sports bracket, with a top speed of 127 mph. The 350SL has power-assisted disks all around, removable steel hard-top roof, and fully disappearing soft top. Agility with stability are its two great virtues.

Somewhere between a sedan, a coupe and a station wagon is the 3-door Saab 99L Combi. The makers claim it combines the space of a 5-seater sedan and the tailgate and load capacity of a station wagon. With a British ancestry, the single-carb 2-liter 4-cylinder power unit gives 100-bhp and 100-plus mph. The construction is still typically Swedish—with slight heaviness owing to thorough steel reinforcing. Latest in the range is the 99GL, with twin carburetors and 108 bhp.

Don't be surprised if you've never heard of this one. Panther Westwinds is a small specialty maker with a plant near the old Brooklands circuit in England. The Panther sports roadster and Panther de Ville are two similarly audacious "replica" designs in wood and steel and chrome evoking memories of Bugatti, Hispano Suiza and other 1928 exotica. A 6- or 12-cylinder Jaguar unit is housed in a mock-classic body that gives the impression of just warming up to beat the Orient Express from London to Istanbul. The Panther packs a solid punch, however—that Jaguar engine will take an unwary driver into the illegal velocity bracket all too quickly. Not, of course, for the economy-minded.

Renault's star of the year was the new 30TS, powered by the "co-op" 2.7-liter V-6 light alloy engine designed by Volvo/Peugeot/Renault. The front-wheel drive 30TS is aimed at the executive market and has a number of built-in safety devices new to the make. In line with current European fashion, it claims a top speed of 110 mph—although the number of countries in which a vehicle is permitted to reach this speed must be rapidly diminishing.

A sports coupe with high performance and tight handling, the Opel Manta for 1976 offered a new aerodynamic shape in the contemporary mode. In five versions, the Manta has a 1.6-liter unit as standard, with a 1.9-liter optional. The new model precisely confirms the design talent of the German company.

Panther de Ville (GB).

Turbo-charging and K-Jetronic—the combination of exhaust-driven supercharging and continuous direct fuel injection—must add up to the most modern engine investment yet, and the Porsche Turbo has both. Although new in concept, the Turbo is no leap in the dark. Flagship of the 911 range, the experience behind the car, with its well-known 3-liter 6-cylinder opposed piston unit and construction techniques, the Turbo is pure Porsche—robust, reliable, enormously flexible, and entirely practical.

As suppliers of small and medium sports cars, from MG Midget to Jaguar E-type, British Leyland continued in the tradition during 1976 with the Triumph TR7. A complete departure from previous styling, the TR7 complies with all current and anticipated emission laws. A true 2-seater, it has eschewed the "shoe-horn" 2 + 2 form and has, consequently, comfort and space for driver and passenger. High performance is provided by a 2 liter electronic fuel-injection single ohc unit fitted (in the USA) with twin Stromberg 175 CDSEV carburetors.

Fresh for 1976 in Europe from Japan's Toyota was the 2000 sedan, and from the US point of view, right in line with current thinking—power unit 2-liters, with room for "five six-footers", as the company claims. The single ohc engine produces 116-bhp at 5,000 rpm using a single 2-choke carburetor.

Porsche Turbo (D).

Chevette (GB).

With major manufacturers clubbing together to produce a "co-operative" engine for their common use, it is no surprise to see General Motors planning a small car for construction in several countries. Based on GM's "T" floor plan, and owing much to the Vauxhall Viva 1300, the hatchback Chevette from Luton is shorter than either, giving the car a totally new look for very small styling changes other than at the front end. Its 1,256-cc engine can give up to 50 mpg when driven with care.

Volvo of Sweden has been known as one of the most conservative European auto manufacturers, but with the 240 and 260 series, a major step was taken into the future. The latest, the 264 GL, has the advanced 2,664-cc V-6 all-alloy engine designed in concert with Peugeot and Renault, and built in France. A completely new safety innovation is "Day Notice" lights—in effect, higher intensity parking lights that are active whenever the car is moving, to warn pedestrians that the car is in motion. Rear seat belts are also installed; Volvo maintains that the main danger to front occupants in a head-on crash are the rear passengers.

AC's ME3000, in production for Britain in 1976, became available for export in 1977. The car is powered by a Ford V-6 3-liter engine mounted transversely amidships. Bodywork is double-skinned, fire-resistant fiberglass, bringing the weight to about 1,800 lbs.

AMC Pacer, 1977 (USA).

The 1977 AMC Pacer—now available as a station wagon—represents advanced thinking and incorporates a number of unusual features. Not the least of these is the asymmetrical doors, the passenger door being 4 inches wider than that on the driver's side. Powered by the AMC 232 C1D six, both the sedan and the wagon offer the 258 C1D six as an option, and, interestingly, the wagon utilizes compressed gas cylinders to aid the operation of the tailgate. Sign of the times: you can have the interior trim in Levi's denim!

Winner of six "Car of the Year" awards, the Audi 80 range suffered the disadvantage of being launched on the British market right at the start of the oil crisis in 1973. It weathered the storm successfully. In GTE gas-injection form it is one of the fastest-accelerating 1,600-cc production sedan cars and was restyled for the 1977 year. All Audis in the range incorporate the self-stabilizing steering system pioneered by the firm. Audi's flagship is the new 100LS announced for 1977. Aimed at the executive market, the 2-liter sedan employs the same overhead-camshaft 115-bhp engine as the Porsche 924 and combines a top speed of 111 mph with 30 mpg fuel economy overall. A 5-cylinder 2.2-liter version with Bosch K-Jetronic fuel injection was promised for later in 1977 (it was delivered, too—right on schedule). Unlike those developed by Ford and Rover, Audi's is the first 5-cylinder gasoline engine to achieve general production.

The BMW "5" range, redesigned for 1977, sports a new grille and hood line and realigned rear lamp clusters. Both of the 6-cylinder models, the 525 and the 528, have redesigned combustion chambers and altered carburetion, boosting output by 5-bhp. A new "piston" support of the rear-axle damper contributes to a much quieter car, and instrument visibility is enhanced by a new steering wheel. BMW's "3" series offers the 320, an 109-mph 2-liter, two-door sedan that accelerates from 0 to 60 mph in a creditable 10.2 seconds. Now available as the 320i with a gas-injection engine, a top speed of 113 mph is possible. And one more BMW—the new 3.3-liter 633 CSi, first production car to boast a pre-drive safety check. By pressing a button on the instrument panel, seven lamps light up if there is no fault in engine oil level, radiator water level, brake fluid, windshield washer, rear lights, stop lights and brake-pad thickness. The all-steel two-door bodies are built by Karmann for BMW and the model is available with manual transmission or with ZF automatic transmission. With a 6-cylinder engine of 3,210-cc inherited from the 3.0 CS, the gas-injection CSi is capable of 133 mph.

Supposedly the most successful car ever to bear the Chrysler nameplate, the Cordoba for 1977 sported new front and rear styling, including a chrome-plated grille of formal design, more rectangular opera windows, and the option of the successful "T-bar" roof that appears on other Chrysler products. Engine: 400 cu in V8, with the "Lean Burn" electronic system. Cordoba is also available with a smaller 318 cu in unit.

BMW, 1977 (D).

Chevrolet Monza, 1977 (USA).

Chevrolet's 1977 Monza Spyder is a two-door hatchback coupe with a low profile and a sporting image. With a small "beard" in front and a larger spoiler at the rear, it projects an image of a competition ancestry. Supplied with a 5-liter V-8 unit or a much smaller 4-cylinder 2.3-liter power pack, the Monza is versatile, handsome and functional.

Heralding the phase-out of the Volkswagen Beetle after over a generation of production (prototypes were seen as early as 1936), the 895-cc VW Polo has a transverse front-mounted engine, is a 4-seater (almost), and is simple to drive, pleasant to handle, and looks *nothing* like a Beetle.

The first-born directly attributable to Citroën's marriage to Peugeot (upon whose 104 it is based) the LN hails from Citroën's Aulney factory where it is produced alongside the CX. Designed to "strengthen Citroën's position at the bottom end of the market", it is difficult to see the logic of this, with the legendary 2CV, Ami and Dyane models already dominating that sphere. Even though fitted with the most powerful of the Citroën flat-twin engines, it will have its work cut out to compete with the above-mentioned VW Polo or the FIAT 127.

290

The new luxury model of the Chrysler Alpine, the GLS is one of the first all-British assembled Alpines since Fench-assembled cars ceased to be imported in mid-summer 1976. Identical mechanically to the 1,442-cc Alpine S, the GLS features built-in head restraints, tinted glass, electric window lifters, and headlight washer-wipers. Another British Chrysler, the Avenger 1600 Super, while capable of 100 mph, is a thoroughly conventional car that has changed little in basic specifications over the past two years, although performance has improved. Its ohv engine with chain-driven camshaft still relies on the Stromberg 150CD3 carburetor and develops maximum power at 5,000 rpm. Coil-spring suspension all around results in a some-what lively ride over all but the smoothest surfaces, but generally the car is without vices and behaves as one would expect at this stage of development.

Available with the standard "1600" as well as the more powerful "Astron 80" 2-liter engine, Japan's Celeste retains the 92-in wheelbase and general layout of the Colt Lancer, although the fastback body is new. With 5-speed transmission (direct on fourth) the Celeste is capable of 110 mph on low-grade fuel, but at the expense of a rather harsh ride, because of the use of semi-elliptic springs at the rear.

Chrysler Alpine, 1977 (GB).

Dodge Royal Monaco, 1977 (USA).

Complementing Dodge's successful compact Aspen range at the top-of-the-line for 1977 is the Royal Monaco. Also offered in brougham form, it acquired a smaller sister in the mid-sized Monaco, the latter being distinguished by its vertically stacked headlights. With a close eye on Federal emission controls and legislation, the 1977 Dodge lineup features increased availability of the Chrysler Electronic Spark Advance "Lean Burn" engine, with 400-cu in and 360-cu in V-8s supplementing the existing 400.

Combining the front-wheel-drive of the Cherry 120A Coupe with a new and larger three-door body shell, Datsun's 1977 Cherry F.11 Coupe utilizes the transverse-mounted 1,171-cc engine adapted from the old 120Y Sunny unit (more than 4 ½ million produced) and all around independent suspension, incorporating coil springs and rear-mounted McPherson struts.

The Ford Pinto for 1977 is sportier than earlier models, and stiffer rear suspension provides it with more positive road handling. Standard power team is the economical 2.3-liter ohc 4-cylinder unit with manual four-speed transmission. A 2.8-liter engine is available to all versions except the Pony.

The Argocat (GB).

No, it's not a dune buggy. It's a genuine all-terrain amphibious car, and it's built in Kent, England by Crayford Auto Developments. You can have it in either six- or eight-wheeled form, with a choice of the American Tecumseh 2-stroke single-cylinder or Japanese Chapparal 4-stroke single-cylinder engine. Police and the military are using it, and so are farmers. And if you insist, you can have it as a Snowmobile. One more item—a non-rust body of polyethylene—virtually indestructible.

During the pioneer days of the automobile, motor car makers blatantly copied the Mercedes shape. Today's makers might do well to take their slide rules to the most popular car in Britain—the 1977 Ford Cortina Mark 4. Dating back to its introduction in 1962, it has been a sales winner from the outset, and it continues to top the charts. With its new lines and ageless look, it should stay on top, and with a 17-model option embracing four power packs from 1300-cc to an ohc 2,000-cc, it covers mid-range European requirements ideally. Another British Ford, the Fiesta baby car represents a brave step by Ford. The car combines three schools of thought—one Anglo-German, one American, and one from Ghia of Turin. A true European car, its production is a joint effort shared by factories in no less than four cities: Valencia, Dagenham, Saarlouis (Belgium) and Cologne. All except Cologne will play a part in its final assembly.

Cougar, 1977 (USA).

A successful year brought a fistful of new-look Lincoln models in 1977. The Continental Mark V follows the prestigious IV, and the division's redesigned intermediates all carry the Cougar motif in 1977. As well as extensive restyling, Lincoln-Mercury adopted the DuraSpark system in 1977—a sophisticated second-generation ignition that gives higher plus voltage during the starting and running cycles—and improved catalytic converters. The 1977 Cougar Brougham pictured is powered by the standard 302-cu in V-i engine (351 in California).

Ironically, the last of the GM family to introduce a version of the T-car, which was originally based on an Opel body design, Opel's Kadett City uses the Opel 4-cylinder engine and 4-speed transmission and is available with GM automatic transmission. The City has an 1,196-cc engine, with a smaller 993-cc unit available. The larger-engined model with compression stepped up to 9-1 (and known as the Strasbourg) offers automatic as an option. In its fastest form, the City achieves 87 mph. Another Opel, the Ascona, offers a choice of two- or four-door models and three engines on a longer wheelbase. With the larger 1.9-liter unit, the Ascona can deliver up to 104 mph from the 90-bhp under the hood. Automatic transmission is available on all models.

294

Lancia, 1977 (I).

Celebrating the 70th anniversary of the founding of the house of Lancia, a new high-powered luxury sedan was launched on the international market. Designed by Pininfarina, the body displays advanced styling, and an even more spacious interior is achieved by the use of front-wheel drive. The use of a 2,484-cc flat four engine—an area in which Lancia has plenty of experience—adds to the compactness of the design, and twin overhead camshaft allied to an overall advanced specification result in a top speed of 120 mph. The Gamma is available in sedan and two-door coupe.

Coming at a time when British Leyland badly needed a potent weapon in the prestige market, the Rover 3500 is the success story of the year. It offers 125 mph, five doors, five gears (with genuine true overdrive on fifth), five seats and a 3 ½-liter engine of thoroughly sporting demeanor and astonishing fuel frugality. The result of a five-year gestation period, the steel monocoque body bears a frontal resemblance to the Ferrari Daytona.

295

Plymouth Gran Fury, 1977 (USA).

Functional elegance is the stamp of the Plymouth Gran Fury Brougham, pictured in two-door hardtop form. Automatic transmission, power steering and power-assisted front-disk brakes are included in the package. Buyers have a choice: the 400- or the 440-cu in V-8 engine, with the Chrysler electronic "Lean Burn" system giving improved acceleration and response. Available also as a four-door sedan and in Suburban station wagon form, the 1977 lineup dropped the Custom model from the range.

Renault for 1977 included the 5GTL, a 3-door fwd sedan which converts to an estate wagon (fold-away rear seating). The engine is 4-cylinder with a light alloy head of 1,289-cc and a eyepopping 60 mpg. Polyester bumper shields can take a 4 mph impact without damage. The Renault 14, a middle-range car uses a transversely mounted engine. 1.2-liters, fwd, nearly 90 mph. Very compact—only 13 feet, 2 inches overall—it has five doors and five seats (the rear seats are adjustable). Lastly, the Renault 20 TL gets 90-hp from its 4-cylinder, 1,647-cc engine with fwd and all-independent suspension. The 20 TL is a spacious five-seater designed to fill the gap between the 2.7-liter V-6 30TS and the 16 TX. Offered with 4-speed manual or three-speed automatic transmission, it has a top speed of 102.5 mph and commendable fuel consumption of from 25 to 31 mpg.

TVR, 1977 (GB).

The rear view of the British TVR 3000M shows the unconventional rear end, redesigned to give improved airflow. A new air intake involving reshaping the front end has decreased air resistance, and the intake also acts as a spoiler apron, giving the low-lying sports car more ground adhesion at speed. Its 2,994-cc unit will take the car up to 120 mph, and the 0 to 60 acceleration figure of 7.7 seconds is rapid enough to satisfy the expert sporting driver.

Originally set up in 1953, and concentrating on FIAT designs, SEAT of Spain have by now developed an individuality of their own, and even include a Mercedes-engined model in their range. The 1200 Sport boasts an 1,197-cc east-west configuration engine, and with front-wheel drive, brings home 67-bhp at 5,600 rpm. Suspension is independent—McPherson—and a respectable 100 mph is maximum.

Speaking of Mercedes, the 450 SEL is the most powerful and expensive car in the 1977 line. Top speed: 140 mph; acceleration, 0 to 60 in 7.4 seconds. Fitted with an ohc 6.9-liter, V-8 engine, it is supposed to be virtually maintenance-free for the first 50,000 miles (except for oil changes). Torque convertor automatic transmission, and Mercedes' very-own-designed power steering. Super luxury, as expected.

Now—The Seventies: 1970-1979

Styled by Guigario, like most of the current VWs, the Golf is the complete opposite of the old Beetle. The Golf has fwd and a water-cooled engine. The engine, in either 1,100- or 1,600-cc, is transverse-mounted. Either three or five door models are available. A high-lift tailgate and folding rear seats make for quick conversion; the transmission is filled with oil and sealed for life; and the chassis, steering rack and door locks require no lubrication. All this, 35 mpg and a top speed of 100 mph (on the 1,600-cc LS variant) makes the Golf another worthy successor to the Beetle.

Some notes from Toyota for 1977: their Crown Custom Estate is a new verion of the Crown with seven-seat accommodation and other specifications almost identical with the 2.6-liter Crown Super Sedan, plus top-hinged tailgate. Over 15 feet long, this estate car is spacious by any standard. Going from big to small, Toyota's peewee is the 1000, in two-door sedan or estate version. The 993-cc front-mounted (rear-drive) inclined four-power unit is extremely economical and runs happily on low-grade fuel. Like most Japanese cars, the 1000 offers a high level of initial equipment, including radio, reversing light, reclining seats and inertia-reel seat belts. Suspension is unsophisticated, with rear semi-elliptics allied to McPherson struts at the front.

Volkswagen, 1977 (D).

Volvo, 1977 (S).

The direct result of the marriage between the car-making interests of DAF and Volvo, the Volvo 66 is basically a DAF66 with re-styled front end and an uprated specification in line with Volvo's more exacting standards. While the Variomatic drive is retained, the old centrifugal clutch is supplemented by a vacuum servo-operated unit, and Volvo's rubber-covered bumpers are fitted. Produced in 1,100 and 1,300 form, the 66 gives Volvo a valuable foot in the common market and a badly-needed economy car in their range. Another Volvo, the 343 DL was designed to fill the "mid-range" between the aforementioned 66 and the 240 series. The 343DL places a strong accent on safety while still providing a spacious three-door, five-seater sedan with very little less passenger area than the 240. Equipped with trans-axle automatic transmission, the top speed is 90 mph and the 1,397-cc engine, with chain-driven camshaft and carburetor built into the engine block, returns a commendable 32 to 35 mpg.

Vauxhall's Cavalier was designed to fill the slot between their Magnum and VX ranges. In two- or four-door sedan form, or as a coupe (the latter with 1,897-cc cam-in-head ohv engine) the standard 1977 Cavalier wears a 1,584-cc ohv engine and four-speed transmission, although GM automatic transmission is an available option with both engines.

Ford Fairmont, 1978 (USA)

Ford relied heavily for the 1978 model year on its new mid-size Fairmont, introduced as a car with ''mid-size roominess at a compact price''. Optimistically, they hoped it will outsell the first-year record sales of the Mustang. (419,000—a first-year-model high for Ford.) The car was offered in two- and four-door sedans and wagons with a standard 2.3-liter engine and the larger 3.3-liter six and 5.0-liter V8 as options.

Ford ran the gamut from Pinto and sub-compact Fiesta (German-built by Ford) through Mustang II, Granada, LTD II, LTD, Club Wagon and the top-of-the-line Diamond Jubilee Thunderbird with Ford's biggest standard engine, the 5.0-liter V-8. If you insisted, you could be optionally supplied with a 5.8- or 6.6-liter power plant.

As with most American makes, Ford's options, either in packages or singly, were almost bewildering in their complexity and variety. Even Thunderbird, which appeared in only two body styles, (four-passenger coupe or Town Landau) had at least 14 options, ranging from a Sports Decor group to a heavy-duty towing kit.

300

Ford Granada, 1978 (USA).

Ford Diamond Jubilee Thunderbird, 1978 (USA).

Now—The Seventies: 1970-1979

Like the parent company (Ford), Lincoln-Mercury hung a lot of hopes on a new car for 1978. The compact Zephyr, which replaced the Comet, had an exhaustive test history—320 hours in wind tunnel testing alone—that dated back to 1973. Zephyr was offered in two- and four-door sedans, a station wagon and a 2-door sports coupe—just 4 of the 28 models in 9 lines on the Lincoln-Mercury agenda, which began with the sub-compact Bobcat and proceeded thru Capri (German-made), Zephyr, Monarch, the intermediate Cougar, Marquis, Lincoln Continental, Continental Mark V and the Lincoln Versailles. The latter was scaled down as a rebuttal, no doubt, to Cadillac's Seville.

One of the most imaginative innovations for 1978 emerged as an option on the Mark V—a "miles-to-empty" indicator on the dash which lights up in a bright orange when a button is pressed. Controlled by sensors in the gas tank and transmission, the figure shown updates every minute, taking into account road speed, type of driving (long hills, etc.). When positioned, it is directly underneath the fuel gauge.

Engines ranged from the 2.3-liter 4s on Bobcat, Capri and Zephyr to the big 7.5-liter V8s, optional on the big fellows.

Zephyr, 1978 (USA)

Lincoln-Mercury Marquis, 1978 (USA).

Lincoln-Mercury Diamond Jubilee Continental Mark V, 1978 (USA).

Chevrolet Monte Carlo, 1978 (USA).

For the most part, nothing radical was attempted by Chevrolet for 1978. The emphasis was on cosmetics, weight reduction, and on some models, more headroom and legroom. Four hatchbacks (two of them new) were offered in the Chevette, Monza and Nova ranges. In all, Chevrolet for 1978 offered approximately 30 body variations in seven models: Chevette, Monza, Nova, Monte Carlo, Camaro, Caprice and Corvette. Practically every car in the entire Chevrolet line was offered with engine options ranging from the 1.6-liter, 4-cylinder unit on the subcompact Chevette to the 5.7-liter V-8 power plant used optionally for the Nova, Camaro, Caprice and Corvette.

The most dramatic change in body styling was the use of a large wraparound rear window on the Corvette, giving what has been called "America's only true Sports Car" a more suitably fastback look. Adding sharply to its cruise range, Corvette's gas tank capacity was increased by some 41%—from 17 to 24 gallons. The T-Bar roof with lift-out tinted glass panels was another option for those who like air coming from all directions, made available on Corvette, Camaro and Monte Carlo.

Chevrolet Nova, 1978 (USA)

Chevrolet Corvette, 1978 (USA).

Pontiac Grand Am, 1978 (USA)

Pontiac completely redesigned the mid-sized LeMans and Grand LeMans for 1978 and re-introduced the Grand Am (out of the line in 1976 and 1977). These two items, plus a general overhaul for improved gas mileage, interior room and weight reduction and a bit of face-lifting here and there were Pontiac's major thrust for the 1978 models.

Pontiac's 1978 engines ranged from the 2.5-liter, 4-cylinder plant used for the sub-compact Sunbird and the compact Phoenix to the hefty 6.6-liter V-8's under the hoods of Firebird Formula and Trans Am, Catalina and Bonneville. In a burst of welcome candor, Pontiac listed its engine sources as Chevrolet, Buick, Oldsmobile and, of course, Pontiac.

Grand Am, billed by Pontiac as a European-style touring car, was offered in two-and four-door models. A total of five station wagons and two hatchback versions were available in LeMans, Grand LeMans, Sunbird, Catalina and Phoenix.

For the trailer home contingent, there were three trailer towing packages capable of handling tow weights of from 2,000 to 6,000 pounds.

306

Pontiac Grand Prix, 1978 (USA).

Pontiac Sunbird Sport Coupe, 1978 (USA).

Oldsmobile Cutlass Supreme, 1978 (USA).

Oldsmobile, like Chevrolet and Pontiac, devoted a good portion of their efforts for 1978 to the areas of weight reduction, interior design for greater leg and head room, and improved gas mileage. One model, the intermediate Cutlass, has been completely redesigned. To achieve more trunk space on the Cutlass, Oldsmobile took an interesting route: a new "compact" spare tire—described as "a 15-inch small cross-section tire that comes already inflated, weighs about half as much as a regular tire and wheel assembly and can safely be driven for at least 2000 miles".

Oldsmobile now offers twenty-five models (down two from 1977) in six lines—Cutlass, Starfire, Omega (the Omega LS is a small luxury limousine), Delta 88, 98 and Toronado.

Perhaps their most important item for 1978 is the availability of the GM 5.7 V-8 diesel engine on three models: the 88s, the 98s, and their largest wagon—the Custom Cruiser. With a 27.3 fuel tank, the diesels, used for the coupes and sedans, will have a cruising range of more than 600 miles. Factory testing indicates a fuel economy improvement of up to 25% over comparable gasoline engines.

308

Oldsmobile Delta 88 Royale Sedan Diesel, 1978 (USA).

Oldsmobile Toronado Brougham, 1978 (USA).

Now—The Seventies: 1970-1979

Buick, for 1978, managed to display the largest number of body styles of any GM line—thirty-four in all—in eight series: Skylark, Skyhawk, Century, Regal, LeSabre, Estate Wagon, Electra 225 and Riviera.

Heavy emphasis was laid by Buick on the intermediate Century; a total of nine body styles, including two station wagons were presented. As with the other three GM lines, (Cadillac is the exception in GM thinking—it plows its own stately, luxurious course) fuel efficiency and weight and size reduction were features.

Four hatchbacks were available, plus the two Century station wagons and something Buick is pleased to call an "Estate Wagon"

A new emission control system was to be available on some Skyhawk models sold in California, employing an oxygen sensor in the exhaust, an electronically controlled carburetor and a rhodium / platinum catalytic converter. The "temporary use" lightweight spare tire was standard on all Century and Regal models.

Buick LeSabre Sport Coupe, 1978 (USA).

Buick Century Sport Coupe, 1978 (USA).

Buick Park Avenue Coupe, 1978 (USA).

Cadillac Coupe de Ville, 1978 (USA)

Every 1978 Cadillac except Seville used the same engine—an ohv 7.0-liter V8. Seville, billed as Cadillac's "international size" car, uses the V8, but in a slightly smaller (5.7-liter) size.

The use of aluminum in a few marginal areas was Cadillac's only concession to weight reduction, and the weight loss was minimal. The only emphasis the maker placed is on, in their own words, "subtle design refinements and consumer-oriented engineering benefits."

As usual, Cadillac's complete line was the shortest in the GM stable—a total of seven regular models and two "Special Editions". The latter were a sportier-looking Eldorado called "Biarritz", and the Seville "Elegante" pictured.

Also as usual, Cadillac's two limousines were monstrously long—over 20 feet from bumper to bumper.

312

Cadillac Eldorado Biarritz, 1978 (USA).

Cadillac Seville Elegante, 1978 (USA).

AMC Concord 2-Door Sedan, 1978 (USA).

American Motors, with a much more Spartan lineup than the Detroit Colossi, still managed to touch most of the bases for 1978—even up to and including their own new car, the Concord.

Concord, said AMC, was designed as a luxury compact, for those buyers stepping down a peg from the gas-guzzlers. Four body styles: two- and four-door sedans, hatchback and wagon. A 232 cu in six, manual shift was standard on all models. If you wanted to pay for it, you could move up to automatic and a larger six or a 304 cu in V-8.

Gremlin looked as pixy-ish as ever in its sub-compact form. Plenty of options, lots of cosmetics.

AMX was suitably (as pictured) sporty for the younger set. The larger six with four-speed floor-mounted manual shift was standard, with the V-8 optional. (Yes, the "Levi" interior trim was still an option.) Pacer still featured the huge glass area and asymmetric doors for easy "in-and-out".

The Matador was the big boy in the line, looking quite impressive as a standard or a wagon.

314

AMC Gremlin X, 1978 (USA).

AMC AMX Hatchback, 1978 (USA).

Toyota Cressida 5-Door Wagon, 1978 (J).

Toyota added one more "C" for 1978. To the ongoing Corolla, Corona and Celica, came top-of-the-line Cressida, available in two models—a four-door sedan and the five-door wagon pictured. Featured were a 2.6-liter, 6-cylinder engine and a four-speed overdrive automatic transmission which was alleged to have a solid upward impact on gas mileage.

Celica shaved off up to 75 pounds and went in for some redesigning—a sloping hood and more glass were the highlights. A transistorized ignition system promised maintenance reduction due to the elimination of point and condenser replacement.

Toyota was still the number one import (since 1975), expecting sales around the half-million mark in 1978. This is in contrast to their sales of 2,893—total—for their first four years (1958 through 1961) in this country.

Toyota Corolla 2-Door Sedan, 1978 (J).

Toyota Celica GT Sport Coupe, 1978 (J).

Now—The Seventies: 1970-1979

The number one arrow in VW's quiver for 1978 was the Rabbit—seemingly no less prolific than its namesake: 13 varieties of Rabbit were available, ranging from the bare bones 2-door hatchback (all VW Rabbits are hatchbacks) thru the 4-door Deluxe with automatic. Additionally, 4 models were available with diesel power.

Sporty Scirroco was back, with some decor improvements and a slightly smaller, slightly more economical engine. VW's midsize Dasher, available six ways, also had some lipstick and eyeshadow treatment—the styling by Giorgetto Giugiaro of Turin.

VW's big one—the Bus—was again available in Station Wagon, Campmobile or Kombi versions.

And yes, Virginia, there was still a Beetle—in a 2-door, 4-passenger convertible—one of only two such ragtops still being sold in the U.S.A.

Volkswagen Rabbit "L", 1978 (D).

VW Bus, 1978 (D).

Datsun B-210 GX, 1978 (J).

Datsun 280Z, 1978 (J).

At a suggested retail list price of $3,198, Datsun's B-210 two-door sedan was the lowest-priced item on Datsun's 1978 shopping list. At $9,278, the 280Z 2+2 was far and away the highest-priced. And those prices did not include destination or handling charges, or state and local taxes.

Nestled amidships of the line was the new 510 series, replacing the 710. The new body comes in two-door hatchback or sedan, and four-door sedan and wagon versions. On the same basis as the above, it was in the $4,000-$5,000 range. As seems to be the case with the entire industry, Datsun talked about more room inside, despite reduced outside dimensions.

The entire Datsun range included the B-210 in four models (including a new 48 m.p.g., "GX" federal car), the 200 SX (coupe), F-10 wagon and coupe (front wheel drive available), the 810, a luxury sedan and wagon series, and the 280Z's—coupe and 2+2. Fifteen models in all.

Peugeot 504 SL Station Wagon, 1978 (F).

Peugeot 504 SL Sedan, 1978 (F).

No one was bewildered by any vast Peugeot assortment in 1978. Two basic models—604, a six cylinder sedan, and 504, a 4-cylinder sedan or station wagon. Quality, *oui;* variety, *non.*

Of course, you could have one other choice with 504: both models came with conventional gasoline or diesel engines.

504 was a four-seater; 604 seated five, and was billed as comparable in size to Cadillac's Seville. Transmissions for both were manual shift, four-speed synchronized with three-speed automatic optional. Power-assisted rack-and-pinion steering was standard on both. Decorative styling by Pininfarina characterized both models.

An added thought: Peugeot is the oldest automobile manufacturer still in continuous existence in the world. They began operations in 1889. It gives rise to a suspicion that they must be doing *something* right!

320